Signs in Use

An introduction to semiotics

'Unique and thorough, this is one of the best introductions to semiotic theory and method I have ever seen.'

Marcel Danesi, University of Toronto, Canada

'Successfully overcoming the semiotic "cold war" between the American and French schools, 'Signs in Use' offers a complete picture of the whole discipline of semiotics. Larsen and Johansen's book is an original contribution to the field.'

Kristian Bankov, New Bulgarian University

All organisms, from bees to computer networks, create signs, communicate, and exchange information. The field of semiotics explores the ways in which we use these signs to make inferences about the nature of the world.

Signs in Use is an access introduction to the study of semiotics. Cutting across different semiotic schools, the book introduces six basic concepts which present semiotics as a theory and a set of analytical tools: code, sign, discourse, action, text, and culture. Moving from the most abstract and simple concept – the code – to the most concrete and complex – culture – the book gradually widens the semiotic perspective to show how and why semiotics works as it does.

Each chapter covers a problem encountered in semiotics and explores the key concepts and relevant notions found in the various theories of semiotics. Chapters build on the knowledge gained in previous chapters, and can also be used as self-contained units for study when supported by the extensive glossary. Written in a student-friendly style, the book enables its readers to use these concepts to analyse texts from different media. *Signs in Use* is illustrated with numerous examples, from traffic systems to urban parks, and offers useful biographies of key twentieth-century semioticians.

Signs in Use is an essential text for students of semiotics.

Jørgen Dines Johansen is Professor of Comparative Literature at Southern Danish University, Odense.

Svend Erik Larsen is Professor of Comparative Literature at Aarhus University, Denmark.

Signs in Use

An introduction to semiotics

**Jørgen Dines Johansen and
Svend Erik Larsen**

**Translated by Dinda L. Gorlée and
John Irons**

London and New York

First published 2002 by Routledge
11 New Fetter Lane, London EC4P 4EE

Simultaneously published in the USA and Canada
by Routledge
29 West 35th Street, New York, NY 10001

Routledge is an imprint of the Taylor & Francis Group

This translation of *Tegn i Brug* is published by arrangement with
Amanda/Dansklærerforeningens Forlag.

Danish edition originally published 1994 by Amanda/Dansklærerforeningens
Forlag as *Tegn i Brug*.

English edition © 2002 Jørgen Dines Johansen and Svend Erik Larsen

Typeset in Baskerville by Keyword Publishing Services Ltd
Printed and bound in Great Britain by The Cromwell Press, Trowbridge, Wiltshire.

British Library Cataloguing–in–Publication Data
A catalogue record for this book is available from the British Library

Library of Congress Cataloging in Publication Data
A library catalog for this book has been requested

ISBN 0-415-26203-8 (hbk)
ISBN 0-415-26204-6 (pbk)

Contents

Figures

Tables

Acknowledgements

Figures

Fig. 2.1 Drawing by Gunna Larsen.

Fig. 3.5 Brask, Peter, 'Model Groups and Composition Systems', *Danish Semiotics* (ed. Jørgen Dines Johansen and Morten Nøjgaard) (Munksgaard Publishers, Copenhagen, 1979).

Fig. 7.1 from *Touch the Wild* (Zimbabwe, Africa) advertisement.

Text

Aerestrup, Emil, 'What do they mean . . . ', from *Digte I–II* (Hans Reitzel, Copenhagen, 1962).

de Troyes, Chrétien, 'Eree et Enide', from *Lettres gothiques* (ed. Jean-Marie Fritz) (Librairie Générale Française, Paris, 1992).

Dos Passos, John, *The 42nd Parallel* (Signet, New York, 1979).

1 Introduction

What is semiotics about?

A summer day at the beach. A boy decides to play ducks and drakes. He finds a likely stone, tests it with his fingers, looks at the water, waits for a moment – and then throws. A dog runs next to him. It stops suddenly, sniffs a clump of seaweed, stiffens and runs off. A mosquito arrives, circles above the boy's shoulder, lands and sticks in its proboscis. Smack! Curtains!

A series of semiotic processes has taken place here. The boy, dog and mosquito have perceived certain phenomena in such a way that they refer to something else than themselves: *the stone* refers to impending small skips across the surface of the water; *the smell of the seaweed* refers to something that the dog cannot actually see; and *the shoulder* refers to mosquito-food for the mosquito, while an *irritating itch* tells the boy that a mosquito is at work. The things become *signs*. Some of these processes are shared by living organisms, others are specifically human. We intend to concentrate mainly on the latter in this book. But since not only humans have semiotic competence, we will always be prepared to broaden our horizon.

Let us begin by looking at what the boy does. He starts by choosing a stone. With reference to its possible flight-path it gains a particular meaning, i.e. its suitability for stone-skimming when thrown. Next, the ripples of the waves are read as indications of wind and current conditions, so they gain the meaning of being favourable for stone-skimming. Separately, the stone and the water each refer to something else (wind and current), possibly to something which is as yet not present (the game of ducks and drakes). As signs they have acquired *meaning*, making it possible to orient one's behaviour as a result. The surroundings have become an environment for human activity.

The dog, too, has semiotic abilities. With its sense apparatus it has selected a clump of seaweed as being especially interesting, possibly with reference to food or to a rival marking of territory. A closer sniff, however, reveals that it has interpreted the sign incorrectly: it obviously meant potential danger, and the dog took fright. When one perceives things as being signs, there is no guarantee that one does so correctly, or that one perceives all the consequences of the sign-making process. Consider the mosquito. Its registration apparatus reads a phenomenon as a reference to food. It acts accordingly. But this causes a new sign – a painful or itching sting that refers to the mosquito itself. This is read, localized and interpreted by the boy. He identifies the mosquito as a manageable enemy and goes into action.

Even though the processes might seem identical, they do not in fact coincide. Neither the boy nor the mosquito can do what the dog does. Indeed, they would scarcely be able to register what the dog has scented. But with a special, elementary ability to change things into signs, each of them describes a circle around their life. They change their surroundings into an environment within which they can orient themselves accurately. They have to be able to perceive things as signs for food, danger, others of the same species, preferably those of the opposite gender, and they must also be able to perceive things as signs for possible movements, e.g. direction, the layout of the terrain, etc. Otherwise, they have no environment in which to live. That is the first function of semiotic competence: to change things into signs that, together, form an environment in which the organism can live. Even though the three creatures belong to each other's environments – since they can perceive and identify each other – their environments are not identical. Their circles merely overlap.

The boy makes the stone and the water signs by making a number of *inferences* on the basis of selected material qualities in things. This sorting process takes place with the aid of a *code* he is familiar with. Using it, he rejects characteristics that are unimportant in this particular context (e.g. the colour of the stone), linking others (e.g. the weight of the stone, the movement of the water) to a meaning that has to do with stone-skimming. He undertakes an *interpretation*. In principle, the dog and the mosquito do the same within their universes, and with the codes they are familiar with.

Because of this, the stone, water and boy cease to be isolated phenomena. In the act of interpretation they are bound to each other in such a way that they are integrated in a number of realizations and actions which are *repeatable*. The sign starts a regular activity, an inference; it is thus that the stone as a sign through its meaning, its suitability for stone-skimming, refers to a future action that can be carried out precisely because the code indicates that here we can use the rules established via previous experience. The single instance acquires a general, rule-directed nature, and thereby a collective nature. That is the second basic function of semiotic competence: it ensures that phenomena can be repeated, remembered and stored in habits, so that we can use the signs to make inferences about the nature of the world. Semiotics is about our engagement in this basic process as living organisms and as humans, and its consequences for our attempts to make the world around us *our* world.

In the next two chapters of the book, we deal with these fundamental semiotic functions: in the second chapter we outline the *codes* by means of which phenomena are structured in such a way that we can interpret them as signs. In the third chapter we give a presentation of how *signs* occur and are kept apart from each other as different types of signs which act together in complex sign-wholes. The remaining chapters deal with the consequences.

In its broadest sense, semiotics comprises all forms of formation and exchange of meaning on the basis of phenomena which have been coded as signs. Whether this information belongs to the entire biosphere from cells to dinosaurs or only in the world of humans, or whether information is formed and exchanged in machines, robots, etc. as electronic signals, in organic or inorganic materials, whether it belongs to a novel or a down-to-earth every-day conversation, is a matter of indifference to such a broad interpretation. We intend, however, to narrow the definition, emphasizing that semiotic competence is bound to sign-linked intention-determined actions, conscious or subconscious. For us, semiotics belongs to the living world. Sign-processes in machines, etc. are only of semiotic interest when they are integrated in sign-processes in an environment where intentions are possible. Sign-processes in such a context are referred to as *discourses*. This is the subject-matter of Chapter 4.

This narrowing of the semiotic perspective does not necessarily mean that human use of signs is something that enjoys special status – although the truth of the matter is that it does. Let us see what happens when the boy has returned home from the beach. He is alone in the house and potters about for a while before going to bed. Later, he wakes up with a stomach-ache. He calls out. His father arrives on the scene, frantically consults Spock's guide to parenthood, has a quick look at *The Home Doctor* and happens to look into a biscuit tin that shows a catastrophic, illicit loss of its contents. He is faced with a composite phenomenon that has to be read as signs. The father must arrive at the correct conclusion about what object the sign – expression of pain, calling out and cramped lower stomach – refers to. Is it appendicitis, which means calling for an emergency service doctor immediately? Is it merely stomach-ache after excessive, illicit consumption of biscuits that are reserved for adults after the child's bedtime? In both instances the father has to carry out the same semiotic process as the boy did down on the beach. But now he furthermore has to be able to isolate a valid context for the sign, while making his own inferences about what it refers to. He has to anchor these in a situation which is not only given, but which he has to define. Otherwise all inferences will lack a conclusion and validity.

The type of sign we are dealing with in both interpretations is a signal, i.e. a sign which via an inference is linked to a cause, independent of any human intention. If the sign is a signal for constipation, we have to broaden the interpretative framework so that we can include intention-determined actions to understand the coming into existence of the sign: the boy's urge to eat biscuits. Not if it is appendicitis: the biology of infection is indifferent to intentions. But it could also be that the boy's stomach-ache is a message to the father. Perhaps the child intends – conscious or subconsciously – to tell his father that he has been too busy creating his own semiotic environment, so that the boy's sign of pain refers to a sense of lack. In that case, the sign is no longer just a signal with information about a causally determined relation to an object; it is also an act of communication – a subconscious nervous pain, possibly based on compulsive eating. But, on the other hand, it can also be the result of more direct human ingenuity: what if the boy, sneaky fox, only pretends to have a stomach-ache because he knows the sign always works? The father rushes to the scene, maybe egged on by a touch of bad conscience. The sense of lack is just as real in both cases. So there are many possibilities for anchoring the sign in a situation.

People have a number of ways, however, to get themselves out of this multiple-meaning jam. The mosquito senses food, creates a new sign which refers to itself, but is unable in time to register the sign for the possible smack. The dog goes straight to the clump of seaweed and discovers its mistake, so to speak, experimentally. The father, on the other hand, can construct a narrative as an imagined framework around the sign-process: he imagines that the boy has come home, has been alone, has cried a bit, taken biscuits from the tin and got a stomach-ache. And he can ask the boy, who can confirm the story, or take evasive action and tell a new story. The *construction* of narration or narrative structures is a way of placing signs in a context, so that it becomes possible to interpret signs as determined by intentions and to link intentions and action with certain subjects who may have carried them out. *Interaction and narration* is the subject of Chapter 5.

However, the father can call the emergency service doctor who, with the aid of various implements, can confirm whether there are signs of impending appendicitis, or whether a cup of camomile tea or a laxative tablet will do the trick – or whether one can completely exclude the sign being a signal that refers to physical pain. It may be simply the child's imagination, a narration of suffering, pain and lack that the boy tells with his body and the nocturnal dramatization, with the father as co-actor. The father, and then the boy, can then narrate further. The semiotic competence of humans gives us a greater liberty than animals to construct an environment and to orient ourselves – but it also makes this environment more unstable and open to interpretation.

Signs not only share the context of other signs; but the meaning of the sign, its credibility and validity, rests on a number of often indirect assumptions concerning the actual context between signs. This means that signs are constituted in *texts*. This is the subject of Chapter 6.

It would seem to be a fundamental trait that humans equipped with semiotic abilities are not only able – like the dog and the mosquito – to adapt to nature-given surroundings and convert them into an environment they can survive in. We can to a great extent also modify the given surroundings and, in a number of instances, widen the boundaries of this environment. Not all, of course; there are biological and mental conditions which define our species, parts of the material surroundings we are not able to change. But via an ongoing modification process our environment is changed and becomes historical. Such a historicized dynamic universe is what we call *culture*. To the extent that the cultural process is linked to semiotic processes it is the subject of cultural semiotics as presented in Chapter 7.

What is this book about?

The aim of this book is threefold:

1 to introduce the reader to an understanding of how humans create and exchange meanings through signs;
2 to introduce concepts to do with this process which will aid the analysis of texts from different media and sign systems; and
3 to reveal semiotics as a specific theory and practice in our understanding of human culture.

In accordance with a well-established method in 'structuralism' and semiotics – proceeding through 'differentiation' – it may prove useful both to underline what we set out to do in this book in order to reach our goals and what the readers can *not* find in this book.

We do not claim that semiotics today is a *tabula rasa* where introductions have to start from point zero. There are plenty of books that introduce separately the specific schools of structuralism, of European semiotics, of American semiotics and of post-structuralism, and open specific fields of investigation such as film, literature, architecture, mass communication, computer studies, biology, philosophy, linguistics etc. in a theoretical and analytical perspective, some of them more preoccupied with the limits of semiotics than its potentials. Many of these books date from the 1960s and 1970s and are still valid in their fields. They have continued to foster new discussions up to the present day. This book is one such discussion. Fortunately, their achievements have to a large extent been included in a series of available and important dictionaries and encyclopedias, of which we list the following:

Greimas, Algirdas Julien and Joseph Courtés (1979 and 1985). *Sémiotique. Dictionnaire raisonné de la théorie du langage*. 2 vols. Paris: Larousse. 1st vol. *Semiotics and Language: An Analytical Dictionary*. Bloomington: Indiana University Press, 1982.
Colapietro, Vincent (1993). *Glossary of Semiotics*. New York: Paragon House.
Sebeok, Thomas (gen. ed.) (1994). *Encyclopedic Dictionary of Semiotics* (2nd edn). 3 vols. New York/Berlin: Mouton de Gruyter.
Posner, Roland (gen. ed.) (1997–). *Semiotik/Semiotics. A Handbook on the Sign-Theoretic Foundation of Nature and Culture*. 3 vols (2 have appeared). Berlin: Mouton de Gruyter.
Bouissac, Paul (ed.) (1998). *Encyclopedia of Semiotics*. Oxford: Oxford University Press.
Mey, Jacob (ed.) (1998). *Concise Encyclopedia of Pragmatics*. Oxford: Elsevier.

Nöth, Winfried (2000). *Handbuch der Semiotik* (2nd edn). Stuttgart: Metzler. *Handbook of Semiotics*. Bloomington: Indiana University Press, 1990.

Danesi, Marcel (2000). *Encyclopedic Dictionary of Semiotics, Media and Communications*. Toronto: Toronto University Press.

Cobley, Paul, (ed.) (2001). *Routledge Companion to Semiotics and Linguistics*. London: Routledge.

The present book is situated in an already existing semiotic landscape and, like most introductions in other fields, should be used together with such handbooks and their rich bibliographies.

Therefore, we do not introduce in great detail specific schools or specific fields merely because they exist. Instead this book unfolds a basic argument on semiotics through a limited number of basic concepts shared by most semioticians. We are more concerned with focusing on how to present a semiotic argument using such concepts than presenting all existing varieties of their interpretations and usages. Each chapter is devoted to one such concept and demonstrates the arguments it can be used for, only integrating existing theoretical trends in semiotics to the extent that they, it is hoped, make the argument clear. Therefore, we do not reproduce extensive bibliograhies already published in handbooks and encyclopedias, but offer a select bibliography. The order of presentation of the chapters makes the book itself an unfolding argument on the role of signs in human culture, moving from the most abstract and simple, the code, to the most concrete and complex, the culture. We aim to introduce a way of working with signs.

Although we do not intend to introduce specific schools or domains, as we have stated, our book, unlike most introductions, emphasizes the importance of bridging between European and American semiotics based on the theories of, respectively, Ferdinand de Saussure and Charles Sanders Peirce. And, as in most introductions, we have only been able to use a few analytical examples to enable the readers to generalize them and transfer the argument to other domains they may be working in. Therefore, this book is not only addressed to those who work in language and literature and cultural studies generally, but also to those who work with the understanding of all types of signs in use in human culture.

We have constructed the book so that the chapters gradually widen the semiotic perspective. Even so, each offers rounded presentations of an independent semiotic issue. It is thus possible to read them separately and, with the aid of cross-references, glossary and biographies, to relate the individual chapter to the book as a whole and the wider semiotic context.

An introduction to semiotics at the present time must have as its point of departure a basic argumentative structure and a limited number of basic semiotic questions. We focus on those that have the common denominator *signs in use*, and hope readers will agree with us – in using the book.

2   Code and structure
From difference to meaning

Code and meaning

Structural code and processual code

Let us observe a painter in front of his easel. He chooses different colours from his palette, mixes them, and applies them with repeated brushstrokes to the canvas. After finishing the painting, he places his signature on it. We have here watched a process in which colours and, finally, letters have been selected, combined and distributed – a process in which a given material becomes a complex cultural sign, a work of art.

This process is a rule-bound activity, even though the rules may be ambiguous or used unconsciously. The rules governing the selection and combination of elements are known as *codes*. Because all codes are not semiotically pertinent, a general definition of code is too broad to be directly useful for semiotics. Nevertheless it may serve as our point of departure in approaching the field.

Let us imagine that we have two phenomena which may be separated from one another. If it is possible to establish a rule for the relation between them, the most elementary condition for the existence of a code has been fulfilled, namely that the code and the rule are identical. If the elements are characterized by merely one distinctive property, e.g. a straight line and a curved line, and if the rule determines their size, distance, repeatability, as well as their horizontal and vertical position *vis-à-vis* one another, we can generate most of the letters of the Latin alphabet by *combining* these elements according to the code. This, to return to our painter, was indeed what he did when he signed his painting.

These elements may also be more complex, and be determined by two or more properties. They may, for instance, have form (straight, wavy, open, closed, etc.) as well as colour; or they may be characterized by several colours occurring simultaneously; or by several forms. Such features are not created by the code, since the latter presupposes the former. What the code does create is their *relevance* (also called *pertinence*). This enables us to choose among the various features, so that some of them become relevant and others not. Through the pertinent features the given element acquires a *specific iden-*

tity, and may then be separated from other elements. In some cases this relevant distinctive feature may be colour; in others, it may be form. Although form and colour are commonly present in all cases, it is possible that the qualities of an element's form are irrelevant to its overall identity. This means that the relevance of the chosen features (i.e. the identity of the element) depends upon the context in which the element is placed; and the combinations of different elements which are found there are governed by a code. Moreover, these elements will often have different features which can become relevant in different rule-governed contexts, without needing to be relevant at the same time. The fact that the elements can be coded in more than one way is known as *overcoding*. This is the case with most of the phenomena in our everyday life: we mostly choose our good old winter shoes because they are warm and not thin and cold, or sometimes because they are black and not white; now and then because they are cross-country boots and not trainers; on other occasions we do not choose them, maybe because they are sturdy and inelegant. Our shoes are ostensibly characterized by more properties – or by an absence of certain properties – than are relevant in individual cases. Only few things, if any at all, are exhaustively coded by such binary oppositions as +/−, on/off, yes/no.

If, in the painter's view, the only relevant combination is one of form, he will produce alphabet characters. His signature on a contract is valid, regardless of whether he uses a blue, green, or red pen. If he chooses to make colour the relevant feature, the coding process will certainly not involve writing, but maybe a work of art with blurred forms, like Jackson Pollock's paintings. If both a specific form and a specific colour have been chosen as essential features, the painter may place his signature in the corner, or he may paint a particular detail on the canvas.

When described in these terms, the artist's creative talent appears to be disconnected from the creative process itself, and the creative process appears to be deprived of its artistic value, trivialized, even robotized. First the artist selects the elements to use, whereupon the codes function automatically. This reduces the role of the painter to that of the paintstore clerk operating the paint-mixing machine to produce one particular colour of paint, using the colour chips provided by the manufacturer.

There are two types of codes: *digital* and *analog* (see Wilden 1972: ch. VII). Both types are operative when dealing with colours and/or forms, but their relative dominance may vary. Digital codes are based on the ability to differentiate clearly between the entities which are selected and combined: they follow the *either–or* principle. Primary colours like red, yellow and blue are defined by not being mixtures of one another, but are each unique; they are therefore susceptible to being digitally coded. In the paintstore, for instance, exactly measured quantities of different paint colours are mixed in standard combinations. This procedure enables the satisfied customer to take home paint colour no. 305 and apply it to his/her wall. If the paintstore clerk changes, however minimally, the quantity of one ingredient colour, the resulting colour will no longer be the same. All chromatic variants are the result of a digital code, based upon numerical principles. The Latin alphabet contains digitally coded forms, such as straight and curved lines. For instance, the letter C consists of a curved line, and the letter I consists of a straight line, P of one of each type of line, B of one straight and two curved lines, M of several straight ones, etc.

Colours can also be coded analogically. This process takes place when paint colours are mixed on a palette. In this case, the code does not govern the relation between the colours, but their relation to the object represented in the painting. The colours of this object can be reproduced to be more or less similar to the real-world colours of the object represented. On the canvas, the green colour can be mixed to approach the colour of grass. Here the code is analog: it follows the *more-or-less* principle. Though the letters of a signature are digitally coded *vis-à-vis* each other, thus enabling us to see them separately, a forged Picasso signature is analogically coded in relation to the master's own handwriting.

In the paragraphs above we have discussed the subject of codes in general, semiotic and/or otherwise. We have seen that a *general code is a rule for the selection and combination of relevant properties belonging to elements with predefined properties*. But after the painter finishes his/her painting, having selected and combined colours and forms according to complex and sophisticated combinations of analog and digital codes, and after having signed the painting, s/he has thereby created a new and meaningful object. This painting has a conventional meaning, because it is a particular kind of object, to wit, a work of art. But as an individual work of art, it also has a meaning which is open to interpretation, and can in turn become conventional – e.g. by being taught to others in a school situation – and this conventional meaning can become the commonly recognized interpretation of it. Through this interpretative process, the codes used in this particular work of art may become normforming, which again means that the work of art is part of the canon. When this happens, the codes have created *meaning*, changing the perspective in a semiotic direction. What has happened here and how has it happened?

The basic requirements for operating semiotic codes involve more than the presence of two elements, each with one distinctive feature, and a rule governing their combination. A combination of the elements O and X in a series according to the rule that each element must alternate with the other generates the following cluster of elements: OXOXOXOXOXOX . . . , but without necessarily creating meaning for that combination. In order to create meaning, there must be at least two *sets* or *groups* of elements, the essential features of which have been selected in advance, and combined into a code. One such set can be O and X held together by the alternating code; another set can consist of two persons whose relation is coded in the same way, so that they alternately choose O and X. By interrelating these two internally organized elements together by another code, something new happens: the person who is the first to score three successive elements in a series wins the game. The result of

the combination between the elements of both sets is an independent phenomenon, a tick-tack-toe game (noughts and crosses) in which O and X have
become pieces and the persons have become players. The whole has become
a social activity, which is code-bound and may be repeated. This combination
of structrual codes is illustrated in Figure 2.1 for the game of chess.

For those taking part, the game can receive a strictly context-bound meaning, e.g. by referring to victory and defeat. Independently from the individual
players and the associative meanings they may give to objects and phenomena in their environment, the board game *Monopoly* can thus refer to basic
features of the free-market society that invented it. Social activities like games
and play can further refer to culturally determined and possibly ritualized
differences between adults and children, work and leisure; they can express
moral standards regarding their binding or not-binding nature; or they can
exemplify fundamental socializing operations, stages in the psychological
development of humans.

If we again use colour and form to define a set of elements, they may be
coded according to a fixed order of three elements (red, yellow, green) and
defined as traffic-light elements. Another set of elements is defined by three
properties, which are digitally coded in fixed pairs and are thereby defined as
a set of elements relating to road users: movement (stop/go), source of movement (motorized/non-motorized), and spatial location (road/pavement). If a
dynamic code is established to interconnect both sets of elements, the systematic change between the three colours of the traffic lights will order the road
users to stop or go. In other words: since this code process is a repeatable
social activity, it can become meaningful. A closer examination of the further

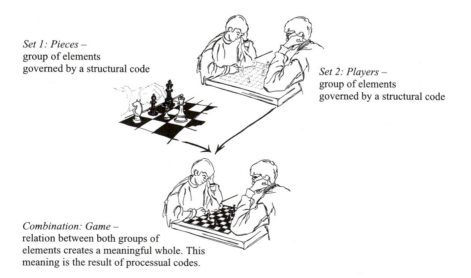

Set 1: Pieces –
group of elements
governed by a structural code

Set 2: Players –
group of elements
governed by a structural code

Combination: Game –
relation between both groups of
elements creates a meaningful whole. This
meaning is the result of processual codes.

Figure 2.1 Structural and processual codes: a game of chess.

conditions and real-life occurrences of this possibility for meaning naturally leads to an examination of the relevance of codes for semiotics.

As argued above, semiotics operates with codes on two different levels, which are simultaneously active. On the first level, we have codes connecting a set of elements into a well-defined but not necessarily closed system – pieces and players, traffic lights and road users. On the next level there is a code connecting at least two such systems. The first are called *structural codes*; the second, *processual codes* (cf. Eco 1984: 164–88). Semiotics is only marginally interested in the build-up of systems according to structural codes, but semiotics commonly takes for granted the existence of collections of elements that have a more or less clear structure, and are capable of creating meaning – possibly new meaning – through the use of processual codes. Processual codes can be viewed as a kind of translation from one structure into a different one. O and X can be translated into human action, and vice versa, thereby becoming a game. A series of three colours can be translated into interaction, thereby controlling the flow of traffic. The processual codes are semiotic codes proper; therefore, they will simply be called 'codes' in what follows.

The task of processual codes consists of establishing a hierarchy of elements, which are chosen from the two pre-established structures. This may mean that, during a game, the elements can change place in the hierarchy. The same is true for the painting process: colour, or form, or certain colours together with certain forms, can graduate from a subordinate role to a highly meaningful position. The hierarchization may be described as follows:

1   some features receive *priority* (e.g. the form of the pieces used in certain games, the players' skill, their rating or, in golf, their handicap, that regulates players' formal access to competitive playing);
2   other features are placed in a *subordinate* position (e.g. in some games, the form of the pieces is of minor importance and a missing piece can be replaced by whatever object the players may decide; another example is the uniform colours of the players' clothing, which can be changed if necessary to avoid confusion – this happens in soccer when both teams are dressed in similar colours);
3   again, other features are *excluded* as irrelevant (e.g. the material from which the pieces are made, the players' mood and eating habits, and so on).

Such a processual code focuses on a particular meaning-domain within a universe full of meaning-potentialities, many of which remain ineffectual in a given situation. The semiotic process never operates with the code in its totality, but with a segment of it. While everything can be coded, not everything that is coded is actually relevant at the same time.

The *linguistic sign* illustrates how a processual code works semiotically. In language, structural codes organize a series of elements, arranging them into an expression structure with clearly identifiable elements. Other, partly iden-

tical, structural codes organize a series of units, arranging them into a semantic structure, or content structure, with certain identifiable content entities. A
phonetic, or letter, aspect is combined with a lexicon, in short: the alphabet
versus *Webster's Dictionary*. The expression level is a closed whole: we only
have a limited set of expression elements (vocals, consonants, written characters) with a limited set of properties (voiced, voiceless, rounded,
unrounded, made up of curved and straight lines, etc.). The lexicon is
open; though there is no exhaustive list of meaning possibilities within a
language, this does not mean that the meaning of language is a chaotic affair.
Though it is possible to compile dictionaries, any attempt to define meaning
units, however thorough, must remain incomplete because there is a steady
stream of new meanings, not to mention the fact that the lexicon is anchored
in the whole cultural encyclopedia (cf. Eco 1984: 46–86).

A linguistic sign is the result of semiotic, processual codes connecting an
expression and a content. In a game of noughts and crosses, each player is
supposed to choose the same element every time, and each element is connected to one particular player. This creates a one-to-one relation between
piece X and player X, and between piece O and player O. The language
situation is different: the combination of letters 'i-c-e' may form a noun
meaning 'frozen water', a verb meaning 'to cover with icing', a word fragment, as in 'slice', or a suffix, as in 'notice'. Likewise, the meaning content of
'female person' can be realized, on the expression level, by many different,
even sometimes unflattering combinations of alphabet characters. Both structures are semiotically connected by a processual code, which excludes a one-
to-one relation and always has a provisional character (Larsen 1993a). This
makes their relation a dynamic process: expression level and content level are
subject to shifts *vis-à-vis* one another, comparable, in geology, to the movements and interrelations of tectonic plates. This implies that meanings may be
changed, and may be translated from one semiotic system into another,
thereby giving a content a new expression. This also implies that different
media of expression have different ways of marking how cultural meanings
are expressed and developed, such as when the so-called verbal culture competes with non-verbal, pictorial culture to express the fundamental meanings
of a particular period (Hess-Lüttich and Posner 1990).

The scope and use of semiotic, processual codes is therefore a complicated
affair. John Fiske (1990: ch. 4) has described its complex nature using five
basic features (which we have slightly modified to allow a better understanding of the problems involved in the use of processual codes in semiotics), thus:

1 The codes presuppose the existence of *two or more already structured sets of
   elements*, whereby the codes establish the rules that enable us to select one
   or more of these elements and combine them into a whole. The rules
   governing the combination of a set of pieces, O and X, with two persons,
   create a game.

2 The codes create a *meaningful whole*, in which the selected elements are placed in a hierarchy. Thus the whole can refer to something other than itself – e.g. a game referring to social experiences, to victory and defeat, to moral, aesthetic, and psychological values.

3 The codes are transmitted by *appropriate media of expression* and channels of communication. There still may be different media operating simultaneously: a game may be played with words as well as with gestures. But each code functions differently in each medium. For this reason, semiotic codes are never purely formal, but must be partly dependent on the presupposed elements and the distinctive material characteristics of the medium of expression.

4 The codes depend upon an *agreement* among their users. If the rules of the game are not followed by all players, there is no game. And a not insignificant number of linguistic and bodily reactions can result. The codes presuppose, but may also contradict, the shared cultural background which serves as their framework.

5 The codes perform an *identifiable social or communicative function*, even if they may raise doubts in our minds: 'Are you fighting for fun or is it serious?' we may ask when things in the children's playroom are heating up.

Let us in what follows exemplify how codes work in practice. When we ask ourselves: 'What is going on here?', this generally means that we are only able to see the codes in the light of some, but not all, of the five above-mentioned items, preventing us from using and understanding the codes. Most often we are able to see that some persons are engaged in some rule-bound activity, but we may not understand which rules. We are usually able to see that some meaning is conveyed, but which meaning may not always be clear, and we can also see that players receive information through various channels of expression, but not exactly from which ones. It is not sufficient to have a general acquaintance with rules, nor to have knowledge of certain codes, nor to trust that semiotic codes depend upon a consensus. We can never be sure that this consensus is known or acknowledged by all, and should always be prepared to modify and adapt the way we use codes.

Streets and codes

A woman is standing on a street corner in a medium-sized American town. She is a foreigner. Like any American city intersection, two streets of the same size cross each other at an angle of 90°, not just there but all around her, since the whole street pattern forms a uniform grid, a network of straight horizontal and right-angled lines. The traffic moves in an orderly fashion, yet there are no traffic lights. The cars approach the intersection from several streets at the same time, in a slow-moving flow. Without stopping long, they intertwine and separate again: not a honk, a scratch, or a curse. The drivers are apparently familiar with the code which regulates the order in which they may cross the intersection. The foreign pedestrian needs to cross the street but, unlike the drivers, does not understand the code. And since she would like to reach the other side of the street in one piece, she must find out first how the system works. The traffic is too heavy for her to wait until all cars stall or no cars are left at the intersection, and there is no pedestrian crossing.

How does the foreigner proceed? She could of course go a bit further down the street. With some luck the traffic may be lighter there, and the semiotic code she is trying to work out less rigorous or even irrelevant elsewhere, so she is let off the hook. But the street pattern at the next block has an identical intersection, so the detour is not of any help. She has also the possibility of challenging the code, of flinging herself on to the street hoping that the drivers' code includes rules about how to handle situations such as a violation of the code, or an encounter with different codes.

The knowledge she is about to acquire about the semiotic codes must include all five points mentioned above. She can learn them in three ways (Fiske 1990: 77):

(a) She can use common traffic *conventions* which derive from supposedly shared experience; e.g. she may act in a way that is familiar to her, assuming that her behaviour will be understood in the foreign environment; that is, she starts with (4) and (5). This method relies on conformity with local practice which she is not sure of, and is for this reason a dangerous hypothesis with no guarantee of success.

(b) She can use direct *information*: she may ask an American to explain the whole system and instruct her how to behave in that system; that is, she may ask a native to translate a meaning content from one medium – traffic conduct – into another – language. If she uses this method, she is relying on (2) and (3).

(c) She can decide to decode herself the *signals* sent by the traffic situation; that is, she can proceed through indexical signs (Larsen 1991b). But since all Americans drive cars, she finds herself alone on the pavement, without being able to receive information about the traffic conventions from anyone. She will have to start with (1) and find out which sets of structured elements are present. So she must try to work them out on her own.

It is not hard to see that one of the structures that is relevant to the situation under investigation is the *static* street grid, which is based on the difference between two elements – the pavement and the road – and the relationship between them. The pavements never cross the roads, and generally are, like the roads, at right angles to each other. Another structure consists of *moving* elements: road users, both motorized and non-motorized. The code we are looking for is that which regulates how motor vehicles should move together, and how pedestrians should stay safe from motor vehicles. Some of the codes involved are easily recognizable as conventions: motorized road users always drive on the right side of the road, while pedestrians can move in both directions on all pavements. Violations of the car-direction rule are penalized: horn-blowing, cursing, and possibly paying a fine. All this allows us to say that the code controlling the movement of vehicles and pedestrians defines the situation as a whole as the phenomenon known as *traffic*; and that it conveys meaning in the form of social organization, use of the road, etc. So much for (1) and (2) on Fiske's list.

But this does not suffice. The features and codes which the pedestrian on the American street has selected do not yet solve her problem of crossing the street safely. Since we are dealing with city traffic, we know that there must at least be some rules, but we still lack proper codes, perhaps both structural codes (the right elements and their relevant distinctive features) and processual codes (the relevant movement codes). Without them, it remains a difficult task to turn the traffic flow into a meaningful hierarchical whole.

We need to find the basic clue to decoding the traffic situation, the code that regulates the shift between stop and go: go car, stop pedestrian; go pedestrian, stop car. We may first look at the structure of static elements. As in many other places, the relevant signals may be part of the material structure of the street. Painted road markings reveal that main direct roads and through-streets grant drivers the right of way against local cross-traffic. However, the American situation often differs, having many uncontrolled intersections with neither painted signals nor traffic lights (cf. Johansen 1993a: ch. 8). The pedestrian happens to be at an uncontrolled intersection. Looking up and down the street, she notices that the next ones are of the same kind. So she will have to look for the relevant signal in the second structure, that of moving elements such as automobiles and pedestrians, who are her fellow road users. If so, it might perhaps help her to wave her arm and thus give a signal – unless, of course, the drivers are only supposed to notice each other. But her waving has no effect. Hence there must be some clue in the cars: their size? the driver's appearance? the licence plate? the speed? We are now checking (3) on Fiske's list, concerning the medium in which the code is expressed.

She really needs to observe the warning to drivers according to *The New Jersey Driver Manual* from 1992, especially the final strongly semiotic advice: 'Watch for uncontrolled intersections where there are no lights or signs. Do not think that a roadway is protected because it is wide, smooth or busy. If there are no traffic signals, there is no traffic control. Avoiding accidents is up to you. Look. Listen. Think' (*Manual* 1992: 69).

Now let us imagine that our pedestrian suddenly gets a bright idea: the drivers probably take into account who arrives first at the intersection. First come, first served: a solid, respected social convention. This idea can be tested in two ways. One can step out on the street in the hope that the cars will stop to let one cross. If one gets hit by a car, or creates chaos in the flow of traffic, this approach has proved to be wrong. Or else one can wait a while and observe the traffic. After having seen about a dozen times that the car which arrives at the intersection first also goes first, one begins to believe that this is indeed what happens. And if one is able to see that the drivers seem to remember the order in which they arrive, and respect this order, even if they have to wait in line before crossing the intersection, the procedure which they follow should be clear. At this time, our pedestrian is convinced that the processual code, 'first come, first served', is operative in American traffic; according to (4) and (5) this code depends upon an agreement among its users and performs an identifiable function. By looking, listening and thinking she has reached the same conclusion as the *Driver Manual*: 'Yield to the other driver if he is already in the intersection' (ibid.: 55).

On seeing that the car in front of her has arrived last, and therefore has to wait the longest time, she safely crosses the street. She did not realize that the pedestrian almost always has priority, a dangerous hypothesis for a trial-and-error test. But she is safe now.

Code and structure

Code and law book

Semiotics has often been identified with 'structuralism'. Structuralism has many faces, but the common denominator with semiotics is that both fields consider the relations connecting things more than the things themselves, whether the elements thus taken together convey meaning or not (Petitot 1986; Larsen 1998b, 2000). Briefly defined, a structure is a network of relations connecting interdependent elements. Within structuralism, such a closed whole is called an object. The definition of a structure implies the identification of the object. By this token, atoms together form a structure: a molecule. Similarly, an ice crystal has a structure, a sentence has a structure, and a city also has a structure. In other words, the notion of structure is synonymous with what has previously been referred to here as a structural code – namely, the rules linking the parts of a closed whole.

The notion of natural language as a structure has enjoyed considerable popularity in the twentieth century. Since semiotics has taken structural linguistics as its model, many scholars have not drawn a clear line between semiotics and structuralism.

We speak of a 'structural code' and not simply of a 'structure'. This is because, within semiotics, the concept of structure cannot stand alone but depends upon other mechanisms, processual codes, in order to convey meaning. Semiotics is not based on the concept of structure but on the concept of the *sign* that results from the cooperative action of various structures. Structure, like code, is a central concept within semiotics, but it is too general to qualify as its cornerstone (Larsen 1992).

Within semiotics, the concept of structure refers not only to various interacting components, which together form a sign. It can also be used to characterize the relationship between signs and the reality to which they refer.

What knowledge do we gain when we conceive signs as structures that refer both to each other and to their environment? We gain an *epistemological* perspective (Derrida 1967). On the other hand, the concept of structure has also given us analytic criteria. How do we proceed when analysing something which can be considered as a structure? (e.g. Greimas 1966). This is a *methodological* perspective.

Raymond Boudon has addressed both these perspectives in his book, *A quoi sert la notion de structure?* (1968). Here the notion of structure is disengaged from its traditional identification with static, closed structures. Through Boudon's argument we can place the concept of structure within the history of the concept of code. Hereby, he fine-tunes and clarifies the association of structure with code, which in the received view is as closed as it was vague. At the same time, his analysis underlines the permanent relationship between code and structure in the history of the concept of code. He makes us see that the lack of precision in the definition of this relation is not only due to the shortcomings of researchers, but is essential to its history. His analysis enables us to understand that today a clear differentiation between code and structure is necessary to give both concepts a well-defined, relevant place within semiotics.

Historically, the word *code*, like the word *book*, refers to the wooden surface upon which the characters were originally written. Code comes from Latin *caudex*, hence *codex*, meaning 'trunk of a tree', 'wood tablet'; book comes from Old English *boc*, meaning 'beech wood'; Greek *byblos*, 'papyrus', is the etymological origin of the Bible, the Book. Since it was, for practical purposes, particularly important to write down laws, *code* or code came to mean the law book as well as its content, the law itself. *Code Napoléon*, the French legal code, still refers today to the legal code introduced by Napoleon in 1804, as well as to the material form, the actual law book, in which it is codified. A code is thus a *content-directed* set of rules which govern the relation between a general body of social norms and concrete facts involving human behaviour. This broad definition also includes the rules of conduct given in an etiquette book, which are not enforceable and fall outside the legal domain.

However, when we refer to a coded text, more often than not we think of the material surface of an object or phenomenon as something that must be read like an enciphered text, which needs to be decoded, deciphered, or interpreted, to discover its underlying meaning. This implies that a code is a regulating mechanism which can be *abstracted* from its material manifestation, such as a book, and from the phenomenon it aims to regulate, such as a form of human conduct. In this way, a code becomes an abstract organizing principle that can be transferred from one phenomenon to another, and is capable of characterizing it without taking its material manifestation into consideration. At this point the code approaches, and is assimilated to, the modern, formal concept of structure.

This semantic slide is equally an epistemological development, a development in the theory of how we 'know', which occurs in tandem with the move away from the old conception of the immanent order of Nature, as illustrated by the medieval metaphor, the Great Book of Nature (Blumenberg 1986). Nature as we perceive it is written like a law book. It possesses an internal order, which is a message from God to humanity, written in a code. The Bible serves as our aid to uncovering and understanding Nature's order. Once one has deciphered the law of Nature, it then serves as a law for one's own life and for human society. This means that the code of Nature operates in two directions: (1) it is the order creating and maintaining the world humans inhabit, and (2) by recognizing and using this agreed code in their own personal and communal lives, humans link it back to the God-given order. For the creation of meaning no distinction needs to be made between structural code and processual code; nor need there be two or more differentiated sets of elements linked by a processual code. In the final analysis, all these phenomena could be considered identical.

This may be exemplified by Abbé Morelly, an Enlightenment writer associated with the production of the French Encyclopedia. In 1755 he wrote a book titled *Code de la Nature*, meaning *Law Book of Nature*. Reading in Nature's 'law book', Abbé Morelly attempts to find the hidden order which he believes to be the very essence of Nature and to act as the code which man uses to deal with it. Subsequently, he tries to formulate this code so that man can apply it to his own moral and social life. He offers, among other things, a master plan to build a city and to organize life in it. Nature's law can be translated into language, moral conduct, or urban planning, but all remain identified by Morelly with the immanent order of Nature.

When Boudon puts forth a notion of structure, belonging to the context of *intentional* definitions, he identifies structure with the immanent order of things. Structure is not an aspect of the thing, but the thing itself. The intention of a phenomenon or object, according to Boudon, is referred to when we inquire about the phenomenon's own inherent purpose, what it means according to its nature. In this early view, the structure found in an object expresses its intentionality, its own nature and purpose, abstracted from the situation in which it is placed.

Before the publication of Abbé Morelly's book there were already some philosophers who questioned this approach. How can we judge an object using language, logic, and more or less fallible perceptions and instruments, and how can we then reach an insight into its inner and true nature? And, further, how can we be sure that there will ever be a complete identity between the object's structure as it appears to us, and the rules generated by this object from its immanent structure? The structure as we perceive it might as well result from the language and other instruments used to analyse and describe it. And in the course of the process of transforming an immanent structure into the object as we perceive it, the structure may undergo radical changes. This is, for example, the case with a map or chart: the geometrical structure which a surveyor applies to an area disregards the earth's curvature and distorts Nature by projecting features from a round body on to a flat surface.

About 150 years before Abbé Morelly's work, a different conception of the book of Nature was advanced by, e.g., Galileo Galilei and, somewhat later, by Isaac Newton. Instead of representing it like a message written in a meaningful language, they put forth the view that the book of Nature was written in geometrical and other mathematical sign-systems and was ruled by the mechanical rules of Nature. These rules can be abstracted not only from Nature but also from meaning, thereby becoming semantically empty formulas used to describe gravity, causality and other natural phenomena. When Galilei claimed that Nature's book was written in geometrical language (Galilei 1953: 121), he thereby stated that this language had been constructed by us, and that we had done this to understand the workings of Nature. For the linguist Viggo Brøndal language is a geometrical grid with which we cover the world, enabling us to orient ourselves in it (Brøndal 1948: 35). Geometry competes here with the old metaphor of Nature's book.

Boudon's own concept of structure, which is connected to the geometrical metaphor of the order of Nature, is placed in what he calls a context of *effective* definitions. The basic assumption which serves as his point of departure is looser than was the case in the context of intentional definitions. We simply assume that there are phenomena which show traits that invite systematization in different ways, although no specific system is yet defined. Boudon calls such phenomena *system-objects*. Their *structure* is a construction we make based on a selection of the traits which can be systematized. Thus the structure defines the object through a specification of the systematic possibilities of the system-object, the structure being only one of several possible specifications, none of which provides the final truth about an object. Instead, they give it an identity which enables it to function in a specific context and on specific explicit conditions. This is why Boudon uses the expression 'context of effective definitions'.

It is relevant to distinguish, on the one hand, between the construction process specifying the object (processual codes) and, on the other, their building blocks (elements organized by a structural code into system-objects with an as yet unspecified order). This opens the way for structural codes and processual codes to play an active and independent role in the creation of meaningful objects.

Types of structure

To return to our example of the pedestrian standing on an American street corner, she felt no need to identify the essential structure of American traffic rules, nor, for that matter, of the American way of life. She wanted to find out the structure of the traffic flow, so that she might safely cross the street. Instead, the woman might have structured the systematizable features of the traffic as a system-object by studying the relationship between the number of male and female drivers, or the relationship between cyclists, pedestrians and automobile drivers, and take the result as a basis for cultural studies comparing gender role patterns and transportation habits. It is equally possible to make a traffic count and build a structure upon it. Whether one or several of these alternative structures that defines the object will be accurate or not, and to what degree, will, however, depend upon the properties of the object(s) studied and the context in which the object(s) must function. The concept of structure in a context of effective definitions is predominant in semiotics.

Within the context of intentional definitions there is only one structure: the object's own structure, which is merely repeated in different forms before referring again to itself. In a context of effective definitions, Boudon distinguishes between four different *system-objects*, each of which build upon structural codes allowing for construction of different *structures* (see Table 2.1).

1   Some system-objects are built of interrelated elements with a finite number of distinctive features. The three-coloured traffic lights will serve as one example of this; another illustration is the marriage system in some Native American tribes in South America, which is determined by kinship relations. Here we have a finite number of roles (mother, brother, father, sister, uncle, etc.) which together form a system in which the interrelations decide which marriage is allowed and which not. Both the structures constructed on the basis of possible marriages, and those based upon possible light signals for drivers and pedestrians, can be tested directly or empirically in social reality.

2   There are also system-objects built of elements that are defined by an infinite number of distinctive features, which are only delimited for particular purposes. This happens, e.g., when the results of an opinion poll or a questionnaire about consumer behaviour are used to structure the population statistically. Such structures can also be confirmed or invalidated empirically.

3   The case of the traditional literary genres – epic, lyric, drama, with their various respective subdivisions, such as the novel and the comedy – is significantly different from (1) and (2). Here we have a system-object with a finite number of distinctive features, which are formulated within a particular literary theory. While different theories will use different criteria to focus on different features, no theory can deal exhaustively with the full body of literature. This is why there is an ongoing debate, and indeed controversy, about the validity of the principles of literary

Table 2.1 Types of system-objects and structures

	Finite definition	*Infinite definition*
Direct test	1. Traffic lights or marriage system	2. Opinion poll
Indirect test	3. Literary genres	4. Psychological structure

classification: the failure of a given structure does not entirely depend on its lack of capacity to account for certain literary works, but also on the degree of coherence of the argumentation given by the literary theory. This means, for instance, that if two literary scholars use the same body of novels to exemplify and support the existence of the novelistic genre, they need not necessarily refer to the same concept of literary genre. In this case, the truth-value cannot be decided empirically (cf. Boudon 1968: 176f.) and the validity of each theory is determined by its own internal coherence, which in turn determines which empirical perspective the scholars adopt. Literary genres as system-object allow for structure that must be tested indirectly, non-empirically.

4   Finally, the fourth type of system-object must be mentioned here. This type is defined by an infinite number of distinctive features and delimited according to particular circumstances. It may be exemplified by the treatment, within psychoanalysis, of a patient's network of associations as they emerge in the course of the therapeutic analysis. The structure of such a network can only be tested indirectly, and its truth-value can never be confirmed to be 'true', only 'not false' or 'not yet true or false'.

The idealized concept of structure advanced by classical structuralism and structural linguistics only covers type (1): a closed system of interrelated elements. Meanwhile, Boudon has demonstrated that type (1) does not occupy a privileged position within the context of effective definitions; it is only one of several possibilities. However, by placing the concept of structure put forth by semiotics – that is, the collaborative union of structural codes and processual codes – within this context, it becomes clear that the structural code is not necessarily a closed system; it is a perceptual framework composed of elements with a meaning-creating potential, and no more.

The closed structure has so far been *methodologically* predominant, both within semiotics and within the long list of disciplines which have turned to linguistics for their model. One semiotic system – natural language – is thereby taken as model, which makes other semiotic systems – such as film, theatre, pictures, fashion, food, sports events and architecture – linguistic systems, or linguistic *analogies*. To use this procedural method, two analytic steps must be taken:

- first, the phenomenon must be divided into an expression aspect and a content aspect. For example, a building is the expression – through the architectonic elements used in its construction – of a number of functions, while the content, or meaning, of the building consists of its spatio-functional possibilities;
- subsequently, a classification must be made of elements on both sides, in such a way that they form opposite elementary structures. Within architecture, the expression aspect is based on the relationship between openness and closedness, big openings and small openings, height and depth,

light and dark, and so on; and the content aspect is based upon the relationships inherent in certain functions. These may be symbolic functions, such as power; they may be social functions, such as family life; or they may also be psychological functions, such as intimacy.

This methodological basis has been widely used to develop a semiotics of architecture, a literary semiotics, a visual semiotics, a semiotics of culture, of cinema, of the theatrical arts, a psychosemiotics, a biosemiotics, etc.

It must be underscored that semiotics addresses not just one but all four types of system-objects as well as the structural code they build upon. If we take as our object of study a theatre performance, we find it to be a highly complex phenomenon consisting of many different system-objects: light, sound, movement, gestures, dialogue, props, costumes, and so forth. All such elements cannot be understood as a meaningful structural whole on the basis of a verbal, linguistic model alone and of the methodological analogies produced by this model (Johansen and Larsen 1990; Helbo *et al.* 1991). For this reason it is important that linguistics and its closed conception of structure be used, but only as one of a number of sources of inspiration.

This also implies that general semiotics needs to modify the principle applied by structural linguistics, that the sign has a predominantly conventional, or arbitrary, relation to the reality it refers to during the semiotic process. It is of course undeniable that the meaning of the series of sounds, or the series of letters, 'h-o-u-s-e', is only 'house', because there must be agreement in order for verbal communication to be successful, not because houses possess certain properties. And though a child's drawing of a house shows features which are more characteristic of the way children draw than they are characteristic of houses, there are bound to be some common features. General semiotics must operate with more types of signs than just those provided by linguistics.

The child's drawing shows that the semiotic view of the relation between structure and reality should steer a middle course between the various classical epistemologies, or theories of knowledge, which are all radically dichotomous. This we have illustrated by the different ideas of Nature's book as developed by Abbé Morelly and Galilei. Semiotics is not, as suggested by Galilei's reading of Nature's book, a purely *nominalistic* field of research; that is, semiotics does not adhere to the idea of structure as an arbitrary order we impose upon the world from the outside, and which is valid as long as we agree upon it, regardless of how the world actually behaves. Neither can semiotics be exclusively identified with the kind of *realism* defended by Abbé Morelly; that is, supporting the idea that the identity of an object's structure repeats, and is a direct reflection of, the identity of the object itself.

In addition to the above it must, however, be stated here that nor is a purely *extensional* view on the object congenial to semiotics. From a semiotic viewpoint, an object's structure is not identified solely by stating it to be a member of a particular class – that is, by establishing the so-called extension of its structure. This was what Galilei and Newton recognized: that Nature belongs to the kind of things which obey mechanical laws, and that all things which fail to obey such laws are either supernatural or unnatural. If we recognized a butterfly by a structured set of properties, we would, in an extensional perspective, still not know anything about what a butterfly was: we would only know that it belonged to the kind of things with properties which were organized by the same structural code. But having said this, it must be emphasized that neither does semiotics analyse its object of study entirely from an *intensional* viewpoint. Following Abbé Morelly's intentional approach, this would mean that the object in itself is shown by its supposed relevant features constituting its essence: in other words, by building a city in accordance with Morelly's law book, his natural code, it would naturally become a natural city.

Semiotics adopts a predominantly realistic *and* intensional position. Semiotics acknowledges that semiotic systems have a conventional character, and that they can be used to make objective classifications of the elements populating our reality. Yet semiotics emphasizes and concentrates on the fact that the relevant features found in system-objects are real; that is, that their existence in reality is independent of the semiotic system used to organize and structure them. Semiotics stresses that these features must be relevant because they are instrumental in making the object meaningful, in giving it a meaning that determines a description of what it is without exhausting the range of possible descriptions. Semiotic systems are themselves part of the world they refer to, and semiotic codes are equally an integral part of the world they are supposed to organize. Thus the purpose of a semiotically relevant distinction between types of code and types of structure can only be to enable us to account for how codes and structures are integrated into reality.

3 Signs
From tracks to words

Zadig and the doctrine of signs

In Voltaire's amusing tale *Zadig or Destiny* (1747), the queen's eunuchs are in despair after discovering that her lapdog has disappeared. They ask Zadig to help them find it:

> 'Young man,' cried the Chief Eunuch, 'you haven't seen the queen's dog, have you?' – 'It's not a dog,' answered Zadig modestly, 'it's a bitch.' – 'That's so,' said the Chief Eunuch. – 'It's a very small spaniel,' added Zadig, 'which has had puppies recently; her left forefoot is lame, and she has very long ears.' – 'You haven't seen her then?' said the Eunuch, quite out of breath. – 'Oh, no!' answered Zadig. 'I have not seen the animal, and I never knew the queen had a bitch.'
>
> (Voltaire 1923: 9)

Likewise, Zadig is able to describe the king's horse, who has disappeared from the stables and whom he also claims never to have seen. Believing him to be a liar and a thief, the court sentences Zadig to be flogged and banished from the kingdom. However, the royal pet is soon found, and after some further troubles, Zadig finally seizes the chance to explain how he was able to describe the dog so accurately without ever having seen it:

> I saw an animal's tracks on the sand and I judged without difficulty they were the tracks of a small dog. The long shallow furrows printed on the little ridges of sand between the tracks of the paws informed me that the animal was a bitch with pendant dugs, who hence had had puppies recently. Other tracks in a different direction, which seemed all the time to have scraped the surface of the sand beside the fore-paws, gave me the idea that the bitch had very long ears; and as I remarked that the sand was always less hollowed by one paw than by the three others, I concluded that our august queen's bitch was somewhat lame, if I dare say so.
>
> (Voltaire 1923: 10)

Not surprisingly, the court is awestruck by Zadig's powers of observation. Voltaire here presents semiotic analysis in one of its earliest forms: the use of signs in order to track an animal. This process is an integral part of the hunt, which forms the foundation of most primitive tribal societies (a more detailed analysis of hunting as a semiotic process has been made by Ginsburg, who also mentions *Zadig*, in Eco and Sebeok 1983: 81–118; see also Johansen 1999).

Voltaire's story illustrates two essential – perhaps the most essential – properties of a sign. According to the American semiotician Charles Sanders Peirce, a sign is 'something by knowing which we know something more' (8.332).[1] We learn something more by comprehending a sign, because it stands for something else. The ancient Scholastics defined a sign as *aliquid stat pro aliquo* (something stands for something else); and this representative function appears to be the only feature all signs have in common. Signs allow us to *infer something* that is not evident, something hidden or absent, based on the presumption offered by the sign. The ability to use a sign in order to infer and form hypotheses about something else, namely what the sign represents, is the second characteristic of the sign. Zadig's explanation of how he inferred the dog's physical properties is an amusing example of a detective's reconstruction of an unknown and absent object, based on the traces it has left.

Signs are phenomena that represent other phenomena. Anything can function as a sign, since signs do not have predetermined, prototypical properties like, say, a bird or a sewing machine. Instead, the properties of a sign are defined in terms of their relation to what is represented (see Johansen 1993b). For instance, the slant of the trees is a sign of the dominant wind direction, a red nose is assumed to be a sign of drunkenness, and old photographs are interpreted as images of deceased relatives. Tourists wandering around an unknown metropolis trust a city map to be an accurate representation of the streets and their relation to one another; they rely on it to find their way. An actor's expression of sorrow or joy can be interpreted in either of two ways: as a fictitious person's reaction to actions and emotional expressions, or as the actor's convincing (or, for that matter, unconvincing) imitation of emotions. We also encounter signs that we fail to comprehend, such as someone else's strange behaviour or emotional expressions; gestures used in foreign cultures; or long and cryptic words that make us reach for a dictionary. Upon finding, inserted into a hotel room Bible, a scriptural quote in 25 different languages, at least seven or eight of those will appear to us as simple scribbles on paper, while at least eleven other versions will be equally incomprehensible to us, even though they consist of linguistic signs from our own alphabet.

---

1 Reference is here made to C.S. Peirce (1931–58), *Collected Papers* Vols I–VIII (C. Hartshorne, P. Weiss, and A. Burks, eds), Cambridge, MA: Harvard University Press. References to the *Collected Papers* will be given in the text by volume and paragraph number; for example, 8.332 indicates Vol. VIII, paragraph 332. References to other writings of Peirce will be given as they occur.

Thus we encounter phenomena that we assume to be signs, even when we are unable to determine their representative function. We fail (to our benefit, it should be said) to interpret a large number of phenomena in our environment as signs. We do not attempt to establish their representative function or meaning, since they are familiar objects or events that we relate to on an everyday basis, and therefore escape our notice. In other words, even though anything can function as a sign, we do not need to grasp every phenomenon's semiotic potential. The semiotic potential of signs is of interest to us only when we, for instance, read a newspaper, or study a phenomenon in order to answer relevant questions about it, e.g. when we interpret someone's behaviour and speech as a sign of his or her feelings toward us, or when a detective investigates a crime scene for tracks of the perpetrator. In other words, signs are both an inconspicuous part of our everyday existence, such as the linguistic signs we use in common idle gossip, and they are things we detect and investigate, such as is the task of the hunter, physician, detective and scholar.

What does the sign represent?

In Voltaire's *Zadig* and the other examples mentioned above, the sign represents (i.e. *stands for* or *refers to*) an object, event, action, repeated process, state of affairs, an emotional situation, and so on. These different kinds of referents (i.e. things that are referred to) can be real or imaginary. For instance, the queen's bitch and Zadig's ingenuity are both fictitious, products of Voltaire's imagination. What they have in common is that they are objects, processes, or states that exist or occur in a physical, historical, or fictitious universe. In other words, signs can represent relationships in the real world as well as in an imagined universe. Although this is both correct and important, it nevertheless remains insufficient, because the element still lacking here is what Peirce calls the 'interpretant'. This semiotic component can be extrapolated from Zadig's reasoning for his success in describing the queen's dog. For example, he declares that, 'The long shallow furrows printed on the little ridges of sand between the tracks of the paws informed me that the animal was a bitch with pendant dugs, who hence had had puppies recently.' Zadig here interprets and translates some characteristic marks in the sand and the relationship between them (the furrows between the paw imprints). Thus the phenomenon (the furrows in the sand) only becomes a sign when it allows for interpretation (the furrows as tracks of the bitch's dugs). This means that signs not only imply a representative or referential relation to objects, states, and processes in a universe, but also point to a possible meaning (see Johansen 1989).

To use Peirce's terminology, we can say that the SIGN, in the broad sense, consists of three interconnected elements: (1) the *sign* in the narrow sense, also referred to as the *representamen*, i.e. that which represents something else; (2) the *object*, i.e. that which the sign stands for, that which is

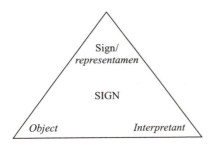

Figure 3.1 Relationship between the three elements of the sign.

represented by it; and finally (3) the (possible or potential) *meaning* the sign allows for, which may materialize as its translation into a new *sign*. Peirce refers to this as the *interpretant*. In Zadig's case, the furrows in the sand are the sign (*representamen*); the queen's bitch is the represented *object*; and Zadig's interpretation and translation of the furrows' meaning (potential) is the *interpretant*. Figure 3.1 illustrates the relationship between the sign's three elements.

In his best-known definition of a sign, Peirce offers the following explanation of this triadic relationship:

> A sign, or representamen, is something which stands to somebody for something in some respect or capacity. It addresses somebody, that is, creates in the mind of that person an equivalent sign, or perhaps a more developed sign. That sign which it creates I call the *interpretant* of the first sign. The sign stands for something, its object. Its stands for that object, not in all respects, but in reference to a sort of idea, which I have sometimes called the ground of the representamen.
>
> (2.228)

Even though Peirce reserves only a minor role for the notion of *ground* in semiotics, it should be noted that the sign represents specific properties of the object. The furrows in the sand enable Zadig to infer that they were made by a female dog, that she recently gave birth to puppies, that she limps on one leg, and that she has long ears. However, the marks in the sand give him no clues to, say, the dog's colour or the sharpness of its teeth. It is, in fact, impossible to determine how many properties of the animal the sign does *not* provide information about. Therefore, Peirce distinguishes between two objects:

1 The *immediate object*, the object as it is directly represented in and by the sign (in this case, Zadig's reconstruction of the dog based on the tracks it has left);
2 The *dynamical object*, the object that lies outside the actual sign relation (in this case, the lost dog) and may be represented by an infinite number of different signs.

A portrait photograph represents a picture of a person at a certain point in time, seen from a certain distance and angle, in a certain light, and photographed with a certain camera focused in a certain way, with a certain film, developed and processed a certain way. These are all properties that determine the immediate object. On the other hand, the person represented in the photograph, its dynamical object, can be the source of an indeterminate number of representations, i.e. signs that each contain or refer to an immediate object, including our visual and mental representation of the person when we see him or her *in persona*.

Semiotic competence

Even though we most often speak of signs when confronted with substitutes for the dynamical object or effects of the dynamical object (like the photograph, which can be both a substitute and an effect), what we perceive are signs created on the basis of processes in our own sensory and nervous systems. In fact, we can only perceive immediate objects through signs, and we can only see the dynamical object in the shape of a concrete immediate object that is mediated by our mental processes, and by those signs that appear to our consciousness. In this sense, our relation to the world around us and to our own physical body is always mediated by signs. This becomes particularly obvious in those cases where neurophysiological disorders, congenital disabilities or illnesses thwart the normal construction of signs. Blind people, for instance, are unable to form visual representations of external objects, while colour-blind individuals lack the ability to distinguish certain characteristics of the visual image (colour vision).

The sensory input from the external world, it should also be noted here, is processed differently by each animal species – including humans – because each species' neurophysiological functions are unique. Even though all species inhabit and interact within the same physical universe, each occupies its own specific environment or what has been termed as *Umwelt* (we shall return to this issue below; see p. 153). In addition, animal species (not including humans) are, to a large extent, genetically programmed to react to certain signs in certain ways.

Let us briefly illustrate this with ethologist Niko Tinbergen's fascinating accounts of the mating behaviour of the three-spined stickleback (Tinbergen 1951). Here we have to limit ourselves to the central role that the male fish's red belly plays in the mating process. First of all, both male and female sticklebacks display a hereditary reaction to this colour (Tinbergen showed this by isolating individuals from as early as the oval stage). Second, the reaction to the male's red hue is gender-specific: males display an aggressive reaction to the colour while females, if willing to mate, respond by following the male to the nest. Third, the reaction of both sexes is specifically focused on the red colour. Well aware of this, Tinbergen used a number of dummies of the red-coloured male in his celebrated experiment (see Figure 3.2):

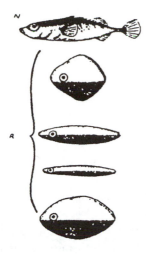

Figure 3.2 Tinbergen's stickleback models.
Source: Tinbergen (1951).

Models of males release the same response, provided they are red under-
neath. A bright blue eye and a light bluish back add a little to the
model's effectiveness, but shape and size do not matter within very
wide limits. A cigar-shaped model with just an eye and a red underside
incites a much more intensive attack than a perfectly shaped model or
even a freshly killed Stickleback which is not red . . . . Size has so little
influence that all males which I observed even 'attacked' the red mail
vans passing about a hundred yards away; that is to say they raised their
dorsal spines and made frantic attempts to reach them, which of course
was prevented by the glass wall of the aquarium. When a van passed the
laboratory, where a row of twenty aquaria were situated along the large
windows, all males dashed towards the window side of their tanks and
followed the van from one corner of their tank to the other.

(Tinbergen 1951: 66–7)

Tinbergen's description of the experiment is relevant to semiotics for several
reasons. One is, of course, that his observations demonstrate the existence of
semiotic processes in nature, where they play a crucial and integrated role,
even in something as fundamental as the reproductive cycle. The male's red
underside has a potential meaning, or *immediate interpretant*, which is male
sexuality. Among other members of the species it elicits a genetically determined and gender-specific behavioural pattern, or *dynamic interpretant*. Among
sexually mature males, the red colour displayed in the mating season (off-
season, the belly fades to a brownish colour) can be understood as a meto-
nymical sign (i.e. based on contiguity), or more precisely as a synecdoche (a
part signifying the whole) for species-specific male sexuality, as it is part of the
whole (*pars pro toto*) of male sexuality. Among sticklebacks, the reaction to the

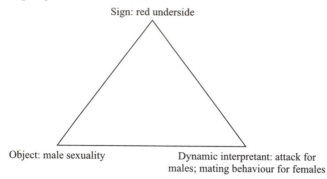

Figure 3.3 Dynamic sign-process incorporating three sign-elements.

red colour from the females and from the other males is a hereditary interpretative mechanism that ensures that the message is transmitted. All this
forms a complete, dynamic *sign-process* or *meaning-process* incorporating all
three sign-elements (see Figure 3.3).

Tinbergen, experimenting with a variety of dummies, also found the red
colour to be the specific factor that triggers the behaviour. Both the other
males and the females (some of whom even agreed to mate) are deceived by
the decoys. The dummies' red 'belly' is of course not metonymically *connected*
to male sexuality, but is instead *similar* to the males' most prominent sexual
characteristic. A large number of other ethological observations and experiments have confirmed that hereditary behaviour, within the relevant context,
is triggered by the presence of specific characteristics, while the absence of
such features slows the behavioural pattern, or blocks it entirely. In other
words, Tinbergen found semiotic regularity; if the males and females decided
to stop responding to the triggering force of the sign, the species would
quickly run itself into extinction (see also Johansen 1993a: 124–44).

The genetically programmed behaviour of humans is negligible in comparison to other species. Instead, our programming capacity, that is to say our
learning capacity, is greatly developed. This difference between humans and
other species can be seen as a difference in *semiotic competence*, which can be
understood as:

1 the ability to *perceive* phenomena in our environment as signs, i.e. to
    understand the connection between present, (partially) hidden, and
    entirely absent phenomena (e.g. the slant of the trees as a sign of the
    dominant wind direction, or the male stickleback's belly as a sign of his
    sexual function);
2 the ability to *produce* and transmit signs, either subconsciously and geneti-
    cally triggered; or as a result of a learning process, consciously and crea-
    tively;
3 the ability to *store* information and form interpretative habits on the basis
    of either genetic programming or memory and learning processes.

Our unique semiotic competence has the following features:

1 It is not limited by our sensory-motor apparatus. On the contrary, we produce instruments of ever-greater precision, and exploit ever-more sources of energy. And since we can be said to produce our own perceptual and motor capacity, we cannot set a limit for which impulses we are able to translate into informative signs (e.g. the electron microscope and intricate astronomical instruments).

2 Further, we not only produce signs (like other animals), but invent and develop a multitude of sign-systems, from the development of speech and language (about which little is known) to an infinite number of semiotics serving specific cognitive and expressive purposes. We also produce unique signs, primarily works of art (verbal and non-verbal art).

3 Just as we extend our own sensory-motor apparatus with instruments in order to provide our senses with appendages enabling us to receive normally inaccessible impulses from the outside world and to translate them into signs, we also extend our own memory. As the saying goes, *Verba volent, scripta manent* (the spoken disappears, the written lasts). One way to describe the development of the human race is by recording our ability to retain and pass on larger and larger amounts of signs, from early oral cultures, which after all could only pass on a limited amount of information, to today's capacity for storing seemingly infinite amounts of information, also known as *exteriorization* of memory.

Such an exteriorization is based on three presumptions: it requires the development of (1) representative systems (semiotics) that – unlike speech, gestures, etc. – are independent of the particular situation in which they occur and can be inscribed on a 'permanent' material (stone, leather, paper, celluloid, mixtures of metals, etc.). It is also requires the development of (2) production and reproduction techniques that ensure the reliable and preferably rapid recording and distribution of signs (it is a quantum leap from the Sumerian and Egyptian tablets of *c.* 3000 BC to today's computerized, paperless word processing). And it requires (3) the creation of conventions that ensure more or less congruent interpretations of the transmitted signs. One of the most fundamental elements of our semiotic competence, *speech* (dating back approximately 200,000 to 400,000 years) has been followed by *writing* and hence reading (no more than five millennia ago). Before going on to examine the different kinds of sign systems, we will account for how signs are able to represent anything at all.

How does the sign represent something?

Earlier in this chapter, we discussed Peirce's definition of a sign as a triadic relation between sign, object and interpretant. The question remains, what binds a sign and its object together and allows us to interpret the sign as referring to that particular object, and not to any other object? In other words, what makes meaning and interpretation possible? Why do we interpret the trees' slant as a sign of the dominant wind direction; an actress's scream as a sign of fright; and a green traffic light as a signal to drive? The conditions for representation and meaning have been thoroughly investigated by Peirce, who introduced the important distinction between *iconic, indexical* and *symbolic* signs, which we will now present. However, we shall change the order in which they will be discussed, and start with indexical signs before moving on to iconic signs (for a more detailed account of Peirce's classification, see Johansen 1988b and 1993a: 90–144).

The indexical sign – reagents versus designations

Since the wind affects the trees by bending them in the same direction, the slant of the trees can function as a sign of the dominant wind direction. In this causal relationship, the dynamical object influences the sign; and without the bending force of the wind, functioning as the dynamical object, the trees would not function as a sign. Peirce refers to such an indexical sign, in which there is a cause–effect relation between dynamical object and sign, where the latter reacts to the former, as a *reagent*. In our example, the immediate object is the 'wind as represented by the trees', while the dynamical object is the 'wind as bending force'. One distinction between the immediate and dynamical object is that the immediate object only reveals a limited amount of information about the dynamical object: the trees' slant enables us to determine the dominant wind direction, but will not provide us with any clues to the wind's normal force, seasonal differences in wind force, and so on. This illustrates that the immediate object is an aspect of the dynamical object.

Two key types of reagents are *tracks* and *symptoms*. Examples of tracks include the paw imprints of a hunted animal, or the imprints that Zadig uses to construct his description of the queen's lapdog. There exists, of course, a physical relationship between the tracks and the animal, between cause and effect. And the information that the tracks provide is, of course, dependent on the experience and knowledge of the interpreter. The relationship between tracks and animal exists regardless of our ability to identify the animal based on the tracks; most people have a hard time identifying any animal from its tracks, but the relationship exists none the less. And this relationship, it should be noted, is specific, namely between an animal and the tracks it has left. While Voltaire may have gone overboard when he had Zadig so cleverly support almost any conclusion about the queen's dog, an experienced hunter can extract a surprisingly large amount of information from tracks – the animal's species, age, gender, speed of movement, and so on.

In a further sense, any marks left by an individual's reaction to the surrounding world can be regarded as tracks. Not just the animal's paw prints, but also broken twigs and tree branches, tufts of hair or feathers, smell, urine and droppings may be considered tracks. All animals, including humans, leave tracks constantly. Like the fictional sleuth Sherlock Holmes, Voltaire's Zadig possesses an incredibly well-developed sense of alertness and eye for detail, noticing what others overlook. And like Sherlock Holmes, Zadig has the ability to formulate hypotheses about connections by reasoning 'backwards', using the dog's tracks as his premise. Observing the furrows between the paw imprints in the sand, he reasons as follows:

0   there are furrows between the paw imprints;
1   a dog does not normally leave tracks between paw imprints;
2   *if* the dog's teats hang so low that they leave grooves in the surface of the sand,
3   *then* it is reasonable to assume that the grooves were produced by the dog's teats.

This is known as a hypothetical (or abductive) syllogism, which can be described as:

If **q** and **p**		If **q** then **p**
q	or	non-**q**
p		non-**p**

It should be noted, however, that there is no guarantee that an 'if–then' hypothesis is true. In fact, the grooves could have been produced any number of other ways. For instance, they could have been caused by two leather flaps on the dog's collar. Zadig may have been, in other words, just plain lucky.

While *tracks* are left by the object and can lead back to it, *symptoms* most often occur at the same time as the object, and form a part of it. In this sense, the red-coloured belly is a symptom of, and is part of, the male stickleback's sexuality. When we speak of symptoms, we usually think of medical disorders. In fact, symptomatology (the study of symptoms) is still referred to from time to time as *semiotics*, the study of signs (of diseases). In ancient times, semiotics was considered a medical discipline; the writings of the Greek physicians Hippocrates (*c*. 460–377 BC) and Galen (*c*. AD 131–200) contain the earliest systematic representations of diagnoses based on signs. Some symptoms have proven invaluable, enabling physicians to make the correct diagnosis and prescribe the proper treatment: *if* the patient has red spots of a particular appearance, *then* the patient has a case of measles.

As a rule, however, both subjective symptoms (e.g. a patient who complains that 'my right arm aches') and intersubjective symptoms (e.g. a cardiogram) are ambiguous, and therefore insufficient to support a diagnosis, i.e. a sure connection to one given object. Symptoms, though, can appear in characteristic combinations known as *syndromes* that can be interpreted as a complex sign suggesting the presence of a certain illness. Such syndromes are a set of *indices*, a collection of symptoms that in all likelihood all refer to the same object.

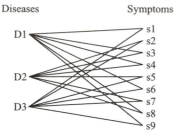

Figure 3.4 Connection of symptoms to diseases.

Until now, we have discussed reagents as having a direct physical relationship to the object. There are, of course, also symptoms of emotional or psychological conditions (i.e. mental disorders). Some elementary expressions of emotions seem to be natural to the human species, e.g. the facial expressions related to joy, fear, anger and pain that spontaneously accompany such emotions unless we make a concerted effort to suppress them. Just as some physical symptoms are connected to certain physical disorders, some behavioural patterns are characteristic of certain psychological illnesses, like persecution complex among paranoiacs, compulsive–obsessive behaviour among neurotics, and psychogenic paralysis and lack of emotions among hysterics. But such psychological symptoms are equally ambiguous, and therefore unreliable, as physical symptoms. To complicate matters, many symptoms may have either physical or psychological causes. Furthermore, there is a grey area between what is physical and what is psychological, and the interaction between these two domains remains largely unexplored territory to medical science.

To illustrate this point, let us imagine that a patient displays nine symptoms that are connected to three different diseases, as in Figure 3.4. In this greatly simplified construction, the relationship between the diseases and symptoms can be described as in Table 3.1. The way this example is constructed, each sign by itself remains ambiguous, since it can be a symptom of two different diseases. In fact, even three signs do not ensure a correct diagnosis. For instance, both diseases D1 and D2 are characterized by symptoms s3, s4, and s8, while diseases D2 and D3 are signalled by symptoms s2, s5, and s7. None the less, each disease has several unique combinations of symptoms. This is equally true for tracks: both the hunter and the detective are often confronted with ambiguous signs that can be interpreted

Table 3.1 Relationship of diseases and symptoms

Diseases	*Combinations of symptoms*								
D1	s1		s3	s4		s6		s8	s9
D2		s2	s3	s4	s5		s7	s8	
D3	s1	s2			s5	s6	s7		s9

in several different ways. In the classic 'whodunnit' story, the plot builds on fundamentally ambiguous signs, in which the appearance of each new clue moves the suspicion from one character to the next, until the final piece of the puzzle is laid and the amount of clues and their interrelationships single out the perpetrator. The determination of the object by the sign, their cause–effect relation, led Peirce to regard reagents as a type of sign that can be used to decide whether a causal relationship exists or not. For those who are able to interpret them, the signs reveal some information about reality. More complex sign-connections that are motivated and/or linguistically mediated, e.g. when we respond to a threat with expressions of fear or anger, or to a break-up of a relationship with expressions of despair, can also be said to have a reactive aspect. Here, however, we are dealing with reasons for behaviour.

The second major group of indexical signs are *designations*, signs that signify by pointing to something. Examples of these signs include demonstrative pronouns, proper nouns, and letters that identify geometrical points or planes. The word *index* is derived from Latin, where its meanings include *index finger*, as well as *informant* or *spy*. Like an index finger, designations point us to an object, drawing our attention to it, as if urging us to '*take a look at that*'.

Designations localize and identify the object in time and space within a given universe, and in relationship to a given system, such as a calendar or the longitudinal/latitudinal grid. *Odense*, for instance, designates a city in Denmark that is located 55 degrees 23 minutes north and 10 degrees 23 minutes east. 'Charles Sanders Peirce was born on 10 September 1839 and died on 19 April 1914' is an accurate description of Peirce's life span, but only according to the Gregorian calendar – not to the Jewish calendar, nor to the Muslim calendar or to the calendar adopted in France in 1793, in which Year 1 began on 22 September 1792, the birth date of the Republic. Nevertheless, Peirce's statistics can be easily translated from the Gregorian calendar into an alternative system of time-keeping.

The above-mentioned indexical systems are intersubjective and conventional, though this does not necessarily hold true in all cases. In language, for instance, *deictic systems* (derived from the Greek *deiktikos*: demonstrative) use the subject as the point of reference. For personal pronouns, *I* refers to the one who is speaking, *you* refers to the one who is spoken to, and *he, she,* or *it* refers to that which is spoken about. Similarly, the *present* is the point in time at which speech takes place. The designations of time and place can be either subjective or objective:

Subjective	*Objective*
yesterday	the previous day
today	this day
tomorrow	the next day
here	at the place where
there	from the place where

The questions regarding deixis in language are complex and manifold (for an excellent summary, see Lyons 1977: II, 636–724), but in the discussion here, it should suffice to note that our existence is recorded in two separate, temporal/spatial coordinate systems, both of which must be used in order to localize and identify objects in our environment. For the individual, the '*I–here–now*' point carries the greatest weight, of course, but the individual's coordinate systems, memory and perspective on the future are short, random and unstable, while those belonging to the collective are long, tradition-bound and stable.

Indexical signs – reagents as well as designations – represent an object through *connection* and/or *contiguity*. Reagents are directly determined by their object, while designations merely serve to point toward their object. In most – but certainly not all – cases, the connection between object and sign includes their *co-occurrence*, i.e. they exist in the same place at the same time. Symptoms are part of a disease, and the part which is easiest to perceive and recognize. Tracks indicate that the animal which left them is still nearby. The label on a medicine bottle or a sign bearing a street name are designations placed in direct connection or promixity to the object signified. The directness of the sign–object relation – from object toward sign for reagents, and vice versa for designations – and the fact that they may be simultaneously present are the reasons why indexical signs, according to many psychologists (such as Piaget and Bruner), are the first type of signs that infants learn to grasp.

Iconic signs

While the ability of indexical signs to represent something else is based on their connection to the object, iconic signs are based on their *similarity* to the object. Nothing would seem more straightforward: the photograph in a person's passport or driver's licence is an iconic sign of that person, because it is like that person. This similarity enables the sign to be used to identify the object, as police detectives use mug shots to identify a suspect. Although there is no reason to question this basic statement, it does require some differentiation and explanation, since *similarity* is a complicated, problematic and controversial concept. This is primarily because anything can be considered similar to something else when seen from a certain perspective. To illustrate, we will borrow an example from the American philosopher Nelson Goodman, one of the harshest critics of the notion of similarity:

B B O
1   2   3

This figure poses the question: which is most similar to the character numbered 2: 1 or 3? Without hesitation, most of us would answer '1', since it appears to be nearly identical to 2, the letter 'B'. However, a mathematician specializing in topology (the study of the relationship between curves and surfaces) may argue that 3 is, in fact, the correct answer, since both 2 and 3 delimit just one surface while 1 delimits two (for a further critique of similarity, see Goodman 1972: 437–46). Goodman's example and argumentation seem irrefutable, and in fact can be supported by a number of other examples. From a theoretical perspective, we are forced to dismiss the concept of similarity because it is too loosely defined. Nevertheless, we constantly make comparisons of similarity in our everyday speech, and have no trouble understanding each other when making comparisons. In doing so, we specify the areas where the similarity may be found; for instance, a husband may tell his wife that their offspring 'has your face, but my figure', or he may state the criteria for the similarity by asserting that, 'His nose is as straight as yours, while my nose is crooked.' The same can be said to apply to Goodman's example: in topological terms, 2 is most similar to 3; but in terms of writing, 2 is more similar to 1. To summarize, similarity can only be considered (1) *in relation to implicit or explicit criteria* (similarity only exists in relation to a specific language of description); and these criteria are themselves (2) selected for their *relevance to the purpose of the statement.*

Images

Aware that similarity only exists for a specific purpose, Peirce differentiated between three types of iconic signs: *images, diagrams* and *metaphors. Images* are iconic signs that have simple qualities in common with the object. When a paint-store customer presents the clerk with a piece of cardboard in the particular shade of red that he wants to paint his walls, the cardboard becomes an image of the desired object, the paint. In this example, it is obvious that the sign and object share just one common property, their colour. Those objects we traditionally refer to as images, such as portrait paintings, consist of a collection of properties shared by both object and sign. For instance, a painter will use her oils to depict the model's facial features, the shape of his head, the direction of his gaze, and so on; in other words, she uses a two-dimensional surface (the canvas) to create the illusion of a three-dimensional object through the interplay of shapes and colours, i.e. different qualities.

If the portrait, be it a painting or photograph, is a good likeness, people who are acquainted with model X will immediately recognize the portrait as being an image of him, while people who have only seen the portrait can use it in order to recognize X at some later date. Police release photographs of missing or wanted persons, often leading strangers to identify them, because the portrait depicts relevant features of the model, that is, the features we focus on, like the eyes, nose, mouth and jaw areas.

In a semiotic sense, images are not only visual or pictorial signs, but any sensory qualities, or combinations thereof, that represent an object. For instance, one can speak of an *acoustic image*. In a radio play, the sound of falling rain or an actress's scream also share (acoustic) qualities with that which is rendered. This also holds true for the other senses. In one incredible but true case, an American woman sued an aftershave company that claimed their product approached a man's natural and sexually arousing smell so closely that it left women unable to resist the charms of any man wearing the lotion. The woman claimed she had run into trouble after being seduced by the dangerous aftershave.

Diagrams

Images share sensory qualities with the objects they represent, while diagrams share relations and structures with their objects. For instance, we can open a travel guide or architectural book and find diagrams and images displayed side by side. A building may be shown as an image that depicts the structure from afar in a romantic sunset; and it may be shown as a diagram that lays out its exact architectural structure. In addition, the book may also include a ground plan showing the proportions of all the surfaces in the building, which one could never observe with the naked eye from any angle, inside or outside the building. Images, in other words, present us with aesthetic experiences, while diagrams provide us with information on the object (see below).

Diagrams possess greater freedom from the individual object (either real or fictitious) than do images. They have a greater degree of abstraction determined by the criteria for what is essential, as well as an intellectualization and generalization. A city map (which, as we have discussed above, also has strong indexical properties) is one example of a diagram, where abstraction and intellectualization on the basis of essential criteria play an important role. On the map, colour is used to differentiate between houses and streets, parks and lakes, based on oppositions like developed/undeveloped, vegetation/non-vegetation, land/water. Similarly, the specific shapes in the aerial photograph on which the map is based are simplified, streets are straightened, and alleys are hidden to join buildings into regular city blocks. This conventionalization and abstraction serves the purpose of the map, which may be to aid tourists in finding their way around town. A high-quality guide will often offer several different maps with different degrees of abstraction, one giving an overview of the entire city, another showing the downtown area in detail.

City maps are connected to an individual object; for instance, a map of Munich is useless to a tourist exploring New York City, and vice versa. Other kinds of diagrams, on the other hand, do not present particular objects. A reference book on anatomy, for example, does not present any particular individual's bones and muscles, but instead presents the generic anatomy of the species *Homo sapiens*, although it often distinguishes between male and female anatomy. Similarly, the classroom skeleton also remains anonymous.

Both examples illustrate that diagrams do not always refer to a specific object, but can also be abstract and general in nature. In addition, a diagram (as well as an image) does not have to represent an abstraction of something already existing. It can be not only a *model of something* (like a map), but also a prototype or *model for something*, such as an architectural sketch or virtual-reality construction functioning as a building plan. Second, a diagram does not have to present relationships that are connected to the material world, but can equally well present intellectual or logical relationships:

All	**M**	are	**P**
	S	are	**M**
	S	are	**P**

This diagram deals with logical relationships. To recall the classical example: all humans are mortal / Socrates is human / *ergo:* Socrates is mortal. As it stands, it should be added, this is a formal inferential scheme (commonly called syllogism) that claims universal validity.

Third, iconic signs, and particularly diagrams, allow for experimentation. This diagrammatic creativity – used by an architect in drawing a building plan, a logician in testing premisses and conclusions, and an author in inventing personages and fictitious events – can flourish because the models allow themselves to be easily modified and reshaped.

Fourth, diagrams – and, to a certain degree, images – are conventional in the sense that the relationship(s) can be presented in more than one way. Peirce gives the following illustration of diagrammatic presentation of a logical relationship, namely, his perception of the relationship between the sign and the three types of signs:

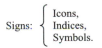

Signs: { Icons, Indices, Symbols.

This relationship can also be presented thus:

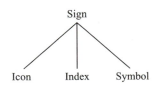

or

sign (icon, index, symbol)

However, we can *not*, in accordance with Peirce's train of thought, write it thus:

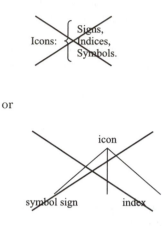

or

or

sign (index, symbol, icon)

The above-mentioned characteristics of a diagram – liberation from the individual object, abstraction, the possibility for generalization, presentation of both intellectual and material relationships, creativity, its function as outline or plan of action, and its use in clarifying the validity or invalidity of inferences – make it a formidable intellectual tool.

Metaphors

According to Peirce, metaphors are signs 'which represent the representative character of a representamen by representing a parallelism in something else' (2.277). Let us attempt to clarify this rather opaque definition. First of all, we are able to observe that a metaphor, according to Peirce, is a relationship between two signs, in which the representative character of the first sign is expressed by the second sign. Fever, for instance, is not an illness but an index, or symptom, of an illness. We take someone's temperature by measuring to what point a thermometer's mercury column has risen. Ignoring the indexical nature of the thermometer (the temperature affects the mercury), we observe that the instrument transforms the heat to a new sign: the height of the column. Naturally, the height of the column corresponds to the intensity of the fever; the mercury therefore represents a parallelism to the temperature in something else, another medium. We use the new, visual sign because heat, after all, can be felt but not seen, while the mercury column can be seen but not felt.

Poetic metaphors, which we usually refer to when employing the term 'metaphor', behave in the same fashion, although the transformation to a parallelism in something else takes place as a transition from one semantic area to another (Greek *metaphora*: transition, exchange). When we describe someone as 'living in the fast lane', we are using a modern variety of the age-old metaphor of life as a journey. The mechanism here is that an equivalent for a large and diffused area of meaning can be found in another (more concrete and well-compartmentalized) semantic area. Traffic and travel is a complex area, but of course much easier to grasp than the whole of human existence.

To further broaden the parallelism, we can add that, 'He is the only one I know who is able to drive that fast', and continue, 'Yes, and hopefully no one will notice that he is ignoring the speed limit', or, 'Yes, driving at that speed has caused many reckless drivers to lose their licence.'

Clearly, reading a thermometer and using a driving metaphor to describe an energetic, frantic and ambitious person are two entirely different things. Nevertheless, it is worthwhile to consider whether (1) the same basic mechanism of meaning, *analogy* (see Johansen 1998b; Larsen 1997a), is at work in both cases; and whether (2) metaphors – as well as comparisons and correlations between different sensory areas and areas of meaning – play a much larger role in our categorization and comprehension of our environment than one would initially assume. A major reason for asserting the importance of metaphors is our flexibility in understanding all kinds of phenomena in spatial categories. In our discussion of deixis, we observed that speech is structured from the egocentric 'I–here–now' point of view. Our ability to spatialize phenomena and relations enables us to strengthen the direct link between our I–here–now perspective and our body. For instance, we experience that something is in front of us, behind us, above us, to our left, or to our right. In a statement such as, 'Without knowing what hit him, he was struck from behind', there is no metaphor at work; it is simply a statement about an event from the perspective of the subject's body. On the other hand, an expression like, 'Her refusal hit him like a ton of bricks' is certainly metaphorical. Similarly, we use spatial metaphors when we say that *prices are low* or *high*; that *stocks are rising* or *falling*; that someone is *falling behind*; or that someone is *on top of the world*. Relationships dealing with power and rank often display a characteristic spatialization, expressed in metaphors such as *to rule from on high* or *to be placed under* someone's command. Let us observe the following list:

> general
> colonel
> lieutenant-colonel
> captain
> lieutenant

The relationships of power and rank are implied in such a vertically oriented diagram, but in fact, the spatialization is metaphoric. And the metaphors, like the diagrammatic positions, can be either valid or invalid:

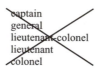

This list is simply wrong: the ranks are randomly arranged, and completely inconsistent with the order dictated by military hierarchy. It would be equally false to claim that prices are *falling* when the economic statistics show the price index jumping 25 per cent from the previous month.

Three important points should be made here. First, metaphors have a much greater sphere of influence than is generally assumed; in fact, they pervade our everyday lives to a large extent (see Lakoff and Johnson 1980 and Lakoff and Turner 1989). Second, the use of metaphors does not mean that the validity of the utterances in which they occur becomes impossible to determine. Just as there are trivial, empty and meaningless metaphors in poetic texts, there are also (as we have previously observed) invalid and improperly applied metaphors.

Third, the use of metaphors is not only a matter of expression and emotion, but can also provide insight and be intellectually productive – creative – as it often is in great poetry. Further, metaphors also have important scientific applications. The transfer of assumptions and patterns of thought between different disciplines can inspire scientists to look at their field of research from fresh perspectives. For instance, when researchers began considering and speaking of the human brain as if it were a computer, a whole new arsenal of knowledge, perspectives and problems came into play. The scientists began by studying the metaphor *the brain is a computer*, and attempted to determine its extent and validity. After several years, they started to speak of the *computer as a brain*, adopting a number of neurological insights and problems. This cross-disciplinary importing and exporting activity plays a decisive role in the development of scientific issues and results. In the twentieth century, for instance, language has been considered as a form of algebra (by Peirce, de Saussure, Hjelmslev, among others), as a generator (by Chomsky), and as action (by analytic philosophers and pragmatists). By importing these perspectives and finding a *parallelism in something else*, they may have limited the validity of their observations but at the same time greatly advanced our understanding and study of language.

The metaphor clearly distinguishes itself from the image and diagram by bringing together signs from two different areas. Images and diagrams, on the other hand, are often near-indistinguishable, since most iconic signs that we refer to as images also contain diagrammatic properties, by presenting relationships as well as qualities. Our earlier example, the red-coloured piece of cardboard presented to a paintstore clerk as a sign of the desired paint, approaches our technical definition of image, although it comes nowhere near what is generally considered an image. We may conclude that the qualitative and relational always belong together. This also means that even simple images (in the common everyday sense) possess a high degree of freedom from the represented object, and that the method of representation is as dependent on conventions as it is on the object.

Symbolic signs

> A chalk mark is like a line though nobody uses it as a sign; a weather cock turns with the wind, whether anybody notices it or not. But the word 'man' has no particular relation to men unless it be recognized as being so related. That is not only what constitutes a sign, but what gives it a particular relation to its object which makes it significant of that particular object.
>
> (Peirce, unpublished manuscript no. L 75, 1902: 149)

Peirce here outlines both the negative and positive aspects of symbolic signs. Negatively, symbolic signs are characterized by being arbitrary, unmotivated, i.e. neither connected to the object nor similar to it. In other words, it is not their own characteristics that make them signs, as with iconic signs; nor is there a natural bond between sign and object, as with indexical signs. Instead, symbolic signs are constructed or agreed upon to be used as signs for given purposes in the internal or external world, i.e. as conventional designations with a referentiality and a meaning that are determined by conventional usage.

Conventional signs can of course be semi-private; for instance, a couple of cheating poker players may agree on a secret code, in which one cough means one pair, two coughs signifies two pairs; and a coughing fit means full house. Such semi-private, randomly selected, and highly specific symbolic signs exist, of course, in order to satisfy certain needs. In the discussion here, however, we will focus on signs that are based on generalized social conventions, forming sign-systems.

The most important of such symbolic sign-systems is language. The word *windfall*, for example, bears no similarity to a tree felled by the wind, nor is it affected by stormy weather. Although the joining of *wind* and *fall* seems particularly meaningful, the sign is built up of elements that are connected to the object only by convention, and its reference and meaning must be mediated by the use of a new sign functioning as the (dynamical) interpretant of the first sign. Saussure expressed this relationship in the following terms:

> The idea of 'sister' is not linked by any inner relationship to the succession of sound s-ö-r which serves as its signifier in French; that it could be

represented equally by just any other sequence is proved by differences
among languages and by the very existence of different languages; the
signified 'ox' has as its signifier b-ö-f one side of the border and o-k-s
(Ochs) on the other.

(Saussure 1959: 67–8)

Saussure here argues that natural languages are also conventional, because
the same reference and meaning can be mediated by two different signs, each
belonging to a different language. In this passage, he also addresses the
sequential nature of the acoustic word-signs, stating that a characteristic
feature of these signs is that they are made up of smaller elements.

Signs and non-signs

Even though it can be shown that indexical and iconic signs are often also
built from smaller units that, in and by themselves, have no reference or
meaning, symbolic signs distinguish themselves by consisting of a finite number of systematically structured elements. This is clearly evident for sign-
systems that are constructed for a specific purpose, such as traffic signs, but
also holds true for natural languages, perhaps the most important of human
sign-systems.

The expression substance of the linguistic sign, its acoustic form, possesses a
so-called *double articulation*. The *first articulation* is the division into an indeterminate number of small *meaningful* units (also known as morphemes). These
minimal signs can be what non-linguists refer to as words (e.g. *hall* and *sun*),
but they may also be prefixes and suffixes – that is, parts of words, with an
independent meaning. For instance, the word *unconcernedness* consists of four
meaningful linguistic elements, that is, four signs: the negative prefix *un-*, the
verbal root *concern* (cf. to concern), the verbal/adjective suffix *-ed*, and the
substantive suffix *-ness*. It is generally thought that the root has an independent meaning, while prefixes and suffixes, as their etymology suggests (Latin
figere: to fasten), only become meaningful by attaching themselves to other
signs. This distinction is probably of a relative nature; a verb, after all, is
generally attached to a subject in order to specify its meaning. The crux here
is that all four elements of *unconcernedness* have a meaning that can also be
applied in other contexts: *un*-real, *concern*-ing, blurr-*ed*, lazi-*ness*.

The characteristic feature of language, however, is the *second articulation*, the
division into the smallest units of sounds, that are not meaningful but serve a
meaning-distinctive function. Consider this list:

t **a** n	n a t (= mat, straw mattress)
t **e** n	n e t
t **i** n	n i t (= egg of louse)
t **o** n	n o t
t **u** n	n u t

Each of these words takes on an entirely different meaning as the vowel between the *t* and the *n* changes. The vowel has no meaning in and by itself, but by altering it (a process known as commutation) we get a new word that holds a different meaning. The example also shows that, in natural languages, the order of phonemes is equally decisive; for example, if we reverse the order of the consonants, e.g. from *ten* to *net*, the meaning changes entirely.

While the number of roots in a living, natural language is infinite and constantly increasing, and the number of prefixes and suffixes is large but limited, the number of phonemes (the phonemic inventory) within a language is very limited, anywhere between 12 and 60 for each language. This means that linguistic signs are built up from a limited, finite number of elements, the phonemic inventory, that serves to separate meaning but has itself no meaning. In other words, linguistic signs are made up of non-signs.

Modern linguistics extends this idea even further by proposing that phonemes consist again of smaller elements, so-called *distinctive features*, numbering between 12 and 40 and ordered into opposing pairs, such as vowel/consonant, aspirated/unaspirated, nasal/glottal, voiced/unvoiced. According to this sweeping thesis, all existing languages show such features, and languages distinguish themselves by the way in which they select and combine them into phonemes. Phonemes, following each other like letters in a linguistic chain, are themselves the result of the simultaneous articulation of several distinctive features taken from several of the above-mentioned oppositions; for instance, the phoneme *p* is both a consonant and unvoiced, and it may be both aspirated and unaspirated.

There is no doubt that linguistics has made great strides in analysing the expression substance of the different languages. Analysis means *fragmentation*, and the possibility of segmenting larger units into their more basic elements stresses an important characteristic of language and symbolic signs generally. The distinguished Danish linguist Louis Hjelmslev noted that any linguistic analysis crosses two borders. One of these runs between an infinite and a finite inventory of elements. For example, the number of words in a language's vocabulary is infinite, while the number of derivative and conjugative suffixes in that language is finite. The second border runs between signs and non-signs, i.e. between morphemes and phonemes. Hjelmslev expresses his view of the nature of language thus:

> A language is by its aim first and foremost a sign system; in order to be fully adequate it must always be ready to form new signs, new words or new roots. But, with all its limitless abundance, in order to be fully adequate, a language must likewise be easy to manage, practical in acquisition and use. Under the requirement of an unrestricted number of signs, this can be achieved by all the signs' being constructed of non-signs whose number is restricted, and, preferably, severely restricted. Such non-signs as enter into a sign system as parts of signs we shall call

here *figuræ*; this is a purely operative term, introduced here for conveni-
ence. Thus, a language is so ordered that with the help of a handful of
figuræ and through ever new arrangements of them a legion of signs can
be constructed. If a language were not so ordered it would be a tool
unusable for its purpose. We thus have every reason to suppose that in
this feature – the construction of the sign from a restricted number of
figuræ – we have found an essential basic feature in the structure of any
language.

(Hjelmslev 1961: 46–7)

Hjelmslev's argument appears valid as long as we occupy ourselves with the
expression substance of language, its sound structure. The question remains,
however, whether the same border between signs and non-signs exists when
we consider the sign's meaning or content substance. Before proceeding to
address that question, we shall, however, first consider another important
feature of the symbolic sign: its systematic character.

Signs and sign-systems

The relationship between a symbolic sign and the object it represents is
conventional, functioning on the basis of an interpretative habit agreed to
by consensus. Here, the sign–object relation is unmotivated (radically arbitrary), i.e. neither the quality of the object nor its structure nor its dynamics
can be used to explain the form of the symbolic sign (see our earlier discussion
of the word *windfall*). Since the symbolic sign does not have a positive motivated relationship to its object, it must instead be supported by a clear
differentiation between the symbolic signs themselves. Swiss linguist
Ferdinand de Saussure, stressing the systematic relationship between linguistic signs, stated that

in language there are only differences. Even more important: a difference
generally implies positive terms between which the difference is set up;
but in language there are only differences *without positive terms*. Whether
we take the signified or the signifier, language has neither ideas nor
sounds that existed before the linguistic system, but only conceptual
and phonic differences that have issued from the system.

(Saussure 1959: 120)

The difficulty with this famous passage is, among other things, its radical
nature – its refusal to challenge the materiality of linguistic signs and their
communicative function. Whether such a formal and abstract point of view is
useful for semiotics and linguistics is doubtful, to say the least. Nevertheless,
Saussure was successful in accounting for the properties and surprising effectiveness of symbolic signs.

Table 3.2 Four basic types of traffic sign

	Red/white	*Blue/white*
Triangle	Warning	—
Circle	Prohibition	Positive injunction
Rectangle	—	Guidance

Saussure's views can be illustrated by the well-known everyday phenomenon of traffic signs. In Denmark, one can categorize the traffic signs into four basic types according to their shape, colour, and location, using a digital structural code (see further p. 8 and p. 201). Both warning and prohibitive signs are (with some exceptions) coloured red or white, but distinguish themselves through their shape. Warning signs consist of a white, equilateral *triangle* framed by a red edge. With the exception of highway signs, all the warning signs point upwards, so that the lower edge runs parallel to the surface of the road. Prohibitive signs, on the other hand, consist (again with some exceptions) of a white *circle* framed by a red edge. In both types of signs, the white inner area contains different signs – legends and/or pictographs – to communicate the specific warning or prohibition.

Both critical regulatory signs (stop, yield, turn) and informative guidance signs (lane and curb usage, speed regulation) consist of a blue background with additional signs in white, but no frame (again, there are some exceptions). However, while the signs giving critical rules are *circular* like the prohibitive signs, the shape of the informative signs is *rectangular*. Again ignoring exceptions, the four basic types of traffic signs can be classified as in Table 3.2. In this table, a certain *content* is linked to a certain combined (colour and shape) *expression*, both organized along simple, digital structural codes. This can also be presented as follows:

Expression:	*triangle + red/white*	*circle + red/white*
Content:	warning	prohibition

Expression:	*circle + blue/white*	*rectangle + blue/white*
Content:	positive injunction	guidance

Both presentations clearly show the systematic use of shapes and colours in relation to the class of message, or content. Furthermore, we can extrapolate from Table 3.2 that some combinations (triangle + blue/white and rectangle + red/white) are unused. One can safely assume that traffic signs are based on the differentiation between providing prohibitions and injunctions, so-called critical rules, and offering guidance and information. The critical rules either order or forbid a certain action, i.e. they are either *mandatory* or *prohibitive*, as exemplified by the two traffic signs below:

Both the warning and the guidance signs claim that something is the case, and sometimes the differences between them are negligible; for instance, *traffic lights ahead* is a warning sign, while *highway ends* is a guidance sign. A pedestrian crossing can be marked with both a warning sign and a guidance sign, but they will be placed at different distances from the crossing, and the warning sign will be primarily directed at motorists. The difference between them, however, is that the warning signs not only inform about traffic problems, but are directed at all traffic participants, because the situation requires careful behaviour, while the guidance signs signal a change in traffic conditions that either present no danger or only affect some traffic participants (e.g. *parking zone* or *gas station ahead*). The expression substance of the system does not appear to indicate the difference between commanding and informing as taking precedence, but rather the difference between *warning* and *informing*, because the maximal expressive difference can be found here (triangle + red/white versus rectangle + blue/white). A warning can be strengthened and become a command (circle + red/white). Expression and content are connected through processual codes for different speech acts, but are based on one-to-one relationships between expression and content (for an extended semiotic study of traffic lights see Johansen 1993a: 311–42).

The above example serves to demonstrate the applicability of Saussure's views on symbolic signs. The traffic signs confirm that the differences are created by and within the system itself. Warnings, prohibitions and commands also exist outside the traffic sign-system, of course, but become apparent through the relation between the system's conceptual and expressive articulation. Further, the relation between expression and meaning is unmotivated, arbitrary. There is no natural reason why a triangle means a warning and a circle means a command, just as there is no reason why informative signs are rectangular, which is simply distinctive, practical, and well learned by traffic participants. A system of symbolic signs such as traffic signs becomes more effective by being consistent: all warning signs should be red and white triangles, and all prohibitive signs should be red and white circles, etc. Hereby, the sign's expression substance – its material and formal properties – is no longer determined by the object represented, but is instead determined by its relation to the other signs in the system.

Saussure appears to have given little thought to traffic signs, of which there were few on the roads around the turn of the last century. Instead, his focus was on language as the prototypical system. Language – which is collective and governed by internalized rules used well-nigh unconsciously – is in several important ways built just like a purposely planned system, such as traffic signs. This not only holds true for basic linguistic elements like phonemes and distinctive features, but also for larger differences of meaning, like the difference between different types of sentence, such as a statement and a question. Phonemes, for example, are ordered as a series of opposing pairs:

	A	B
(a)	p	t
(b)	b	d

where A: bilabial, B: labio-dental and (a) unvoiced, (b) voiced. Thus, *p* can be defined in relation to the other elements in the microsystem (here an expression paradigm): in relation to *t* it distinguishes itself by being a bilabial and, in relation to *b*, by being unvoiced.

For many structuralist linguists, it has been the accepted view – and vision – that a sign's meaning content can be analysed just like its expression, i.e. that it can be divided into non-signs, content figures, etc. (cf. Hjelmslev 1970: 66–7) in the same way as expression figures (e.g. phonemes). According to some structuralists, the words *woman, man, girl* and *boy* can be analysed in a similar fashion to the phonemes above, within the dimensions species (1), gender (2) and age (3):

	A	B
(a)	**woman 1, 2, 3**	**man 1, −2, 3**
(b)	**girl 1, 2, −3**	**boy 1, −2, −3**

where A or 2: female versus B or −2: male, (a) or 3: adult versus (b) or −3: child. If we add to this the important and indubitable fact that all four belong to the human race (within the spaces marked by (1)), we are presented with a useful diagram, which can be expanded further: Danish structuralist Peter Brask, for instance, has shown how other oppositions can be fitted in (see Figure 3.5).

Such analyses of meaning as a system of oppositions are important both to linguistic and literary studies. The so-called thematic analysis of literary texts can be said to rest on the description of the different oppositions found in the textual structure, as well as their (inter)connections and the changes they undergo in the course of the text. These examples of content analysis, however, do not show that we have already reached the limit of signs as far as their meaning content is concerned. Clearly, we have dissolved the word *woman* into three components: *human, female* and *adult*; but these components

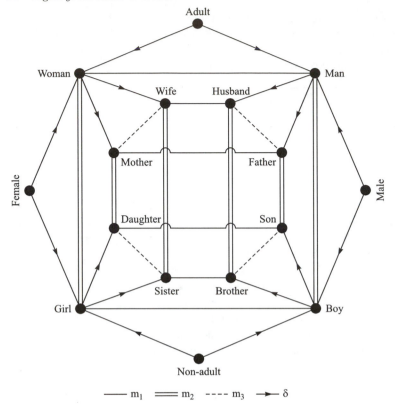

Figure 3.5 Analysis of meaning as a system of oppositions.
Source: Brask (1979: 210).

are, after all, signs themselves! As concerns the meaning of the sign, we will make the following statement: content categories serving to differentiate meaning (e.g. male versus female; adult versus child) are themselves always meaningful. If we take this to be true, we shatter the structuralists' vision of reaching basic content units (figures) that are in and by themselves meaningless, but together construct the meaning of the sign. However, this does not challenge the systematic study of the meaning components which signs possess; it simply means that the components themselves are in turn signs, i.e. that signs should be explained in other signs that function as their interpretants (see also Johansen 1986a and 1992b).

Both traffic signs and our linguistic examples demonstrate the crucial role that internal and systematic differences play in the analysis of symbolic signs, their message and their usage. One important characteristic of symbolic signs, from a Saussurian point of view, is that they are *that, which the others are not*, i.e. *differentially determined*. This is how signs in general, and symbolic signs in particular, are essentially two-sided. They have an external and an internal aspect: on the one hand, they are connected to the object(s) they represent, while on the other, their expression/content substance is also determined by the distinction between them.

Semiosis: the sign-process

We have up to now proposed three different ways in which signs can designate and signify: through *connection* and possibly through *interaction* with the object; through *similarity* to the object, i.e. by sharing certain qualities or structures with the object; or by being tied to the object by virtue of a *convention*. Based on this three-way classification, we speak of indexical, iconic and symbolic signs, respectively. However, it would be erroneous to believe that signs occur in pure form, i.e. that they must be viewed as either indexical, iconic, or symbolic. Peirce was perfectly clear on this point:

> We say that the portrait of a person we have not seen is *convincing*. So far as, on the ground merely of what I see in it, I am led to form an idea of the person it represents, it is an Icon. But, in fact, it is not a pure Icon, because I am greatly influenced by knowing that it is an *effect*, through the artist, caused by the original's appearance, and is thus in a genuine Obsistent relation to that original. Besides, I know that portraits have but the slightest resemblance to their originals, except in certain original conventional aspects, and after a conventional scale of values, etc.
>
> (2.92)

In fact, the portrait is not primarily iconic but indexical, since the cause–effect relation between the original and the image is the determining factor here, as Peirce states. The portrait does have (indeed, must have) iconic features; for instance, a photograph of one-half of a one-egged pair of twins is only an indexical sign of the twin that was photographed, but can in practice also function as an iconic sign of both twins. Similarity only becomes apparent through the conscious or unconscious acceptance of some conventions regarding pictorial representation.

It must be stressed that not only images have indexical and symbolic elements; both indexical and symbolic signs also contain elements of the other two types of sign. Whenever a sign enters into the semiosis, the dynamic process in which it signifies a given object and produces an interpretant, all three mechanisms – connection/interaction, similarity and convention – help establish the meaning of the sign. Therefore the designations 'indexical', 'iconic' and 'symbolic' simply indicate the sign's dominant, but never sole, mechanism of the standing-for relation.

We have here dealt with three types of signs in the sequence indexical–iconic–symbolic because – according to Piaget-based theories on cognitive development (see Bruner 1966, and Piaget and Inhelder 1969; see also Johansen 1996a) – this is the developmental order in which children learn to interpret the signs in their environment, and hence to accommodate to reality. In order for very young children to understand something to be a sign of something else, there must be a connection in space and time between sign and object. Piaget mentions, for instance, that infants are able to interpret a plastic nipple, sticking out from behind a pillow, as a sign of the feeding bottle. A little before the age of 18 months, the child makes a decisive leap in its development, growing independent of the connection and co-presence of both sign and object. This is among other things expressed in *delayed imitation* and *symbolic play*. Delayed imitation breaks the chronological connection between original and sign (e.g. the child will imitate the behaviour of an absent adult an hour after the fact). And symbolic play makes an even more decisive break between object and sign by substituting the object with something else, something completely different. A little girl will, for instance, pretend to fall asleep, using the table-cloth as a 'pillow'. Although the pillow and table-cloth are, of course, entirely different objects, the child apparently focuses on their common traits (e.g. both are made of cloth). Delayed imitation and, more so, symbolic play show that the child's intellect has developed the ability to create a mental image and reproduce it from memory, as well as the ability to differentiate between objects and find similarity between them. After the child begins to engage in symbolic play, it soon progresses to speaking and understanding language. This is because the linguistic sign represents the object in a similar fashion to the mental image and substituted object in symbolic play.

The ontogenetic development of our semiotic competence, that is the development of competence in the individual member of the species, can be regarded as its liberation and independence from the infant's need to have both object and sign actually present in space and time. Later, this liberation will progress so far that we possess an infinite number of signs for wholly fictitious objects. Nevertheless, we cannot exclusively regard this mental development as a simple process, in which new meaning mechanisms are acquired and added to the existing ones. The baby searching behind the pillow for the feeding bottle has, in fact, already attained the ability to differentiate between different objects, the bottle and the pillow. And, in this differentiating process, it has also applied rudimentary criteria for similarity.

The fact that all three meaning mechanisms appear to be present from the earliest moment in a child's sign comprehension and sign use does not mean that all three are developed equally. For instance, in the earliest phase, when the child is still dependent on the physical connection between object and sign, its ability to recognize signs also presupposes an ability to perceive some elementary iconic and symbolic properties. These properties alone, however, are at this stage unable to release sign recognition; this is why the indexical aspect still dominates here. At a later stage, the child develops an understanding of signs in which iconic or symbolic aspects dominate. In this way all three aspects of the semiosic process – indexical, iconic and symbolic – constantly support each other; and it is the interrelation between them that makes the production of meaning possible.

4   Discourse analysis
Sign, action, intention

What is discourse?

Sign and action

'Talk more, do less', 'Plenty of words, little action' – this is how we often, somewhat derisively, talk about politicians and planners. No matter whether one feels that this assertion sounds correct from time to time, it is based on an assumption which is incorrect: that there is a fundamental difference between word and deed, between talk and action.

Discourse analysis builds on an utterly opposed underlying view: all signs, including words, are only signs because they constitute an action among other actions. Discourse analysis must account for what kind of action we are dealing with, on what assumptions it is based, and what effect it has. The discourse concept which is at the heart of discourse analysis unifies the characteristics of the sign and its contexts which make it capable of conveying action. Discourse is a action-logic with a textual manifestation (for the meaning of 'text', see Chapter 6).

When both signs and the actions they constitute are bound together in one concept, the discourse concept widens semiotic analysis, potentially threatening any clear delineation of its boundaries. At the same time, however, discourse analysis involves a limitation which may lead to greater precision. Admittedly, it is not always easy to decide between the subject and the intention in a particular context. To begin with, though, it is sufficient to establish that one can ignore contexts of action which, though including signs, cannot be considered to be discourses.

Let us follow two Sunday strollers in the woods. One of them hears some remarkable bird-song and stops to try to find out what sort of bird it can be that is singing. The other stroller stops too, silently watching. He catches sight of something, tugs at the sleeve of his friend and says: 'Look! There's a robin!' 'So there is!' the first stroller exclaims. 'Sshh!' the other one whispers, trying to get his friend to keep quiet. And now both of them have caught sight of the bird.

The sound of the bird is an indexical sign, a so-called reagent (see Chapter 3, p. 32) for the bird which neither of them has yet glimpsed, but which they agree must be there somewhere or other. The song of the bird causes those out walking to stop, i.e. it provokes an action. But not until one of them uses signs (words and a tugged-at sleeve) can we speak of a discourse. For now subjects are involved. They wish to communicate with each other in a dialogue that is based on signs of a type that the subjects have in common – in this instance, words and gestures. And because they have these signs in common they are able to exchange roles in the dialogue, according to what they want to impart or allow the other to impart, and to achieve mutual understanding, no matter whether they agree or disagree with each other. In principle, they can actually go on taking turns at asking and answering as long as other considerations – the power of the one over the other, external factors such as noise or the disappearance of the bird – do not compel them to abandon the dialogue.

Natural phenomena can also, under certain circumstances, be understood discursively. It is most obvious in, for instance, the classical fables, but also in more philosophically oriented lines of thought; for instance in Ralph Waldo Emerson's nineteenth-century transcendentalism, discursive processes are seen as an inner force and structure in nature which ensure a discursive connection between mankind and nature, 'from stars to vegetables':

> But every night come out these envoys of beauty, and light the universe with their admonishing smile. . . . Nature says, – he is my creature . . . . I am part and parcel of God. . . . The greatest delight which the fields and woods minister is the suggestion of an occult relation between man and the vegetable. I am not alone and unacknowledged. They nod to me, and I to them.
>
> (Emerson 1967: 1065ff.)

Through nature, God speaks to mankind of his creation and, through the language of nature, he makes himself visible to mankind as creating subject. He has given nature a form that is particularly sympathetic to mankind, thereby enabling it to perceive its creator and understand that nature's fellowship with mankind is his deepest purpose. At that time, nature was still conceived in the medieval image of a book – the Great Book of Nature – in which man could read about nature's and his own deepest purpose and interrelationship (Blumenberg 1986), e.g. in 'The Voice of Nature' by Emerson's contemporary, British romanticist John Clare (Clare 1984: 185):

> The voice of nature as the voice of God
> Appeals to me in every tree and flower,
> Breathing his glory, magnitude and power.
> In nature's open book I read and see
> Beauty's each lesson . . .

The discursive voice of nature allocates roles, and the division of power in the mutual relationship between God and mankind is also allocated – the positions from which they can speak to each other.

Particular phenomena, such as the crow of the cock, the stars, dawn and even earthquakes, are not once-and-for-all signs within or outside discourse. But they always have the possibility of occurring in universes in which they can become elements of a discourse. Such a universe can be fictive, or can be the object of philosophical reflection, as in Emerson or Clare. But it can also be real, as in the case of our Sunday strollers, with bird-song, a walk in the woods and conversation.

Discourse analysis and discourse

Discourse analysis sees the sign as an action which takes place at three levels at one and the same time. Together they comprise 'discourse', in the semiotic sense of the word:

1 The sign is a *material* phenomenon. This means that the sign can be localized in two respects: first, it is characterized by belonging to a particular sign-system, a material medium of expression. Second, it always occurs in a physical space in a particular location at a particular point in time, where it can have an effect on those who share the use of this type of sign-system. 'Come on!' is called out, the words being perceived as material sound by humans and house sparrows alike, but it only becomes part of a discourse when someone at the same time localizes it as being part of the English language and thereby potentially a call from somebody. Discourse *localizes* where meaning occurs in time and space and in a medium of expression.

2 This call has the form of a possible *dialogue*, despite the fact that no one apart from the person calling out begins to speak or is allowed to do so. It is an action that establishes or maintains certain interconnected roles or positions, possibly positions of power where subjects manifest their intentions concerning each other in such a way that those using the signs can change position and take turns at speaking. 'Where am I supposed to go?' is a possible query on hearing the call 'Come on!' 'Shut up and get moving!' is the dismissive reply. The form is, nevertheless, that of a dialogue, even though the content is a one-way command, since the command – precisely via the dialogue form – is also interlaced with other types of action when someone commands somebody else to do something. Discourse *allocates* subjective positions in the formation of meaning.

3 This dialogue takes place in an institutionalized situation where precisely this allocation of roles is valid, and where the intentions conveyed are understandable. This is referred to as a *discursive universe*. In the same physical space, e.g. the lounge of a nursing home, the expression 'Look at those vegetables!' could be a condescending and objectionable reference to the old people, being based on a hierarchical relationship between the parties involved in the communication. It could, of course,

also be a mark of satisfaction at the healthy ingredients of a meal that is being served at that particular moment. This remark is not necessarily exchanged between people of differing rank. And finally, it could also be a critical comment referring to the not very decorative pot plants on the window-ledge and thus be an indirect criticism of the staff. All these meanings occur in the same material space, though in different discursive universes, i.e. ones where the collectively accepted rules for the division of subjective positions and for access to language use are not identical with the rules that allow the subjects to speak about particular things. These universes are not only demarcated by their material boundaries, but also by the meanings and reactions to meanings that can occur in dialogues involving the use of one or more sign-systems. It is such an institutiona-lized situation, not the material occurrence as such, that determines whether 'Look at those vegetables!' is understood as the first, second or third proposed meaning. And it is via the integration of the meaning in such a discursive universe that one decides whether one's understanding is valid and thereby whether one's reaction is understood and accepted by others. Discourse *demarcates* the universe where meaning can be under-stood, and where one can decide whether it is relevant and valid.

Discourse is therefore defined as a structured semiotic operation which at one and the same time localizes the meaning in time and space, allocates the roles for those producing it (possibly by confirming or denying an already estab-lished allocation of roles such as that between a private soldier and an officer), and demarcates in which institutionalized universe we can understand a meaning and possibly discover whether it is correct or not.

When we no longer imagine nature to be a discursive universe – as did Emerson and Clare – where the Almighty speaks to us, the signs of nature are no longer signs in a common sign-system which enable a dialogue in which subjective intentions manifest themselves. They are still material signs with an effect in a particular space – only they are now outside discourse. One can believe in talking to one's pot plants, as Emerson did with his vegetables, and they may possibly thrive – but no one could call that discourse.

This conception of discourse coincides to a great extent with the etymo-logical meaning of the word 'discourse'. Literally, discourse means 'running back and forth', even though nowadays the tongue does most of the run-ning: discourse means both talking together as a process and the spoken language product resulting from the process. Discourse can also refer to a special way of talking and thus be concerned with the rhetorical effect of speech, often emphasizing an institutional and formal aspect, as, for exam-ple, a legal discourse, a scientific discourse, or a political discourse. It is also used more loosely for jargonized speech, such as a sports journalist-type discourse, a student discourse. Discourse as a purely verbal phenomenon is a conversation which aims to convince someone by the choice of mode of expression.

In continuation of this, some semiotic traditions have sought to advance a discourse analysis solely with a linguistic point of departure, either by linking discourse to verbal language or by conceiving discourse as having verbal language as its primary model. Other attempts than those based on linguistics have, however, been made to extend the analysis of signs in the direction of a discourse analysis. Although these traditions are often at loggerheads with each other, we wish to try to bridge the gap between them, especially as semiotics cannot be content with granting one system of expression the privilege of being its sole foundation. We intend to stress that the traditions mentioned have two common points of orientation: they conceive of signs as discursive actions; and their efforts are derived from the three levels in discourse which we have just outlined:

1   One type of discourse analysis emphasizes that a sign-system not only organizes the individual signs and their interconnections into a static system according to a structural code. It stresses, first and foremost, that – before and independently of every concrete situation – this system organizes the way in which the sign occurs in time and space when it is materialized in a concrete situation. Signs simply cannot avoid being organized in relation to a situation. The verbal sign-system, for example, contains some special elements such as 'I', 'you', 'here', 'there', 'soon', 'perhaps', etc., which inevitably result in the verbal sign never being realized solely as a material object but *always* being so when it becomes part of a situation whose time, space and personal roles are structured by elements of the system used. Other sign-systems have other elements for this purpose. We call this analysis *structuralist* discourse analysis.

2   A second type of discourse analysis stresses the subjective intentions involved in the discursive process. Here it is emphasized that signs in use orientate the subjects in relation to each other in a possible dialogue and in relation to the world around them, long before there are conscious intentions to approach somebody about something in particular. We call this analysis *phenomenological* discourse analysis.

3   A third type of discourse analysis underlines that signs in use define universes that demarcate and make visible the power relationship between the subjects of the dialogue, forcibly linking understanding and validity. This analysis we call *sociological* discourse analysis.

In the following section we intend to analyse each of these three types of discourse analysis in greater detail. But the aim of a semiotic discourse analysis is to get them to cohere (concerning discourse analysis, see the pedagogical anthologies Dijk 1985 and Jaworski and Coupland 1999, the literary Fohrmann and Müller 1988 and Pettersson 1990, the linguistic Coulthard 1985 and Renkema 1993, the philosophical Perinbanayagam 1991 and the sociological MacDonell 1986).

Structuralist discourse analysis

Enunciation

A special form of criticism has often been made against the structuralist semiotics that arose in the wake of Ferdinand de Saussure's conception of the sign and the linguistics of which it was a part. It has been pointed out that this theory only dealt with – and was only able to deal with – the static sign-system, not language in use; only the particular state of language, not the historical changes of the sign-system; and only the sign-system as something arbitrary and immanent, i.e. detached from the objects to which it refers and from the subjects who use it. Louis Hjelmslev's language theory is the most radical example of this sort of structuralism (see Chapter 3).

To a great extent such criticism is justified. It was advanced early on, as soon as Saussure's theory began to become known, as well as later – against those who attempted to realize his ideas concerning a general semiotics based on linguistics by using them on non-verbal sign-systems. Charles Bally, a pupil of Saussure, criticized Saussure's conception of the manifested sign as being ambiguous: on the one hand, the sign was a *fact*, i.e. something whose presence could be understood causally by referring to the physiology of the mouth, breathing, etc.; yet, on the other hand, it was also an *act*, i.e. an action that was linked to an intention to communicate something to someone (Bally 1939).

One of the more recent critics is the French philosopher Paul Ricœur. In his article 'Structure, Word, Event' from 1969 (Ricœur 1974) he claims that the sign is not only defined with a particular meaning by and in a sign-system of differences and similarities. It is defined precisely with the aim of being realized as an event in which meaning is created for someone about some matter or other. It is, so to speak, predestined to go beyond the closed system, to enter into a situation. While Bally wishes to clarify the ambiguity and make clear-cut differentiations, Ricœur wants to retain the ambiguity and its complexity. The sign is a material phenomenon in time and space, but in its material appearance it is to be understood as a process or an event – the sign does not only *exist*; it *takes place*. It is both fact and act. The structure that defines it therefore contains both certain characteristics which distinguish it statically from other signs and other characteristics which at the same time predestine it to be anchored in time and space in relation to certain subjects who seek to communicate. The sign is structurally determined to be a discursive phenomenon. It is this more recent way of criticizing or extending structuralism which is relevant from a semiotic point of view. But how are time, space and subject organized in advance by the structure? Let us take an isolated quotation which we will then gradually place in its proper context:

> This is no night to throw a human being out inter.

This is a blunt assertion which may be reliable or unreliable, correct or incorrect. Naturally, the person hearing or reading it has to be familiar with the English system of expression and English semantics, and to have a certain amount of practical physical and social experience, to be able to understand what is being claimed, and also to detect that 'inter', instead of 'into', indicates a dialect or a sociolect is being used. In any case, the sentence has a reference.

But more than just a reference is needed if one is to understand the utterance, and this 'more' belongs just as much to the special characteristics of the sign-system as do sound and referential meaning. The sign-system contains elements that structure in advance the way in which the utterance is anchored in a situation and thereby make the utterance a special type of event.

The word 'this' in the quotation refers at the same time to the place where one is and where one speaks, as opposed to 'that', which separates these two circumstances. The same applies to the present tense 'is', which has the same function as 'this', since 'is' is not only present in relation to the terrible night but also in relation to the person who is speaking. The clause 'no night to throw a human being out inter' is also a complex part of the utterance. Even though the negation implies an empty reference, it functions nevertheless as a positive definition of the night via the combination with the infinitive 'to throw'. For this establishes a contrast with some other, more hospitable night which the speakers are assumed to be familiar with. The negation stresses that there is a person speaking who, here and now, while the speech act is taking place, already knows something about what is being spoken about. This indirect marking of the position of the speaking subject is further reinforced in this instance by the subjective intentions thematized in the infinitive ('to throw a human being out inter'). As a prerequisite for the utterance to be comprehensible, all three mentioned elements – 'this', 'is', 'no . . . to throw' – locate the content as regards place, time and the speaking subject, even though these three factors are only indicated indirectly. If we were to make these relations explicit, the utterance would almost become incomprehensible, even though its reference would be clear:

> [I now assert to someone who is here where I am speaking that] This is no night [as opposed to some other kind of night which we know something about, or which we have just been talking about] to throw a human being out inter [which neither you nor I could ever contemplate doing].

Long before we know anything about certain subjects or concrete time and space, the language-system being used sees to it that the utterance is built up in such a way that we are forced to determine and concretize these conditions to be able to understand the utterance. The language-system does so via certain elements which refer both to the *reference* of the utterance and to the *action* which brings about the utterance. Such an action is called an *enunciation*. These elements – 'this', 'is' and 'no . . . to throw' – primarily articulate time, space and subject in relation to the moment of the enunciation and the space where the enunciation actually takes place, but which is not necessarily there where the things being talked about are. They place the reference in relation to the now of the enunciation.

Precisely because they belong to the special language-system we know and use, there is no need to over-elucidate them. There is no need to say 'I' to know that now someone is speaking. The elements in question indicate that it is not only in the nature of language to exceed its own boundaries, to refer to something, but that it *always at the same time* will integrate the reference into the actual action, whereby the reference is expressed in language. This contemporaneity means that language cannot help being discursive. It is this contemporaneity between speech and reference which means that we have to ask ourselves whether the speaker is describing the actions he might possibly consider taking, 'to throw a human being out', or whether it is a metaphorical description of the inhumanity of the night. The implicit subject of 'to throw' is problematized by virtue of the contemporaneity of reference and enunciation. And the problem cannot be solved by our isolating the two aspects. Reference and enunciation are mutually dependent in the discursive process.

The linguist Émile Benveniste, in particular, has analysed the verbal enunciation and the way in which it organizes our perception of time, space and subject. And he has notably pointed out that all languages contain elements which stress the different dimensions of the enunciation – but that they can vary considerably from language to language (Benveniste 1974).

Ever since the ancient grammarians, language researchers and language philosophers have speculated on these strange elements in language: 'I', 'you', 'earlier', 'shortly', 'I wonder', etc., which not only refer to things but also to the discursive process which, simply because it comes into existence, gives things or phenomena roles in relation to the moment when speech occurs. 'Shortly' refers to the phenomenon of the future, but only in relation to the moment when speech is taking place. In the same way, 'earlier' refers to the past. The definite form of nouns, the tense conjugations of verbs or pronouns also cause the reference to become organized via the discursive process. In grammar and semiotics the classical terms 'deixis' or 'deictic elements' have been retained for these phenomena (see Lyons 1977: II, ch. 15, Green 1995). But in a wider semiotic context, as we have seen, they belong to the group of *indexical signs* in the sub-group which Charles Sanders Peirce refers to as *designations*. They establish a relation from signs to things, indicate that things can be localized which can be referred to because of the semiotic process itself, but they do not specify further what sort of things or where they are (the second sub-group consists of the *reagents*, which indicate a causal relation between things and signs – the bird-song is caused by the bird, see Chapter 3, p. 32).

Beyond linguistics

The perspective can be widened from a linguistic to a broader semiotic context in two ways. We can either move from verbal to non-verbal sign-systems (images, gestures, etc.), or we can stay within verbal language but go beyond the basic units of linguistics (words, clauses, phonemes, etc.) to larger units, such as narratives.

A precondition for sign-systems being able to enter into discursive processes is that they contain elements that can link time, space and subject to the enunciation. Non-verbal sign-systems have their own special deictic elements and thus their own ways in which the necessary deictic functions are carried out. In a film it is very difficult to make an image of the relative time in relation to the now of the enunciation. What, for example, does 'shortly' look like, as opposed to 'in a while'? Or what does an image of 'perhaps' look like? The sign-system of a film does not, generally speaking, have many possibilities for creating a graded depiction of this relative time-dimension. On the other hand, it has unique artistic effects for creating contemporaneity between the now of the enunciation, the experience and the events. When we see a dream in a film of a surrealistic nightmare, we are right in the stream of events, and the film has to make considerable efforts to make us aware of the difference between the person dreaming and the onlooker of the dream. Use of supplementary sign-systems, such as verbal language or sound, is often called for.

Verbal language manages everything very easily by adding an 'X said', as in this addition which rightfully belongs to the quotation:

'This is no night to throw a human being out inter,' said the older man.

Now the reader knows who is responsible for the utterance: 'the older man'. The past tense of 'said' tells us that there is an overall narrator who places the older man's utterance as past in relation to the narrative tense. And it also tells us that the present of his utterance refers to a present – the present of the older man at a certain point in time – which is encapsulated in a past which is past in relation to the now in which the narrator communicates to us readers. This is rather complicated when one tries to describe the time-dimensions, but amazingly easy to understand when we read about the older man, since this refined time-structure is incorporated into the language-system of which we are a part. It is of course not possible on the basis of this to determine whether the older man is a real or a fictional person, whether he is speaking the truth, or whether he intends to throw the other person out into the night. The special structuring of time, space and subject is not restricted to literature; it also organizes everyday-language communications about actual events.

So as a rule it is possible to keep a clear head, even when the chronological time of the narrated events is turned upside down in the well-known and far more complicated constructions of literary texts: the older man might also think back and in a stream of consciousness convey his emotions by remembering a cold, dank night, possibly concretized in parenthetical fragments, flash-backs of childhood scenes where he is thrown out into the dark; or the narrator might look forward and tell the reader that the characters do not yet know that the night is full of misfortune, that a traveller will seek shelter and will threaten the house and bring misery to it; or we could spring to another space where other people are engaged in other actions at the same time, returning once more to the older man, etc. Literature can provide a host of examples of such complex time relationships. But as long as we can determine the now of the enunciation as a zero point in the system of time and space coordinates, we are perfectly able to structure the phenomena.

The differences between the sign-systems often lie precisely in the elements with which they anchor the signs in the situation where an utterance is made – their discursive potential, one might perhaps call it. The sign-system of films requires an extra effort for the contemporaneity of presentation, event and experience to be resolved, assuming of course that that is what is desired. The language sign-system, on the other hand, makes it difficult to conquer the distance between the narrated event and the present of the narrative process: even when the keeper of a diary writes 'I' there is a distance between the I who is narrating and that which is being narrated. Yet verbal language can, as in the above quotation, insert direct speech in the present tense into the midst of a past situation and thereby make the reader contemporaneous with an earlier present in and with the present of the reading – and without that causing us to become confused.

Literary textual analysis links these conditions to the phenomena *narrator* and *point of view*. They are discursive instances that are to carry out a double function: *reference* to persons and events and *anchoring* in the verbal enunciation. In some presentations one seeks to draw a sharp distinction: the narrator emphasizes the distance between the text and the narrated events and characters concerning knowledge and credibility, and is responsible for the choice of narrated details, style, metaphorical structure, etc., whereas the point of view indicates the point in relation to the characters from which the reader can view and assess what is narrated. The point of view is responsible for the reference, the narrator for the anchoring of the seen in relation to the reader's now. In other presentations no distinction at all is made between narrator and point of view: both indicate the point, a narrator's point of view, from which the reader can view and assess what is narrated with the aid of a varied number of textual elements.

For discursive analysis, it is the double function not the distinction which is the most important thing: no discourse without simultaneous reference and anchoring of situation. In certain situations it becomes impossible to tell the narrator from the point of view; in others it is both possible and desirable. In any case, both narrator and point of view can be manifested in the same textual elements.

Let us now present a bit more of the scene with the older man in two variants, before looking more closely at the double function:

1 'This is no night to throw a human being out inter,' said the older man, sitting down heavily in the free chair.
2 It is surely a source of amazement to you, my dear Reader, to hear that the older man was sufficiently rude to threaten to throw people out into the night, while he, like most men of his generation, simply sat down heavily in the free chair, without thinking of anyone but himself.

In the first variant we meet in the direct speech – as in all such – a first-person narrator. The distance to the events is zero, there is maximum credibility: the utterance is rendered precisely as it was originally made. The point of view in this case lies with one of the characters, the older man who says those words. In order to make up his mind about its content, purpose, range, etc., the reader has to know something about the older man from other places in the text. Narrator and point of view are one and the same instance. After the remark, the narrator proceeds in the past tense, thereby marking a greater distance to the events. In various, highly discreet ways the narrator underlines certain selected characteristics of the events referred to: 'heavily' stresses a parallel between the man's own physical tiredness and bearing as well as his distaste at the thought of having to go out on such a night. His remark and his behaviour mirror each other. The use of the definite article in 'the free chair' instead of 'his free chair' or 'a free chair' makes it clear that there is only one free chair and that the man quite automatically has the right to sit in it, even without 'his' being in the text. Despite being tired and having a certain degree of self-pity, he exemplifies men's indisputable authority. This interpretation is, however, not made explicit by a narrator. The reader is readily drawn into the events at the characters' level, and the distinction between the now of the events and that of the characters disappears. We interpret as though we were actually there. The narrator creates a minimum of distance to both characters and reader. All three are brought in under the same point of view.

In the second version it becomes clear that it does not have to be like that. The first-person narrator we have here is neither identical with any single character nor situated at the level of the characters – he is communicating directly with the reader. The narrator airs his knowledge about older men's behaviour and attempts to give his depiction a tinge of objectivity, or at any rate of generality – that's the way men are. The assertion is addressed to a reader, whereby both reader and narrator are referred to a shared basis of comparison, though it does not necessarily cover other fictional characters' knowledge and experience of the universe of older men. The narrator expresses no sympathy for the man, who perhaps is tired, but shows his own moral self-righteousness. So the reader has the possibility of adopting a point of view which does not coincide with that of the narrator, for example by conceiving him to be somewhat overbearing. The point of view can, on the other hand, quite easily find itself within a horizon of understanding that could belong to the level of the fictional characters: the facts and attitudes that are conveyed could perfectly well belong to a person in the room who is also irritated with the man. Nevertheless, the point of view does not belong to a single person – but is located on a transpersonal level beyond the individual characters. Thus the narrator is a transpersonal first-person narrator, but the point of view and the narrator do not necessarily coincide: the reader can look at the narrator from the outside and possibly dissociate him/herself from the narrator's self-righteousness.

All sign-systems which at the same time can articulate a reference and an enunciation dimension and which can keep them separate from each other can create a discourse. Without the aid of such systems other sign-systems would not be able to create discourses. A game of chess is a sort of sign-system, with pieces and rules for positions and moves, but it does not of itself become a process until someone via another sign-system says 'Do you want to play?', or invites others to play by means of a gesture, or perhaps writes a book about chess strategies, etc. On the other hand, the tiniest scrap of recognizable language is, by its very presence, an invitation to meaning – it is, to use psychoanalyst Jacques Lacan's term, evocative (Lacan 1966: 181).

Sentence and discourse

Even if we stay within the area of verbal language, a discourse analysis can nevertheless transcend linguistics. In his article 'An introduction to the structural analysis of narratives' (1988) Roland Barthes argues that discourse must be understood in relation to the sentence. It is neither the sign, its component parts nor the sign-system that constitutes the linguistic model, but the combination of signs into a sequence. Discourse is a 'huge sentence', says Barthes, which means that discourse analysis is interwoven with – and for some is identical with – narratology (see Chapter 5).

Barthes is not the only person to see discourse as a special aspect of narration. In particular, the literary researcher Gérard Genette (1980) and his pupil Mieke Bal (1985) have developed discourse analysis in that direction. Even though differences of terminology occur, most people divide narration into two, distinguishing between the *story* and the *discourse*. The story is the sum of the narrated events in a chronological order, as if they took place in reality. The discourse, on the other hand, is – in this context – the sum of the ways in which the story is organized: the use of shifting points of view, of various narrators, of leaps in time, of various modes of presentation, etc. This division corresponds exactly to the classical division between a logical and a linguistic analysis of the sentence: on the one hand that which one wishes to say and which may be right or wrong, and on the other hand rhetoric, which adds a layer of icing to the message to make it more palatable.

When analysing literature, however, this division is more complicated. The discourse, which in this conception of literature is identical with the mode of presentation, is not only a lubricant which ensures the smooth running of communication; it is also a way of bringing the reader's attention to the fact that we are dealing with literary fiction and not with non-fictional prose. This emphasizing of the special holistic nature of the text is not linked to the individual sentence, but to more general narrative principles of composition, to transverse imagery, to the use of points of view and narrators, etc. And the story, for its part, cannot be reduced to an issue which is true or false, credible or incredible, since it is inextricably part of a fictional world. It only exists on discourse's terms, and that which is narrated can even – especially in very modernistic literature – be the work's own sequence of events. The work can have itself as its own object. We are here dealing with the problem of the division between discursive universes (see later, p. 82ff).

Even though Barthes refers to discourse as a 'huge sentence' and has linguistics as his model, the difference between sentence and discourse is not merely one of size. From Émile Benveniste (Benveniste 1974: ch. X) Barthes learns that language sequences from syllable to sentence are organized by two types of element which work simultaneously – the *distributional* and the *integrative*. They are ordered hierarchically, with the distributional superior to the integrative. The former ensures that the formal requirements of the language system are adhered to, and when the latter is added, form becomes meaning. Thus the sequence of phonemes /-ip/ consists of distributional elements which have a spelling in English, whereas /-knrdt-/ does not have such a form. If /ʃ-/ is now added to the syllable /-ip/, the /ʃ-/ becomes an integrative element, since the whole becomes a sign with the meaning 'ship'. This integration can be taken further, since this sign can now be an integrative element which conveys meaning at a higher level, e.g. in the compound 'ship-0-yard' (0 = zero element). Seen from a formal point of view, this linguistic unit only consists of distributional elements, i.e. when they indicate the form that compounds must have in English: x-0-y. In other languages, like German, an explicit link may be required ('ship-0-yard' is 'Schiff-*s*-werft' in German, but zero elements are also possible, 'friend-0-ship' is 'Freund-0-schaft'). The compound can in turn be integrated into more comprehensive linguistic units, with the sentence marking the ultimate boundary.

Barthes partially modifies Benveniste, so as to be able to characterize the discursive nature of narration with the aid of an alternation between distributional and integrative elements. Let us begin by placing the remark of the older man in its right context before continuing with Barthes. The remark is made in John Dos Passos's novel *The 42nd Parallel* (1930), which is the first part of the *U.S.A.* trilogy (1936). The whole trilogy is a kaleidoscopic portrait of the USA from the turn of the century to the early 1930s. Many of the characters appear in constantly changing contexts throughout all three volumes. One of the main characters in the first volume, Fainy O'Hara McCreary, is a poor boy who works for the crook Doc Bingham, an almost

Dickensian figure. He publishes and sells books, sometimes pornographic, sometimes religious, surrounding himself with an artificial atmosphere of eloquence, breeding and learning. He has rented a horse and cart and has now arrived, with Fainy, at a farm, where he is trying to find shelter for the night and to sell a book to the two women of the farm, who prove to be alone in the house. The following long quotation (with some omissions) constitutes the textual basis to which we will return during the continued analysis of the concept of discourse in the rest of this chapter (Dos Passos 1979: 64ff.):

'Good afternoon, ma'am.' Doc Bingham was on his feet bowing to a little old woman who had come out of the door. . . . 'Come inside, mister . . . maybe you'd like to sit beside the stove and dry yourself. Come inside, mister-er?' 'Doc Bingham's the name . . . the Reverend Doctor Bingham,' Fainy heard him say as he went in the house.

He was soaked and shivering when he went into the house himself, carrying a package of books under his arm. Doc Bingham was sitting large as life in a rocking chair in front of the kitchen stove. Beside him on the well-scrubbed deal table was a piece of pie and a cup of coffee. . . .

'Ah, Fenian, just in time,' he began in a voice that purred like the cat, 'I was just telling . . . relating to your kind hostesses the contents of our very interesting and educational library, the prime of the world's devotional and inspirational literature. . . .'

. . . A booklet dropped to the floor. Fainy saw that it was *The Queen of the White Slaves*. A shade of sourness went over Doc Bingham's face. He put his foot on the dropped book. 'These are Gospel Talks, my boy,' he said. 'I wanted *Doctor Spikenard's Short Sermons for All Occasions*.' . . . 'I suppose I'll have to go and find them myself,' he went on in his purringest voice. When the kitchen door closed behind them he snarled in Fainy's ear, 'Under the seat, you little rat . . . If you play a trick like that again I'll break every goddam bone in your body.' And he brought his knee up so hard into the seat of Fainy's pants that his teeth clacked together and he shot into the rain towards the barn. . . .

'How much are they?' asked the old woman, a sudden sharpness coming over the features. . . .

'Oh, if they're only ten cents I think I'd like one,' said the old woman quickly. The scrawny woman started to say something, but it was too late.

. . . The old woman got to her feet and looked nervously at the door, which immediately opened. A heavyset grayhaired man with a small goatee sprouting out of round red face came in, shaking the rain off the flaps of his coat. After him came a skinny lad about Fainy's age.

'How do you do, sir; how do you do, son?' boomed Doc Bingham through the last of his pie and coffee.

'They asked if they could put their horse in the barn until it should stop rainin'. It's all right, ain't it, James?' asked the old woman nervously. 'I reckon so,' said the older man, sitting down heavily in the free chair. The old woman had hidden the pamphlet in the drawer of the kitchen table. 'Travelin' on books, I gather.' He stared hard at the open package of pamphlets. 'Well, we don't need any of that trash here, but you are welcome to stay the night in the barn. This is no night to throw a human being out inter.'

So they unhitched the horse and made beds for themselves in the hay over the cowstable. Before they left the house the older man made them give up their matches. 'Where there's matches there's danger of fire,' he said. Doc Bingham's face was black as thunder as he wrapped himself in a horseblanket, muttering about 'indignity to a wearer of the cloth.' Fainy was excited and happy. He lay on his back listening to the beat of the rain on the roof and its gurgle in the gutters, and the muffled stirring and champing of the cattle and horse, under them; . . . . He wished he had someone his own age to talk to. Anyway, it was a job and he was on the road.

He had barely got to sleep when a light woke him. The boy he'd seen in the kitchen was standing over him with a lantern . . . .

'Say, I wanner buy a book . . . one o' them books about chorus girls an' white slaves an' stuff like that. . . . I couldn't go higher'n a dollar . . . Say, you won't tell the old man on me?' the young man said, turning from one to another.

(Dos Passos 1979 [1930])

While Benveniste has the sentence as the upper limit of his discourse analysis, Barthes has the sentence as the smallest unit of this analysis, not wishing, for example, to break down the sentence 'This is no night to throw a human being out inter' into linguistic minimal units, as does Benveniste. Furthermore, Barthes only operates with two levels in the hierarchy, not with a continued series, as does Benveniste. He renames Benveniste's distributional elements *functions*, dividing them into two sub-groups, *cardinal functions* or *nuclei* and *catalyses*, while referring to the integrative elements as *indices*, considering them as being of two kinds, *indices strictly speaking*, here called *indices proper*, and *items of information*, here called *information* (see Table 4.1). All texts contain all four types of elements, and their demarcation is arbitrary in relation to the text-manifestation (they can be a sentence, a word, a syntagm, an inflection, a whole sequence, etc.).

Table 4.1 Distributional and integrative elements

Discourse			
Functions		Indices	
Nuclei	Catalyses	Information	Indices proper

Nuclei logically link together the course of events and cannot be altered without the story itself becoming a different story. In the story about Fainy and Doc Bingham the nuclei are their arrival at the farm, the invitation to come inside, the sale of the book, the older man's return, the night spent in the barn. The elements of the course of secondary events, on the other hand, are called *catalyses*. There are several of them: Fainy being sent out for the right pamphlets, the announcement of the book's price, Fainy getting some food, the boy getting a spicy book.

Indices are elements which are not bound together by virtue of the story or which do not contribute to its cohesion, but which are linked at a level above the actual narrative linking: the localization in time and space, the nature and psychology of the characters and the narrative process. The nature of the *indices proper* is often implicit, while items of *information* are normally explicit. We are provided with information about the furniture and equipment of the kitchen, the appearance of the older man, the wind and weather, the nervousness of the women, etc. The items of information are identical with content at sentence level, which is the prime concern of linguists. The indices proper are manifested, for example, in the women hiding the pamphlet, or Doc Bingham's mixed ways of speaking. These textual elements can be seen as indices proper, i.e. indices for the women's fear of the older man, or Doc Bingham's cunning hypocrisy.

The fundamental discursive distinctiveness of a text is for Barthes characterized by the relation between the functions and the indices. From their distribution and emphasis he first determines the typical discursive nature of a text, using this as a base for a subsequent detailed narrative discourse analysis. Texts where functions dominate over indices stress the course of events – folktales, for example. If, however, we meet a lot of catalyses and the elements of the text thereby become parataxical and loosely linked, we are looking at impressionistic texts, such as, for example, the stories of Guy de Maupassant. If, on the other hand, the indices are given the greatest say, we are looking at texts where a state of mind, an ideological message, or something similar is of greater importance than the course of events, such as, for example, in an allegory or a psychological portrait. If there is a stark reduction in the items of information, the very dissolving of a localizable story can be taken to great lengths, as is the case, for example, in William Faulkner's novels, whereas a wealth of information creates a naturalistic discourse, as is the case in Émile Zola.

Barthes retains the same basic idea that we know from the analysis of enunciation: with linguistics as a model the formal structures of the text are examined, enabling one to confirm that part of their structural distinctiveness is that they point beyond themselves, anchoring the text in a wider context. The sign-system has its enunciation-markers, while the narrative structure has its indices. It is these characteristics that discursive analysis seizes on in order to understand what it means to say that form creates meaning.

Phenomenological discourse analysis

Intentionality and subject

However, not all those who are interested in discourse use linguistics as a model. Phenomenology is a branch of philosophy which emphasizes the role intentionality and subjectivity play in discourse. Language is of course an important factor here too, but not as a special sign-system or an oral or written mode of expression – rather as a dynamic part of the process that channels intentionality and subjectivity. And that process is seldom dealt with by traditional linguistic categories in phonetics and grammar. When linguists, on the other hand, do attempt from time to time to understand the relationship between language and intentionality, they are often obliged to fill in a vacuum in language analysis that otherwise escapes linguists' attention. That cannot fail to attract semioticians.

The linguist Viggo Brøndal accepts the division made in linguistics between the language-system on the one hand and the concrete language usage we see and hear in a particular context on the other. In the system the elements are only defined in their mutual similarity and dissimilarity as certain possibilities for use. In most languages the system makes a distinction between singular and plural and definite and indefinite forms of nouns, but the one form is not 'better' than the other, it is simply different. In concrete language usage there are certain rules concerning cohesion between the realized sign-elements: in clauses the negation has to be in a certain position; certain clauses can be put earlier or later in the sentence although others cannot; and in certain cases there is more than one correct solution available for the sequential order of the clauses.

But what sort of logic is involved in our preferring certain of the possibilities of the system rather than others, and certain language sequence structures rather than others? For Brøndal it is *discourse*. This is the regulating mechanism which, like a filter, lies between the system and the actual usage. Unlike system and usage, discourse is not limited to particular natural languages; it is an order which cuts across the individual language-systems and usages, giving them an identity as precisely language phenomena, as opposed to every other conceivable type of system or usage (games, mathematical language, etc.).

In his article 'Langage et logique' (1933) Brøndal defines discourse as an order which makes the language usage *irreversible* (Larsen 1987). This means that each and every language usage is an extension of another one – it comments on it, reinterprets it, expands it, reacts towards it. Even when we say that we are going to start again from the beginning, we do not go back – we repeat what we have said at a new point in the stream of speech. We do not begin from the beginning, we continue to move forwards. Materially speaking, a sentence begins at a certain point, but logically it adds to innumerable previous sentences – and that is actually why it is capable of being understood.

This *irreversibility* is not linked to a formal logic; it results from discourse steering language in the direction of a subject or an object about which it wishes to say something. Brøndal says that discourse thereby provides the language-system with an *intention* which enables there to be anything at all to express and to refer to with the elements of the system. Discourse ensures that elements which cannot be used to say anything disappear from the system, even though they are logical and possible, and that sentence constructions which are formally correct but unintelligible are not put to use. This is why Brøndal claims that intentionality permeates all elements of language and makes it possible for them to come alive, acquire a precise meaning and a personal identity. Intentionality, in other words, ensures that language grows together with *subjectivity* and *consciousness*.

Let us take another look at the old man in the chair: 'This is no night to throw a human being out inter.' There is no language rule which determines in advance that night has to be specified by a negation combined with an infinitive clause. 'This is a terrible night' or 'This is a night to stay indoors' are equally correct from a morphological and syntactical point of view. But by the use of negation plus infinitive the utterance is placed in relation to an assumed knowledge about (1) other, different nights which form a contrast to this one, and (2) that this contrast is a part of the knowledge of the speaking subjects about what it means to be out on such a night or not. Language calls upon a pre-existing knowledge or action in relation to that we are hearing or reading. Literature exploits this effect, whether anything has actually taken place in advance or not, as in the opening lines of Dos Passos's first chapter about Fainy, where the readers are placed *in medias res*: 'When the wind set from the silver factories across the river the air of the gray fourfamily frame house where Fainy McCreary was born was choking all day with the smell of whaleoil soap' (Dos Passos 1979: 30). No matter whether we know in advance or not about the factories, weather, house and smell of whaleoil soap, the repeated use of the definite article creates the impression that we ought to know about these things. That is how *irreversibility* works: assumptions are activated in the discursive process, thereby turning meaning into a continuous process.

Moreover, the older man's utterance forces the reader not only to look backwards but also forwards towards the meaning that is to be made precise: is the utterance a metaphorical description or a concealed command or threat? Will they be thrown out, do they decide to leave for themselves, or do they stay indoors? And which of these and other possible meanings are important? No matter what its form, the utterance cannot avoid pointing at one or more matters which are – or are to be – made more precise. That is its *intentionality*.

But precisely because it is the night that is specified – and not the clothing, money or mood of the characters – a selection has already been made of which particular assumed knowledge is relevant and casts its shadow in front of the utterance. It is not just a question of some meaning or other being determined – but the subject-matter is already in focus. There is a subjective consciousness which conveys that there is one particular area of meaning that is most relevant. And this focusing should preferably be perceived and confirmed. For we are looking at a *communication* from someone to some others about a more exactly demarcated subject-matter.

Whether such a subjective consciousness belongs to a fictional character, a narrator-instance, a single individual or a collective subject in this context is irrelevant. The important thing is that without attention being brought to the fact that there is a subjective consciousness involved, the discursive logic would never be able to bring the language process to a conclusion – for in principle it can go on for ever, with one sentence following on the other and attention constantly being directed towards something new. But when a focusing takes place which makes the usage into a communication, there will come a point in time when the message has been received and understood and there will possibly be a criterion for deciding on misunderstanding and disagreement, or for one being able to say that the discursive process has not only been stopped but also been broken off prematurely. From this point one can begin again. This means that the discursive order in the principle makes all utterances potential *dialogues*: they simply cannot be perceived as meaning unless perceived as being sent from one person to another about a certain subject. The older man, however, does not have to exert himself any further. All subsequent conversation is superfluous. Without further ado, Fainy and Doc Bingham take their chance with the barn.

Brøndal – like other contemporaries from the 1920s and 1930s, such as Roman Jakobson and Karl Bühler – gains inspiration for his speculations from phenomenology, with such names in the twentieth century as Edmund Husserl and the post-war figures of Maurice Merleau-Ponty and Paul Ricœur (Innis 1982). If linguistics is too narrow for semiotics, then phenomenology as a whole turns out to be too comprehensive. Based on an analysis of the way in which the world and phenomena appear to consciousness in the immediate experience, this branch of philosophy seeks to break through to a cognition of what things are. How can we understand things so that their immediate appearance to us *refers* to what they really are, even though we only know them as they appear to us, i.e. when they always are *signs*? Since consciousness in phenomenology is by definition *intentional*, it cannot help addressing itself to things and cannot help asking this question. A consciousness which is not a consciousness *about* something is no consciousness at all. If sense perception has not supplied any sense-impressions, consciousness will therefore imagine them for itself – via language, poetry, dreams, dancing, etc. In other words, consciousness constantly creates signs for the things it addresses. Our relationship to the things which appear to us is thus permeated by subjectivity. They are things in *our* world. But signs have to be intelligible, i.e. shared, so the knowledge we have about the things that appear to us will be *intersubjective*, and will always be able to be the object of a *dialogue* between those who use the signs, possibly as an inner dialogue in their own head. This is why verbal language is so important a sign-system: it is seething with signs which refer to things and at the same time it orders the semiotic process in such a way that intentionality and subjectivity prove to be a possible dialogue (cf. Larsen 1994a).

Intersubjectivity and dialogue are, however, not enough to be able to ascertain whether our knowledge is correct. They are only means to make precise *what* we could consider investigating the correctness of. We must treat with caution the phenomenological project of constructing signs by means of which consciousness can get behind both the signs which things are for us (primarily indexical signs) and the signs we construct ourselves (primarily symbolical signs). For we are not able to wrench ourselves out of verbal language and thereby out of the elements that the analysis of enunciation focuses on: 'I', 'you', 'here', 'now', 'perhaps', verb conjugations, definite forms, etc., which refer to the process we speak *in* as well as to the things we talk *about*. So semiotics has to reduce phenomenology's wider conception of, especially, intentionality to sign-specific phenomena.

That intentionality does not only mean an individual intention, as in the case of the older man, is fairly evident. We intend to operate with five types of intentionality.

1   *General intentionality*: Everyone's attention is directed towards something. Independently of what this 'something' is or whether it can be determined, it is the *sine qua non* for people being able to conceive themselves as being present subjects: Doc Bingham is oriented towards hunger, rest and a quick buck; the women towards the reading of books and fear of the older man; the boy towards a little forbidden pornography; the older man towards ridding himself of the nuisance of the strangers. They all orient their consciousness towards a point of balance, where they both reveal themselves and at the same time conceal something of themselves from the others: the women hide their fear of the man while appearing to be accommodating; Doc Bingham hides the fact that he is a small-time swindler while overtly recommending his printed material; the older man overtly shows hospitality and hides his wish to throw the intruders out. It is this ambivalence in all of them towards which the consciousness of the narrator is oriented and which means that the reader can see them as interrelated subjects in the fiction. Even those who attempt to retire into silence or the dark – or who would most like to do so – are involved, since no consciousness can shut itself in and avoid being oriented towards something, long before it becomes something particular. Such a *general* intentionality that cuts across persons and groups is a prerequisite for being able to perceive that oneself and others are present at all. Therefore we can, for example, talk about the presence of a narrative consciousness in a text, even though we cannot put a name to this narrator.

2   *Discursive intentionality*: Those present convert intentionality into a semiotic process: they persuade, give orders, come with offers of food or

books, characterize the night; they also direct their bodily movements by walking, coming, kicking, eating, hiding, etc. By means of this, general intentionality is able to become directed towards something particular with a point of departure in a subject. This is *discursive* intentionality.

3 *Specifying intentionality*: Even though the characters all help to make the intentionality discursive in a semiotic process, they do not do so in the same way. Intentionality is specified or concretized in various types of discourse (verbal, non-verbal, orders, affirmations, questions, silence, etc.) with different marked-off meanings as a result: some have to do with food; others with other things (chairs, horse-carriages, etc.); and others again with norms (enlightenment, belief, inclination, etc.). By means of this the situation is *specified* as a whole in various part-phenomena, gaining the appearance of a differentiated world.

4 *Situational intentionality*: Specifying intentionality makes precise the meanings which map out the surrounding world. But there is also an orientation towards the situation-determined framework within which the specifications take place. Phenomenologists tend to speculate most about the different reality-status of objects: they can be real, fictive, logical, normative, etc., possibly interwoven as when in Dos Passos and his characters we meet an orientation towards predominantly real objects, but in a fictive space. The semiotician tends to be more concrete and look at the situation or type of situation in which the meanings come into existence. For this situation imposes some important conditions for how the meaning of the specifying intentionality is to be understood. In the quotation we are gathered round a kitchen table, not in a sauna; we are on a farm, not climbing a mountain; we are in a space where residents and vagrants meet, etc. *Situational* intentionality is one way of referring to it.

5 *Individual intentionality*: Some utterances – verbal as well as non-verbal – can be linked to particular individuals who consciously choose to express themselves in a particular way, with a particular intention: 'I wish I could throw you out' is how the utterance of the older man can be translated. But this *individual* intentionality never stands alone. It is also within the framework of certain common conditions for what can be understood and accepted in the particular situation. The older man expresses his authority and contempt by offering the barn as overnight accommodation for both horses and visitors, while excluding any further negotiation by specifying the night in the light of the possibility of one being thrown out into it. The women choose to remain silent about the slightly more generous hospitality they have implied by serving food and buying books, and by suggesting that only the horses be housed in the barn. Individual intentionality can, however, never fully control what is said: while revealing a particular meaning one also characterizes oneself, with or against one's will – the women show their nervousness precisely

because they are offering a hospitality they do not have the complete authority to offer. Individual authority also creates unexpected effects of which one may be completely unaware – the silent boy has sensed that there is much more titillating reading for sale than religious pamphlets and that he can lay his hands on it precisely because Doc Bingham is banished to the barn. The farmer's power over his visitors reduces his power over the boy. And precisely because Bingham is cheated out of shelter at the farm he is able to compensate by squeezing an extra $1 out of the boy. And Fainy, who has riled Bingham by pricing the pamphlet as low as 10 cents, has even so to add $1 to Bingham's assets. In other words: individual intentionality exists on condition that discursive intentionality has established the possibility of these unforeseen situations taking place.

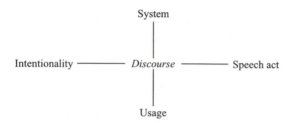

Figure 4.1 Field of discourse.

In discourse the line linking the semiotic system and the semiotic usage on which the linguistic point of view focuses intersects, as does the line linking intentionality and the speech act, which is in the forefront of a phenomen-ological consideration (see Figure 4.1). The *speech act* is our next topic.

Speech act

Many utterances in the long quotation on pp. 66–67 are assertions about facts: 'A booklet dropped to the floor', 'The old woman had hidden the pamphlet in the drawer of the kitchen table' and 'These are Gospel Talks'. Others invite practical actions to be undertaken: 'Come inside', 'Maybe you'd like to sit beside the stove and dry yourself', 'I suppose I'll have to go and find them myself', 'If you play a trick like that again I'll break every goddam bone in your body' and 'Say, you won't tell the old man on me?' Finally, there are others which are slightly less clear-cut, for example: 'Well, we don't need any of that trash here'. This utterance may be an assertion about a fact, i.e. the need of the person speaking. But it may also be a way of calling the religious writings trash simply by the utterance being made – they are herewith called trash. Lastly, the utterance may be a call to throw them into the stove.

Apparently, there are two main types of utterances involved here: some which do not themselves have anything to do with action, but which only refer to it, e.g. mention of the fact that the women have hidden the pamphlets they have bought; and a different type which has to do with action and which, in turn, is divided into two types: one which calls for action after the sentence has been uttered and possibly prescribes what is to be done. And there is a final type, which in itself is a sort of action that is carried out by the very act of speaking. None of these three types is bound to special language expressions, but all three are linked to a particular function. So there is nothing to prevent non-verbal sign-systems from carrying out these functions: when Doc Bingham kicks Fainy it is a call to fetch the books immediately, and by doing so he is also putting him in his place as someone who is in his power, as well as stating that Fainy has made a mistake. A particular verbal utterance, too, can – as we have just seen – perfectly well take care of various different functions at one and the same time.

For this reason, it is impossible to uphold a clear-cut division between utterances that are actions and others that are not. If an action is a material process that can be referred back to a subject with an intention, a demonstrating utterance is also an action. For here there is one person who says '[I claim that] These are Gospel Talks'. And we can either confirm or deny this. In this case the subject is an individual, Doc Bingham, but another subject, the narrator, helps us in denying it – it was '*The Queen of the White Slaves*'. In other instances, '[I claim that] a booklet dropped to the floor', the subject is not individualized. It is the narrator – but it is still a question of the marking of a subjective intention. All three types of utterance become acts, so-called *speech acts*.

The analysis of speech acts comprises in the widest sense the formation of meaning which takes place in human dialogue, its validity and its basis and purpose. Analysis of speech acts arose as a consequence of the recognition that the utterances in which signs refer to objects and facts cannot at any time – as was believed in classical logic – be detached from the situation in which they are uttered and the dialogic structure they have. So how can one determine the conditions for the validity of utterances? In this wide perspective the analysis of the speech act in semiotics belongs together with the account of the concept of text (see Chapter 6, p. 139ff). In connection with discourse analysis we limit the perspective to the role the subjective intention plays in the speech act, with examples from Dos Passos's text.

The English linguistic philosopher J.L. Austin claims that all utterances are speech acts, or *locutionary* acts, which contain a subjective intention (Austin 1962). The difference between them lies in their relation to *time*. The first, *constatives*, are mainly concerned with something which *has* taken place. The booklet has dropped to the floor before we express ourselves. The next, the *perlocutionary*, point to actions that *will* take place in continuation of the utterance. And the last, the *illocutionary*, deal with what is taking place *here and now* while speaking is going on. So we have three types of speech act:

I say that a booklet dropped to the floor
I say that you may come in
I say that I herewith declare books to be trash

When utterances are seen as speech acts in this way, one has integrated the enunciation aspect into their basic definition. They have an interlocutionary force through their anchoring in a subject of enunciation and in the now of the enunciation. This conception is one that the linguistic philosopher John Searle is not all that satisfied with, for it makes all utterances the same in kind (Searle 1969, 1976). For him it is more important to look not at their illocutionary force but at their illocutionary aim: all utterances, by being said, are directed towards a possible receiver who is to be convinced about something. All utterances are structured with a view to a possible dialogue on the basis of an enunciation. In other words: all utterances are discursive phenomena.

Searle extends Austin, classifying five different types of utterance according to their built-in aim:

- *assertives*, which are to convince the receiver of the truth of an utterance ('A booklet dropped to the floor')
- *directives*, which are to get the receiver to do something ('Come inside!')
- *commissives*, which are to oblige the utterer to do something or to avoid doing something ('I suppose I'll have to go and find them myself')
- *expressives*, which are to convince the receiver of the sincerity of a state of mind ('Well, we don't need any of that trash here')
- *declaratives*, which guarantee the receiver that what is being said is valid by the very fact of it being said ('If you play a trick like that again I'll break every goddam bone in your body' = I hereby promise to punish you if you play a trick again).

Searle's analysis makes the speech act into a kind of communication. Even though the speech act is an act among other acts and one which is not bound by particular grammatical forms or particular systems of expression, it is not identical with any act whatsoever, nor does it include all types of communication. In terms used by Jürgen Habermas one can speak of a *communicative act* (Habermas 1987a). A communicative act is one where participants coordinate their efforts so as to reach agreement. At the same time, it is an act in which the participants have the possibility of criticizing the conditions for the validity of this consensus (Honneth and Jonas 1991).

Because of this, communicative acts differ in two ways from communication in the wide sense of the term. It is not sufficient to talk about the exchange of information, as between micro-organisms or in an electronic network. There have to be subjective intentions involved which – possibly under compulsion – express themselves in the common striving to understand or accept the message. Nor is it sufficient to concentrate on the communication process and the content separately, as traditional communication models can tempt one to do. In the communicative act there is a built-in possibility for adopting a stance towards the conditions of the process simply because it is taking place – have the conditions for my wishing to continue to be part of it been fulfilled, and for my being able to understand and accept what is taking place? This knowledge of – and possible control over – the choices available does not simply lie in the exchange of information; it is due to a continuous reflection on the very anchoring the dialogue has by means of the enunciation. Discourse is dialogue that is anchored in a situation. Communicative action is a discursive process.

The speech act must therefore be analysed in such a way that the participating subjects' roles and the conditions for its anchoring in a situation are evident, not in such a way that it is only seen as the manifestation of a particular semiotic system. For that purpose, the linguist Oswald Ducrot (Ducrot 1971) and the linguistic philosopher H.P. Grice (Grice 1975), among others, have looked at some of the conventions that make a dialogue a success, but which of course are also criteria for it possibly being a fiasco if they are not adhered to.

Grice operates with three elements in the dialogue:

1 *The utterance*: 'This is no night to throw a human being out inter.'
2 *Conventional implicit understanding*, which the parties take for granted by virtue of the own rules of the semiotic system and which in this case have to do with actually being able to understand English: we understand implicitly that it actually is night, that it is a bad one to be out in, that we have quick access to it, that the language permits expressions with various meanings, etc.
3 *Situational implicit understanding*, which is linked to certain situational conditions for the holding of the actual dialogue, which are shared by all those taking part in the dialogue, but which are not determined by the semiotic system. Grice lists at this point the conditions that seek to establish clarity in the dialogue: look for areas of common understanding, be brief, concise, candid, etc. He would probably not be content with the older man's ambiguous threat as an example of a successful conversation. But it worked nevertheless.

The utterance is seen as part of a speech act and is linked to a subjective intention – to want to express something. The conventional implicit understandings elucidate the potential meanings and possible ambiguities that the given semiotic system permits. They cannot be chosen, but belong to the utterance in the form they happen to have. The situational preconditions indicate the common rules according to which the dialogue is controlled by those taking part. It is these rules – and neither utterance nor conventions – that finally decide how an utterance functions as a speech act. On the basis of this the speaker can choose between the possibilities that the conventional implicit understandings have placed at his or her disposal, and to follow the situational preconditions or to break them, with differing subsequent consequences for the dialogue.

What this means can be illustrated by another of the older man's remarks: 'Where there's matches there's danger of fire.' According to its language form the utterance could at first glance be understood as what Searle calls an *assertive*, a universally valid assertion about the relationship between matches and fire. Since 'is danger of' also includes a future perspective, the utterance can also be understood as a *directive* ('give me your matches') or a *commissive* ('I'll throw you out if you don't give me your matches'). Finally, the utterance could be understood as an *expressive* ('I am afraid of you guys with your matches'). It is also possible that the older man will put forward a *declarative* ('I hereby forbid the use of open fire'). When deciding which meanings are the most correct, or which is the only correct one, one has to include the situational implicit understandings.

Here this type of understanding is defined by a situation in which someone asks for shelter without being able to demand it formally, but in which, conversely, the unwritten rules make it difficult for the farmer to refuse hospitality. In other words, there is an ambiguous power relationship between the implicated parties. For that reason, Grice's requirements concerning intelligibility, sincerity, clarity, precision, etc. will have to be retuned to precisely this situation. Although the utterances have the form of *assertives* ('This is no night to throw a human being out inter' and 'Where there's matches there's danger of fire'), and although it is possible to conceive of both of them as several different speech acts, the utterance is always understood as a particular speech act in a particular context: in the conversation between the farmer and Bingham they become *directives*, speech acts which bring about other acts: there is no further discussion, and Doc Bingham and Fainy end up in the barn and surrender their matches. The farmer retains the role of host, asserting his formal right to decide things in his own house and to decide who and what may be in it, while not being directly inhospitable: 'You are welcome to stay the night in the barn,' he says, the narrator discreetly reassuring us that 'the older man made them give up their matches'. He observes two non-conventional rules determined by the given situation: be polite; but insist on your rights. In doing so, he turns Bingham's behaviour on its head. During his entire visit he has been polite in order to demand that which he does not have a right to, but he uses a kick to have the services carried out by Fainy.

But is Bingham's kicking really part of the process of carrying out a discursive act? Is he carrying out something which is analogous to a speech act? He expresses himself non-verbally in a way that clearly functions successfully as a *directive*: Fainy does in fact return with the right books. But Bingham violates no less than several situationally determined preconditions for dialogue. And not only by being impolite. When he uses a sign-system that only comprises two elements – to kick or not to kick – there is strictly speaking no possible answer. If one replies by the same sign, it can only be by repeating the first sign, possibly to a higher degree, i.e. a harder kick or some sort of blow. If one reacts by not using violence, one leaves the communication situation. And if one replies in the form of other acts – like fetching the books – one has accepted that no answer can be *chosen*. One can only react by a reflex action. So it is not possible to converse, let alone adopt a stance to the conditions for communication. It is a pure demonstration of power, carried out via bodily and audible – though non-verbal – signs. It can possibly be outbidden by a higher power, which puts an end to the violence, but which precisely excludes the possibility of creating a dialogue. And the verbal signs that Doc Bingham uses when he snarls at Fainy are subordinate to the binary logic of the kicking: there are threats and unambiguous orders that can only be answered by yes or no.

It is not, then, what Habermas would agree to call a communicative act. Nor is it a speech act, in the sense that Austin, Searle and Grice use the term: all situational non-conventional rules are neglected. Is it a discourse? A subject is localized with an intention that can be accommodated within the five types of intentionality we have discussed. The intention materializes in a recognizable and highly direct body language which underlines the anchoring of the sign-process in the now of an enunciation. There is an allocation of subjects in a dialogue: some kick and others are kicked and react to this violence. But throughout such a dialogue the roles cannot in principle be exchanged in a continuing process. So if discourse is supposed to allocate subjective roles which, as I and you, are exchangeable, we cannot speak of a discourse in this case. If, conversely, we accept that every allocation of roles also involves roles being absolutely fixed, in such a way that this division of power is both determined and maintained by the discourse, then we can speak of a discourse also in the case of Bingham's kicking. It is this problem that is addressed by the sociological consideration.

Sociological discourse analysis

Discourse and power

A semiotic system demarcates certain elements in relation to each other, determining thereby certain potential meanings. But the system does not indicate in itself how an exchange of signs must take place, or how the subjects who undertake the exchange must relate to each other. It does not say anything about which meanings are more correct or have more impact than others. The very existence of such systems, including natural language in particular, thus contains the ideal of a communication without supremacy. This is the basis of Jürgen Habermas's conception of discourse.

On the other hand, we have also seen that the system already contains built-in elements which predetermine an allocation of subject-positions – 'I', 'you', 'she', 'here', 'there', etc. But each such division is based on power, the system therefore being designed to forcibly and indissolubly link together conversation, referential knowledge, speech act and meaning-formation. This is the basis of Michel Foucault's conception of discourse (cf. Cooper 1981; Dreyfus and Rabinow 1982).

Foucault's concept of discourse is more described than defined through a series of reformulations during his career; it is at any rate highly unsuitable for an entry in a concept dictionary. It is developed from *Les mots et les choses* (1966) via *Archéologie du savoir* (1969) to *Surveiller et punir* (1977) and *Histoire de la sexualité* (1976 and subsequent years), although it has a cohesive aim and a number of functional characteristics. Foucault's reason for introducing the concept is that he wishes to analyse how power and knowledge are linked and regulate practical actions, not on an individual but an institutionalized collective basis. Discourse is this regulatory mechanism. Discourse is a compulsion we exercise over things, is how it is put in Foucault's published lecture *L'ordre du discours* (1970/1981), where the reformulations of his concept of discourse intersect.

At the beginning of his writings, discourse for Foucault represents a symbolic order which in various sign-systems expresses the common knowledge of an epoch, in such a way that it acquires collectively binding validity and becomes the obvious – but not necessarily conscious – point of departure for possible and permitted actions. The accepted conceptions of sick and healthy, expressed in literature, law texts, paintings, broadsheets, books on medicine, etc., give rise to certain practical relations with and treatment of the sick. So the power of discourse lies in its exclusion of the incomprehensible or unacceptable, in its integration of human beings within the framework of the acceptable and comprehensible and in its hierarchical allocation here of the roles among the participants in the discourse, so that they are adhered to.

But precisely that which is excluded from one discursively determined context can find a place in some other one. Discursive power not only holds sway as a cohesive force within an area; it also does so between discourses on a collision course. An ecological and an economic growth discourse have difficulty in getting along with each other. Even though the one does not give rise to the other, they are nevertheless, by their simultaneous incompatibility, linked to each other. Discourses create continuity and a dominating, controlling power over thought and action; at the same time they create discontinuity and conflict between competing forms of power where none has absolute dominance and which are therefore unpredictable in their outcome. So discourses probably create restrictions and limitations, but at the same time they make it possible for the unexpected and thus unique event to take place and be converted into new knowledge that can possibly be retained. The discursive process moves in such fits and starts and is deposited in history like archaeological strata.

If we now were to allow Foucault to witness Doc Bingham and Fainy's visit to the farm, he would be in no doubt about the relationship between power, knowledge and discourse. Bingham's kicking is part of a power discourse as a corporeal dimension of the power relationships which are otherwise manifested in the speech of the characters. Fainy does not openly criticize Bingham's violence, nor do the women mention the absent farmer, who apparently dictates their thoughts and speech even so, causing them to be visibly nervous. Here power is present as silence in speech instead of non-verbal expression. And when the man – the true centre of power – arrives on the scene, everyone loses control over speech and actions: the women get up; the pamphlets are unsuccessfully hidden; the selling of books ceases; and Bingham's flow of rhetoric dries up. Indeed, not a single word is exchanged between the host and his guests – the man says what there is to be said. All of them are reduced to the status of hired hands, or even of animals by being thrown out to the horses in the barn and given the use of 'horseblankets'. Such is the homogenizing effect of power discourse when the subjective roles are allocated and maintained.

Nevertheless, unexpected effects arise in the wake of the discourse of power. Unlike the silent subjugation of the women, the barn opens up the possibility of another discourse, and thus another subjectivity. Fainy realizes that there is a world that lies outside the reach of Bingham. He experiences happiness at the sound of animals, rain and the smell of hay, and 'He wished he had someone of his own age to talk to' – which then transpires, in the shape of the skinny lad from the farm, who was 'about Fainy's age'. Fainy, however, does not avail himself of this opportunity – he does not even see it. Instead, he foists a spicy book on him as effectively as Bingham himself could have done; he behaves exactly as Bingham would have done: 'Anyway it was a job and he was on the road.' At the same time, the banishing of the visitors to the barn has precisely the effect of allowing the boy to get a chance of breaking the master's monopoly on books and opinions, as well as of getting the pornographic book he wishes to see without being discovered. Even Bingham salvages something out of his defeat – he manages to get one of the books sold that he could not get rid of at the farm – and at a price he would not have been able to get the women to pay. Foucault would see opposing discourses in action here, with the farmer's as the dominating – though not the totally controlling – one.

Jürgen Habermas would not deny the struggle for power, but would rather say that it occurs precisely where discourse stops. He claims that when Foucault makes discourses power relationships by definition, he is drawing the wrong conclusion. Admittedly, Foucault has described and documented a long series of concrete discursive power relationships, but he cannot on the basis of that claim that they are the fundamental characteristic of discourse (Habermas 1987b: chs IX and X). Habermas is of the contrary opinion that discourse realizes the constitutionally – and not historically – developed characteristic of language, i.e. that it enables a coercion-free consensus among those who share the language. So discourse itself is not bound by experience; it represents a possibility in man as a language-using creature to characterize his experience. And since language is taken over and not chosen, everyone belongs to the framework of such a possible consensus concerning the world of experience. Even though, in a concrete situation, one has to give way to power, language affords a possibility in principle for an intersubjectively argued understanding of – and possible going beyond – the conditions of power. Therefore the ethics of discourse is superior to its power (Habermas 1993: ch. 6). Accordingly, Habermas is particularly interested in science and the judiciary as places where this discourse ought to have an institutional framework.

If Habermas had stood next to Foucault, he would not have analysed the discourse as a power mechanism but have looked for the remains of coercion-free conversation or references to the principle of coercion-free conversation left by the tracks of an undistorted discourse. Most of what was said on the farm Habermas would not even consider discourse – rather an expression of power, subjugation, manipulation and dissimulation. Only at a couple of points does coercion-free speech take place – or rather there is the consciousness that such is possible. First and foremost in Fainy's shortlived wish to speak to someone of his own age, i.e. a human being who was his equal and of equal worth. Apart from that, in the rudimentary hospitality shown by the women and which even the older man cannot avoid expressing, although it is here expressed in a negative form: 'This is no night to throw a human being out inter.'

Foucault is able to provide subtle readings of plenty of historical text material – for where does power not operate in and through discursive processes that occur in texts? Habermas, on the other hand, is able with theoretical precision and ethical commitment to analyse the conditions of coercion-free discourse, its ideal requirement and the special decline of the modern period. They represent two depictions of power and freedom in discourse that are difficult to reconcile (cf. Kelly 1994). Although both see discourse as a symbolic order which links subjects with a shared world, and both attempt to determine universes where discourses are valid – Foucault does so from a historical and Habermas from a philosophical angle.

Discursive universes

We have found such a universe in Dos Passos's novel. Until now we have on the whole pretended that the discursive process has created an entire world in which people live, act and think as though it were a real world. We have assumed a number of prerequisites concerning time, space, subjects, social relations, etc. that we know from our own world, these prerequisites having made the text comprehensible. When, in the first sentence of the novel, we read about 'the gray fourfamily frame house', there is no problem about letting it appear in the definite form as, even though there is no previous text to which one can refer, we all know what such a house looks like. The content of a discursive universe is determined by the prior knowledge which enables the meaning to cohere and be linked to our general experience. By means of that experience we fill in the holes between the items of information on the basis of indices – is what Barthes would say in his discourse analysis.

But it's a con. The text is fictional. There are no holes to fill in, because there is no other reality than that which we conjure up on the basis of the text's sporadic items of information and possibilities for interpretation. So it does not suffice to *determine the content* of a discursive universe. One is also obliged to *demarcate* it from others, the discursive universe of the novel from social reality. And one is obliged to give it an *ontological status* – dream, description of reality, fiction, memory, etc. – in order to find out the validity of the discursively produced testimony of the universe. The discursive universe is ultimately what the text is all about. Where are we, what are we talking about and what are we to believe? It is this sort of question that the problem of discursive universes raises, especially in literature, through the use of narrator and point of view.

At any rate, it is obvious that we cannot prevent ourselves from inserting everyday experience into Dos Passos's text, even though we know we are dealing with fiction. The discourse as an act that anchors meaning in a situation with subjects cannot be isolated from the experience which the discourse does not form but simply assumes. This is why there will never be any absolute boundaries between discursive universes, rather gradual transitions – as also between fiction and everyday experience. It is perfectly possible to talk about the same things in the various universes. Even though the demarcation of a discursive universe and the belief one can have in its testimony builds on characteristics which dominate any given universe, this does not isolate it from others. If a discursive universe were isolated from others, we would never be able to understand each other, not to mention the problem of differing semiotic systems and cultural norms. Habermas's point is that we in principle have the possibility of this cross-border understanding by virtue of the built-in potential in language of coercion-free communication, while Foucault's point is that it calls for insight into the mechanisms of power which govern communication and interaction, and which are not only stronger than our capacity to understand but also fixed in the discourses we ourselves practise.

Dos Passos's text mediates between two discursive universes: one in which the fictional characters carry out the discourses in speech, conversation and action that we have analysed, and another in which these characters do not participate but in which they are assumed elements and which are built on the discourse the narrator communicates to the reader – a universe that includes the text as an enunciation. The former is fictional; the latter is real but discursively organized, since the physical person of the reader is only presumed as a bearer of the reader's role that the discursive logic of the text allocates to him. But in the given text these two universes are interwoven.

It is, of course, this interwoven nature of the text that makes reading literature exciting – we feel ourselves transported to another world or gain new angles on our everyday reality. In fact, it is this interweaving of a possible and a real universe which enables us to imagine another reality and to plan for the future. The reading of fiction is only one example of this interweaving. We cannot undertake a complete separation of discursive universes, since we are capable of allowing ourselves to be fooled by the verisimilitude of the presentation or by the sheer weight of real locations and times in documentary novels. As a rule, though, we are able to put a finger on the places where the discursive universes intertwine: that is where we have to make an extra effort to disentangle them.

Let us take a couple of examples from Dos Passos's text. Once more we read '*This* is no night to throw a human being out inter,' said the older man. This *this* is a combined time and place marker not only in the fictional universe (the night which is raging here and now around all the characters) but in the older man's speech act (here and now while he speaks) and in our reading process (here and now, as we read, someone is claiming something about the night). The addition in the past tense, 'said the older man', is not part of this fictional universe's speech act but part of the narrator's communication to the reader about something that has happened, concerning a remark that has been made. By means of this past tense the reader is able to localize something in a fictional universe that the reader himself is not part of.

The indexical signs, designations, not only anchor the utterances in relation to the situation in which they are uttered – as we have claimed in the outline of structuralist discourse analysis. They also anchor the text in such a way that we can distinguish between the discursive universes to which the utterances belong. In this case we experience no difficulty whatsoever in separating fact from fiction in our reading, even without having to think any more about it. The differentiation springs from language's own indexical elements, which define the enunciation exactly as we do in everyday speech. They function immediately by virtue of our unconscious grammatical competence.

Where, at another point in the text, we discover that 'Doc Bingham's face was black as thunder as he wrapped himself in a horseblanket', it is a comparison and exaggeration which does not describe what Fainy can see since, as they do not have any matches in the barn, he is completely unable to see Bingham's face. Nor is it a comparison that happens to belong to Fainy's vocabulary. Lastly, his face does not actually change colour; nor does it begin to emit thunder-like sounds. The comparison is a synaesthetic combination of sound and sight, both on the threshold of what the eye can see and the ear can tolerate hearing. This means that it is an indirect communication from the narrator to the reader that Bingham's feeling of having suffered a defeat breaks the limits of what can be described within the framework of our recognizable everyday sensory experience. Conflicting emotions bring him to the point where he is about to explode. Even though there is no one to pretend to, he controls himself by remaining in the false role of Reverend

Bingham, who complains about the 'indignity to a wearer of the cloth'. By means of this, the description becomes an utterance which refers to the reader's own imaginative world, i.e. to the discursive universe in which the reader's social experience is valid. If the reader is unable to undertake such a separation of the universes, believing that the point is that thunder is black or that the face has acquired black spots, then he has allowed himself to be cheated: the reference is to something wrong, in a wrong universe and with a misunderstood validity.

But in such cases we have no well-known indexical signs to build on: pronouns, adverbs, verb conjugations, spatial indicators, etc. are not sufficient. Misunderstanding is in fact a correct understanding if one only takes such elements into account. So at crucial junctures we need not only to distinguish between discursive universes but to do so in relation to the universe in which we find ourselves. Therefore we have to master a number of more advanced indexical *designator functions* which are common to all sign-systems that function in discourses. They are, however, manifested in widely differing *designator elements* and will often be manifested in several semiotic systems at the same time (Larsen 1991b).

Such functions correspond to those which the philosopher and psychologist Karl Bühler has put forward in his *Theory of Language* (1990), in a different framework and terminology but in a similar argument:

- *Real designator function*, which we carry out when we distinguish the material universe in which we physically are present with the text we produce and the object of which we speak. If one points to a place in the text where it says 'These are Gospel Talks' and say 'It says here "These are Gospel Talks"', then the index finger, the word 'here' and the present tense of 'says' are different designator elements from different sign-systems (verbal language and the language of gesture) whereby we take care of the real designator function. It is correct that it says 'These are Gospel Talks', but not that any books are actually lying there. If we are unable to make this distinction, at least in relation to our own body, we are really in difficulties. With the carrying out of the real designator function we emphasize that we are *present*.
- *Discursive designator function*, which we carry out when we point to what belongs within an already demarcated text in relation to its enunciation, e.g. with the aid of definite forms, verb conjugations, expressions such as 'to look ahead', rhymes, visual repetitions, etc. It is via such designator elements that we turn previously stated meanings into prerequisites for what we are saying now, e.g. when Doc Bingham refers to his own previously stated remarks: 'I was just telling . . . '. In that way, knowledge and meaning acquire a cross-border *cohesion* in a discursive process.
- *Ideal designator function*, which we carry out when we indicate phenomena that are linked across different discursive universes, of which one is our own. When the narrator announces that 'a skinny lad about Fainy's age'

arrives on the scene, and when we later hear that Fainy 'wished he had someone his own age to talk to', we are switching between several discursive levels – within the fictional universe between Fainy's reality and his dream world. Moreover, a relation is created between the internal discursive universe of fictional characters and actions to which Fainy and the boy belong, and the discursive universe that encompasses both narrator and reader. The reader can see the possible relationship between Fainy's dream and reality, whereas neither of the boys can see it. The narrator provides us with knowledge which they do not possess, thereby highlighting the difference between the two universes. As can be seen, there are no fixed designator elements to take care of this ideal designator function. It can reside in the meaning of words ('he *wished* he had someone . . . ') or in a rhetorical figure of speech such as the comparison with black thunder; it can express itself in all the elements known to literary analysis by which the position of the narrator is separate from that which is being narrated (irony, shifts of time and place, shifts of points of view, etc.). Generally speaking, it has to do with our possibility to make what is referred to as a *meta-discourse*: a discourse by means of which we have the possibility – coercion-free, Habermas would say – of adopting a stance towards another discourse, of reflecting on it, of processing it, deciding on the validity of the events that take place in it – possibly of deciding on the power-determined allocations of knowledge and the positions it gives rise to. In that way we are given the opportunity of understanding the *conditions* for our existing in a cohesive universe – and possibly of imagining that things could be different.

5 Action

Interaction becomes narration

Of rats and heroes

The semiotic study of action and plot, narratology, has flourished in the twentieth century, both within research of myths and folktales and within linguistics as a whole: from the work of Danish folklorist Axel Olrik; to Vladimir Propp's pioneering analysis of Russian folktales in his *Morphology of the Folktale* (first published in Russian in 1928); and to the efforts to describe different motif-units as combined in folktales (e.g. Stith Thompson's monumental work *Motif-Index of Folk-Literature*, 1966, first published in 1932–36); from the mid-1950s, the French structuralists' analyses of myths (e.g. C. Lévi-Strauss) and action and plot structures in epic texts (e.g. R. Barthes, C. Bremond, and A.J. Greimas), to the Danish folktale researcher Bengt Holbek, whose dissertation *Interpretation of Fairy Tales* (1987) made an important contribution to our understanding of narrative structure in folktales.

Nevertheless, one can make a convincing argument that little progress has been made within the field of narratology during the past three decades. The field has been dominated by formalistic idling, it could be argued, and has seen the introduction of a long series of dubious models. This is how narratologist and computer expert Marie-Laure Ryan has expressed the problem:

> Rumors of the demise of formalism and narratology may be greatly exaggerated, but it is undeniable that many of the gold mines on which they have lived for the past twenty years are no longer productive. Traditional topics, such as point of view and narrative technique, have been largely exhausted; standard models, such as the semiotic square or generative grammar, never kept their promise of providing a universal and scientific account of textual meaning. The crisis of formalism and of narratology is an urgent need for new sources of ideas.
>
> (Ryan 1991: 3)

Ryan's proposed cure is to import ideas and techniques from the field of artificial intelligence (AI), possible-world semantics, and the experiences gained from computer software development. The problem is, first of all, that the results of such an intellectual import have not progressed much beyond the introductory exercises. Second, the models, notations, and graphical presentations are still growing at a rampant rate. Ryan's book provides an excellent, highly lucid introduction. Instead of its formalized approach, then, we will attempt a non-technical presentation of the ideas on which narrative analysis rests.

Undeniably, concern with narrative structures did not begin just in the last 100 years. The study of narrativity (Greek *mythos*) occupies the lion's share of the work rightly considered to be the first piece of literary theory within our cultural sphere: Aristotle's *Poetics*. Before addressing Aristotle's ideas, we begin with a contemporary interpreter of the classical heritage. Following Propp and the structuralists, classical philologist Walter Burkert has formulated the following radical rule for the basic structure in traditional tales, namely that all narrative functions can be reduced to one simple expression: *to get*, or rather the imperative *get*. According to Burkert, this verb implies

> quite a complicated program of actions. To 'get' something means: to realize some deficiency, or receive some order to start; to have, or to attain, some knowledge or information about the thing wanted; to decide to begin a search; to go out, to meet partners, in a changing environment, who may prove to be helpful or antagonistic; to discover the object, and to appropriate it by force or guile, or, in more civilized circumstances, by negotiation; then, to bring back the object, while it still may be taken away by force, stolen, or lost. Only after all that, with success established, has the action of 'getting' come to its end.
>
> (Burkert 1979: 15)

Burkert not only asserts that the above covers most functions and motives analysed by narratology, but also relates this to biological reality, the processes of life:

> [I]f we ask where such a structure of sense, such a program of actions, is derived from, the answer must evidently be: from the reality of life, nay, from biology. Every rat in search of food will incessantly run through all these 'functions,' including the peak of agitation at the moment of success: then the rat has to run fastest to find a safe place before its fellow rats take its prey away. In the Propp series there is the motifeme sequence called the 'magical flight,' which often constitutes the most thrilling part of a fairy tale, when the magical object, or the bride, has been gained and the previous owner starts a pursuit. This probably is just a transformation of the action pattern described.
>
> (Ibid.: 15)

Naturally, Burkert is bold, even offensive, about human dignity. What is the point of the comparison between the exploits of Heracles and Theseus and the

endless battle for survival of rats? Burkert is of course clear about the difference in level, but this point of view is nevertheless attractive, because it unites
nature and culture in a continuum. Of course, all actions do not have to be
related to or serve the survival of the individual; they can also, for example,
be directly self-destructive or serve the survival of the species (reproduction),
or only its preparatory – but in itself attractive – self-sufficient and biologically based exercises (on literature and desire see also Johansen 1992a). Still,
actions will generally be related to survival and the satisfaction of desires, in
order to achieve what is known as happiness. This is, in any case, Aristotle's
perspective. In his handbook on *The Art of Rhetoric* he writes:

> Men, individually and in common, nearly all have some aim, in the
> attainment of which they choose or avoid certain things. This aim, briefly
> stated, is happiness [Greek *eudaimonia*] and its component parts.
> Therefore, for the sake of illustration, let us ascertain what happiness,
> generally speaking, is, and what its parts consist in; for all who exhort or
> dissuade discuss happiness and the things which conduce or are detri-
> mental to it. For one should do the things which procure happiness or
> one of its parts, or increase instead of diminishing it, and avoid doing
> those things which destroy or hinder it or bring about what is contrary to
> it.
>   Let us then define happiness as well-being combined with virtue, or
> independence of life, or the life that is most agreeable combined with
> security, or abundance of possessions and slaves, combined with power to
> protect and make use of them; for nearly all men admit that one or more
> of these things constitutes happiness.
>
> (Aristotle 1926a: 47–9)

Aristotle then continues by presenting the different elements of happiness as
they appeared to a Greek citizen in his time. We can divide his account into
two categories:

1 Personal goods		2 Social goods
(a) *Physical*	(b) *Psychological*	*Status*
good health	moral perfection	noble birth
beauty	wisdom	numerous friends
strength	courage	
	high principles	wealth
well-developed body	integrity	large and/or successful number of children
	temperance	athletic ability
	good reputation	
	heroism	honour
good old age	good old age	good old age

On the physical goods, and particularly on good health, Aristotle comments: '[H]ealth is productive of pleasure and of life, wherefore it is thought to be best of all, because it is the cause of two things which the majority of men prize most highly' (ibid.: 63).

The very conditions for perceiving, being alive and surviving, and the perception of pleasure, are opposed to being dead, perishing and the perception of pain. Life and pleasure (desire and lust) are related to one another and to the opposition between happiness and unhappiness in a complex way. Even more complex is the relationship between life, pleasure and happiness on the one hand and death, pain and unhappiness on the other, because so many different interpretations of their interrelatedness exist. Naïvely – or as a chosen materialistic and hedonistic position – life can be seen as the prerequisite for pleasure, and pleasure as the prerequisite for happiness, or they can be seen as the minimum and maximum of positive values corresponding to unhappiness, pain and death. However, there are only two non-contradictory ways of looking at this extremely complex relationship. One of the reasons for this complexity is that pleasure is sometimes regarded as one of the parts making up happiness, like good reputation and wisdom, while, at other times, pleasure, and the minimal condition for obtaining pleasure, namely life, may become opposed and in conflict with one another. Pleasure-seeking may lead to death; indeed the very fulfilling of one's lust for pleasure may be deadly. This is even more pronounced for pleasure's opposite, pain, both because pain itself may become a precondition for pleasure, and because pain, although itself a part of unhappiness, may become preferable to other of its parts, e.g. contempt and loss of reputation. Further, pain and death can be interpreted as opposites (e.g. death as liberation (from pain)).

Because the relation between the three opposing pairs can be interpreted in so many different ways, the narrative action in fictitious and other texts – such as news reports – can (nearly) always be described as movements between their different interpretations, within given cultures and time periods. Folktales, such as myths and fairytales, can contain a high degree of consensus on the meaning of the oppositions and the roads leading from one situation to its opposite. Apparently, Burkert believes that folktales all contain the following deep structure:

> The deepest deep structure of a tale would, then, be a series of imperatives: 'get,' that is: 'go out, ask, find out, fight for it, take and run.' And the reaction of an audience to a tale is in perfect accordance with this: under the spell of a thrilling tale, we will ourselves perform one by one the actions described – in idle motion, of course. Thus communication in the form of action sequences, in the form of a tale, is so basic and elementary that it cannot be traced to 'deeper' levels; we may note, in passing, the parallel with dreaming, which also involves action patterns in idle motion.
>
> (Burkert 1979: 16)

For Burkert, then, the fundamental tale is the *quest* or *hunt*, a narrative pattern cutting across genres and a story cutting across cultures. But it is equally clear that Burkert's tale deals with both *hunt* and *flight*; the hunter, after capturing his prey, becomes hunted himself.

In Burkert's and many others' narrative analysis, it is the *prey*, the *object of value* and its circulation among the story's spheres and characters, that creates and shapes the narrative patterns. To the animals and the people who depend on the hunt, it is a question of survival, because the felling (and digestion) of the prey is the elimination of an existing *lack*. The hero of the tale, who fights for and wins the princess, removes another kind of lack, namely a sexual and emotional want and a social inferiority. But to capture or fell a prey implies that someone must give or lose something – either the prey itself, by losing its life, or the monster by surrendering the princess to the knight. Let us imagine, in accordance with Burkert, two rivals – a protagonist (main character or hero) and antagonist (opponent). We can then describe the hunt/flight action programme thus:

Protagonist		**Antagonist**	
1 a lack	vs	possess (non-a)	I
2 a search	vs	hide (non-a)	
3 a find	vs	be found (non-a)	II
4 a pursue	vs	flee (non-a)	
5 a overtake	vs	be overtaken (non-a)	
6 a attack	vs	defend (non-a)	III
7 a win	vs	lose (non-a)	
8 a obtain	vs	relinquish (non-a)	IV
9 a ($1'$) possess	vs	lack (non-a)	

Such an elementary narrative sequence, which resolves lack by winning an object from someone else, consists (at least in our analysis) of 16 different narrative functions, arranged into eight opposing pairs, which together form two parallel chains or sequences of narrative elements that are interconnected. The eight pairs of functions can be arranged into four larger sections:

  I the introductory lack (1);
 II the hunt or quest (2–5);
III the struggle (6–7);
IV the resolution of lack (8–9 ($1'$)).

The construction of such chains of functions, it should be stressed, is neither sacred nor infallible, and from Propp onwards, such divisions have deviated to some degree from one another. The arrangements are formed through an interpretation of the material, based on an understanding of which elements are indispensable and recurrent in certain types of texts (the so-called invariants). Equally evidently, such sequences are 'ideal sequences', in which each individual function does not necessarily occur in every tale. For instance, 2 (non-a) is here called *hide*, though the antagonist does not necessarily have to obscure the object of value. Instead, it can be unattainable in some other way, e.g. the object can be locked up in a seemingly impenetrable mountaintop fortress. In this case, 2a–5a are replaced by another sequence of actions revolving around *penetration into enemy space*. Depending on the purpose of the analysis, the sequences can be defined on various levels of abstraction. In the above-mentioned example, for instance, it is obvious that *hiding*, in the sense of keeping others ignorant about the object's physical placement, is actually a variant on the more abstract *making inaccessible* or *keeping away*. Similarly, II (2–5a and non-a) can be reduced to the more abstract opposition between *seeking contact* versus *obstructing contact*.

Further, it can be seen that the arrangement and its sequential order forms a diagram of the hunting protagonist's aggressive and successful effort to seize the prey from the hands of the antagonist. Yet, in principle, the antagonist has an equal chance of winning (even though this is a very rare occurrence in folktales), or the tale could continue with the antagonist pursuing the hero (cf. Burkert's mention of the motifeme sequence called the 'magical flight'), even though the antagonist in the traditional folktale only rarely succeeds in recapturing the object.

I would if I knew I could

Our above-mentioned example, the hunt, is an elementary sequence of narrative elements, because the hunt or quest for an object plays, in a literal or metaphorical sense, a decisive role in the satisfaction of biological needs and desires. This is necessary both for survival and for obtaining happiness – or some of happiness's elements. Nevertheless, the execution of such a sequence (the victory and capture of the prey) presumes that the antagonist has certain properties (qualifications). To be able to fight for or fell a prey, for instance, the attacking animal generally must be adult, fast, strong, cunning, and possess well-developed hunting and fighting techniques (based on instinct and/or socialization). Of course, the same holds true for the human hunter. This process of growing up and learning to hunt illustrates that one has to qualify oneself in order to execute certain (complex) actions.

Generally, action involves a process that realizes a transition from one state to another: state 1 → process → state 2. However, this definition is too broad because, for instance, it also covers natural phenomena (the earth is dry → it rains → the earth is wet), events (x is alive → roof-tiles fall down → x is dead), and accidents (x is alive → y loses a roof-tile → x is dead). In moral philosophy and law, the definition of human action is tied to the question of guilt and responsibility, and therefore also to sanctions and punishment (see also pp. 97–98). For this reason, the problems involving action have been the subject of much discussion throughout the history of our culture, as attested by the following considerations from Aristotle's *Nicomachean Ethics*. Aristotle defines involuntary actions as those that are either compulsory (fearing a greater evil), or performed in ignorance:

> [A]n act is compulsory when its origin is from outside, the person compelled contributing nothing to it.
>
> An act done through ignorance is in every case not voluntary, but it is involuntary only when it causes the agent pain and regret afterwards: since a man who has acted through ignorance and feels no compunction at all for what he has done, cannot indeed be said to have acted voluntarily, as he was not aware of his action, yet cannot be said to have acted involuntarily, as he is not sorry for it. Acts done through ignorance therefore fall into two classes: if the agent regrets the act, we think that he has acted involuntarily; if he does not regret it, to mark the distinction we may call him a 'non-voluntary' agent – for as the case is different it is better to give it a special name. Acting *through* ignorance however seems to be different from acting *in* ignorance; for when a man is drunk or in a rage, his actions are not thought to be done through ignorance but owing to one or other of the conditions mentioned, though he does act without knowing, and *in* ignorance.
>
> (Aristotle 1926b: 123)

Aristotle's distinctions are important to the moral and judicial appraisal of actions, and can be found in modern criminal law, which takes into consideration whether the action was taken 'knowingly and voluntarily', and whether the perpetrator was in a mental condition that could preclude him from responsibility and/or accountability (i.e. the 'temporary insanity' defence). Aristotle adds that ignorance of particulars of the action's consequences can constitute innocence, while ignorance of the law is not an adequate excuse (no one can avoid a speeding ticket by claiming ignorance about traffic laws). He also notes that legislators double the penalty for drunk offenders who, after all, could have abstained from drinking (ibid.: 147).

To qualify as independent human action, Aristotle's three conditions must be fulfilled. These are expressed in the three modal auxiliaries, *wanting*, *knowing* and *being able*, which correspond to the so-called three modalities – *will*, *knowledge* and *ability* – which are required for any action.

In our hunting example, we presumed that the hunter possessed all three modalities, but in human societies, qualifications are acquired through learning processes (even though they may be rooted in biology); after all, as the saying goes, 'practice makes perfect'. After a learning, practising and testing period, we obtain a diploma, certificate, or commission formally attesting our *will*, *knowledge* and *ability*. Now, we are expected to act independently and responsibly. The practice of our occupation, our professional actions, usually determines our (economic) survival. We also learn to act in non-professional relations, in relation to family members, others, and authority figures, and we learn to act in accordance with laws and customs.

Burkert speaks of biocybernetic programmes (biological control programmes) cutting across the division between humans and animals, and even though the natural part of human behaviour is still the subject of debate among the experts, it can hardly be ignored. The will to act in a certain way can simply be there as part of the protagonist's nature or character. It can be debated whether it can meaningfully be claimed that highly developed animals act (i.e. choose between alternatives), or whether they simply 'blindly follow their instinct'. Without entering into a lengthy discussion of this, it seems to us that when the behaviour of highly developed animals is in fact affected by learning processes, and when they are able to change their behaviour to adapt to new circumstances, there is no reason to place an absolute divide between animals and humans; but we will not draw into question the difference in level of mind. For the purpose of the argument here we will be satisfied with seeing a continuity between behaviour that is released more or less automatically and behaviour that is derived from intelligent deliberation. But so far as the readiness to act is present, whether it is based on biology, habit formation, or culturally created programmes of action, it is evident that the modality *will* will not be an acquired trait (for a broader discussion of human intentionality, see Chapter 4, pp. 69–74).

Frequently, the will has to be aroused, both in life and in literature. And in both the real and fictitious world, there are first-rate ways of making persons act wilfully. In folktales and medieval narratives of chivalry, for example, the hero gains will by entering into a contractual relation of sorts: the successful completion of a heroic feat is rewarded with a particular object of desire; the king gives his daughter's hand in marriage, or the princess gives herself to the knight. The object can also involve goods and gold, social status and power: 'slaying the dragon' in order to win 'the princess's hand and half the kingdom'. It is, however, not a given that the protagonist's will can be expediently led in a particular direction:

> Rage – Goddess, sing the rage of Peleus' son Achilles,
> murderous, doomed, that cost the Achaeans countless losses,
> hurtling down to the House of Death so many sturdy souls,
> great fighters' souls, but made their bodies carrion,
> feasts for the dogs and birds . . .
>
> (Homer 1980: 77)

The first lines of Homer's *Iliad* aptly illustrate the fearsome consequences of Achilles's refusal to take up arms. Only the murder of his close friend Patroclus at the hands of Hector returns him to the struggle against Troy. On a lighter note, Chrétien de Troyes's charming romance *Erec et Enide* (written around 1175) also deals with a lack of will to fight. Erec refuses to leave the arms of Enide, whom he has only recently wed:

> Mais Erec l'aimait d'un si grand amour
>   que les armes le laissaient indifférent
> et qu'il ne participait plus aux tournois.
> Il ne se souciait plus désormais de tournoyer:
> il allait vivre en amoureux auprès de
>   sa femme,
> il en fit son amie et son amante.
> Il n'avait plus en son coeur que le désir
> de l'embrasser et de la couvrir de baisers:
> il ne cherchait plus d'autre plaisir.
>   (de Troyes 1992: 201–3)

[But Erec loved her so much that he became indifferent to weapons and no longer took part in tournaments. And unconcerned with all knightly pursuits he spent all his time loving his wife, who became his friend as well as his lover. Henceforth the only desire of his heart was to embrace her and to cover her with kisses]

This is hardly proper behaviour for a knight! Erec gets plenty of will to fight, though, upon discovering that Enide is ashamed of him. The romance then goes on to tell of their perilous adventures.

The will to act can come from an inner struggle against hesitation, which is caused by unwillingness to take any action whatsoever, or it can appear as a choice of one action over another. In classical tragedy's choice between desire and duty, sometimes the entire play can revolve around one person's will to choose. In Racine's *Bérénice* (1670), the heroine in a single verse expresses programmatically that the lovers have chosen duty over love: 'Je l'aime, je le fuis; Titus m'aime, il me quitte' (Racine 1960: 350) [I love him yet flee from him; Titus loves me yet leaves me].

Finally, there are tales in which the protagonist's fickleness and inconstancy are incurable. The inconstant is a character, a cliché in European literature. For instance, Danish playwright Ludvig Holberg created such a character, Lucretia, the principal character of his comedy *The Waverer* (1723). Another type that has little contact with reality is the fantast. Just how dangerous it can be to lose oneself in fantasy is eloquently shown in Flaubert's *The Temptations of Saint Anthony* (1874).

The will to act, however, is not necessarily a sufficient condition for acting. In addition, one has to know what to do, or, in other words, one has to possess the modality *knowledge*. In its simplest form, the necessary knowledge can consist of a watchword, a shibboleth. The Old Testament provides us with one grim tale of correct and incorrect pronunciation. The Gileadites have defeated the Ephraimites and cut off their escape to the other side of the Jordan river:

> And the Gileadites took the passages of Jordan before the Ephraimites: and it was so, that when those Ephraimites which were escaped said, Let me go over; that the men of Gilead said unto him, Art thou an Ephraimite? If he said, Nay; Then said they unto him, Say now Shibboleth; and he said Sibboleth: for he could not frame to pronounce it right. Then they took him, and slew him at the passages of Jordan.
> (*Judges*, 12, 5–6; from *Authorized Version* [1611]1974: 231)

It is worth noting, from a semiotic point of view, that the meaning of the word itself has no import here; Hebrew *shibboleth* means, among other things, 'ear of corn' and 'stream'. What is decisive here is the difference in pronunciation between *sh* and *s*, a question of life and death. Another example of formulaic knowledge that decides between life and death is 'Open Sesame' from *1001 Nights*.

If the magic spell, charm, or formula is one extreme of the kind of knowledge able to function as a condition for action, the other extreme is the laborious appropriation of knowledge through years of study that qualifies disciples to become masters themselves. This hard-earned knowledge is generally one of three different types. First, there is knowledge as grasp of material, a type of knowledge generally assigned little value in folktales (see, for instance, Stupid Hans's clever brothers). Then there is knowledge as life experience, knowledge about the way of the world. And finally, there is knowledge as religious or occult insight, whether it be held by a clergyman or sorcerer.

Just as the protagonist can be motivated by others to act, so knowledge also is characterized by its ability to be transmitted or communicated. In folktales, the communication of knowledge is so commonplace that it classifies as one of its general features. Often, the protagonist has to solve a riddle; this requires some knowledge, e.g. localizing and identifying an object or a villain; knowledge of certain procedures, e.g. killing a ghost by hitting it with a silver bullet; or simply, as mentioned, magic spells and formulas. Also the more hard-earned knowledge is communicated to the protagonist by one or more people during his years of apprenticeship. In the *Bildungsroman*, there can be one or more persons to watch over the hero's education (e.g. Goethe's *Wilhelm Meisters Lehrjahre*, 1794–96), or they can be guided by their own destiny. In this bourgeois literary genre, the hero as a rule must both qualify himself professionally and mature personally, i.e. acquire both knowledge and experience.

More often than not, the protagonist must prove his worth to receive knowledge, either by his personal merits or through actions springing from those merits. For instance, the hero can show his good nature by sharing his last loaf of bread with an old woman, who then reveals herself to be a friendly witch and instructs him how to slay the dragon. The hero's proof of possessing certain moral, intellectual and physical properties is known, in extension of Propp's analyses of folktales, as the *qualifying test*. Typically, by providing evidence of one or more of the properties *kindness, cleverness, obedience, courage,* or *strength* (cf. Aristotle's elements of happiness), or by simply being *attractive,* happy, or *charming*, the hero or heroine receives the required assistance.

Yet knowledge alone may not be sufficient. If one knows that the dragon can be slain only with a particular sword, or that a wound can be healed only with the spear that caused it, then both are required. The appropriation of the modality *ability* has many aspects in common with the appropriation of knowledge, and is often an extension of this, because one first gains knowledge about the *means* necessary to obtain something, and then receives or obtains it.

The concrete ability that must be obtained in order to act can also be categorized into different types. Like the magic formula, the magic object endows the hero with power and ability. In folktales, it is often strictly instrumental, i.e. it has properties that enable its owner to solve a particular problem. In myth, the magical object can change status from the *means* to becoming the *object of value*. In the epic poem *Gilgamesh*, the plant of eternal youth is, of course, the means by which one can attain immortality, but it is also an object of value in and by itself. Magic spells and religious or occult insights make up a continuum within the appropriation of magical or sacral knowledge, and the magical object within the modality *ability* has the same differentiation. The duplicity of learning and life experience in profane knowledge can be found again here as a division between obtaining specific skills and having a more general social ability in the form of influence and power. Finally, it should be noted that the assignment of ability does not necessarily have to occur as transmission of or growth from the protagonist's personal properties. This is quite likely the most general procedure in the realistic literature of the nineteenth and twentieth centuries, but even here, one can often find (in modified form) *assignment of ability in the form of a helper*, a method so cherished by folktales. The helper either possesses a special skill (e.g. he may be extraordinarily strong or the world's best climber), or he functions as a faithful companion and trusty sidekick who enables the hero to complete his mission. Often, the helper will disappear or be destroyed after the task is completed.

You must not, you will . . .

When Aristotle speaks, in *Nichomachean Ethics*, of voluntary and involuntary actions (see our earlier discussion), he distinguishes between 'three ways in which a man may injure his fellow':

> When then the injury happens contrary to reasonable expectation, it is (1) a misadventure. When, though not contrary to reasonable expectation, it is done without evil intent, it is (2) a culpable error; for an error is

culpable when the cause of one's ignorance lies in oneself, but only a misadventure when the cause lies outside oneself. When an injury is done knowingly but not deliberately, it is (3) an act of injustice or wrong; such, for instance, are injuries done through anger, or any other unavoidable or natural passion to which men are liable . . .

(Aristotle 1926b: 301–3)

These judgements of actions as either morally good or evil, as either legal or against the law, place the individual's actions in a societal context, in which it is either one or the other; the individual is free to choose or disregard them.

Prohibitions and commands can be observed or disobeyed. When Heracles accomplished his twelve labours for King Eurystheos, he obeyed the king's command to perform certain acts, consisting primarily of freeing society from ravaging monsters and fighting agents of death; and in another story (dealing with Alcestis), Heracles even wrestles with Death itself, thereby becoming a culture hero, which is to say that his lofty purpose in life is to secure the limits of human life against monstrous and lethal forces. The myths of Heracles provide more examples of actions following as a consequence of prohibitions and commands. For instance, when Heracles kills his guest Iphitus in vengeance, violating the laws of hospitality guaranteed by Zeus himself, he must atone for his crime by entering the service of Queen Omphalè as her slave, and carrying out any labours, i.e. heroic feats, that she commands.

In traditional tales, myths, legends, fairytales, sagas, etc., the narrative is carried by the relationship between protagonist and society, because the stories deal with the Proppian functions of *lack* and *violation of the law* versus *fulfilment* and *law*. Often, the oppositions will even be interconnected in the course of the narrative, so that the violation of a command or interdiction leads to a situation of lack, which is lifted when the social contract is re-established (this aspect is stressed by the French structuralists, particularly C. Lévi-Strauss and A.J. Greimas). Therefore, the protagonist can cause the situation of lack by violating a law, and then re-establish the social (or religious) contract through his subsequent reparative act, thereby relieving the lack he himself has caused. But the protagonist can also be the stranger who arrives in a country in need, and frees it of a terrible plague. Oedipus plays both parts: as the stranger, he liberates the Thebans by solving the riddle of the Sphinx. Later, his parricide and incestuous relationship with his mother results in a plague that ravages the city of Thebes; upon discovering that he is the cause, Oedipus blinds himself and leaves town so that the plague may cease. But even when a stranger frees the land from a plague, and therefore basically has nothing to do with its outbreak, the plague still often results from a breach of contract that is committed by someone else. In one version of the Oedipus myth, it is Laios (Oedipus's father) who causes the Sphinx to ravage the country, having stolen Pelops's attractive son Chrysippos, whom he prefers to his wife, Iokastè.

In opposition to the three modalities *will*, *knowledge* and *ability*, often tied to the individual action, are the three modalities which serve as social imperatives: *may*, *must* and *should*, and their negatives, which indicate the permissibility, necessity and commendability – or the opposites – of each action. In the narrative development, a violation of the prohibition (must not) is often followed by a forced action (shall) to atone for the crime. The fulfilment of moral norms (should) is often followed by the giving of knowledge or ability to reward morally laudable behaviour, while persons engaging in selfish and permitted yet morally questionable actions often fail to receive the necessary knowledge or ability, or are directly disqualified, thereby losing all their qualifications. In some folktales featuring three brothers or sisters, the eldest two will often behave arrogantly, selfishly and uncharitably, while the youngest sibling will behave in an opposite manner and thereby qualify him- or herself for victory and recognition, while the elder two are disqualified. Of course, there are also examples from literature in which the folktales' wishful thinking and fulfilment of poetic justice are turned upside down. The picaresque story typically deals with the young and inexperienced, poor and socially outcast protagonist who fails to succeed in this world until he masters its crooked ways and turns into a rogue himself (Spanish *pícaro*: rogue).

Error and insight, fortune and misfortune

The relationship between modalities that *qualify action* (will, knowledge and ability) and those that *moderate action* (must, shall and should) also forms the basis for the most meaningful narratological analysis of tragedies. In chapter 14 of his *Poetics*, Aristotle reflects on which actions arouse the spectator's *fear* (or *terror*, Greek *phobos*) and pity (Greek *eleos*). To arouse such feelings is, according to him, the tragedy's mission. Aristotle then states that dreadful and pitiable actions

> must necessarily be the actions of friends to each other or of enemies or of people that are neither. Now if an enemy does it to an enemy, there is nothing pitiable either in the deed or in the intention, except so far as the actual calamity goes. Nor would there be if they were neither friends nor enemies. But when these calamities happen among friends, when for instance brother kills brother, or son father, or mother son, or son mother – either kills or intends to kill, or does something of the kind, that is what we must look for.
>
> (Aristotle 1932: 51)

The poet, Aristotle adds, cannot radically rewrite existing family sagas (on Agamemnon, Oedipus, Achilles, etc.), but should none the less present these tragic actions in an artistically correct way. According to Aristotle (1932: 53), if a tragedy has one family member consciously and purposely murdering another – an act more shocking than tragic – this would be artistically satisfactory if that family member (1) has the purpose and possibility of killing the relative in the belief that the victim is a stranger, but only at the last moment discovers (receives the modality *knowledge*) that the victim is his relative, (2) and then refrains from committing the gruesome act. For example, Iphigeneia believes Orestes is a stranger, but refrains from killing him upon discovering that he is, in fact, her brother. If we formulate the Aristotelian possibilities in relation to Greimas's three individual qualifying modalities *will*, *knowledge* and *ability*, we end up with the following seven possibilities (the eighth being a non-action):

1   + will + knowledge + ability + action: DELIBERATE ACTION
2   − will + knowledge + ability + action: ACCIDENTAL ACTION
3   + will − knowledge + ability + action: ERRONEOUS ACTION
4   + will − knowledge − ability + action: FAILED ACTION
5   − will − knowledge + ability + action: ACCIDENT
6   + will + knowledge − ability − action: DESIRED ACTION
7   + will + knowledge + ability − action: OMITTED ACTION
8   − will, −knowledge, −ability, −action: nothing

In Aristotle's discussion of tragedy, it is presumed that the action is gruesome and causes a reversal (or in Aristotle's term, *peripety*) from *fortune* to *misfortune*. In other genres the presentation of action, and particularly its denouement, is different: e.g. in comedy, the action is supposed to end with good fortune. In the scheme above, where every item allows for two opposite actions, we can mark as a vs non-a, we can therefore distinguish between the (1a) deliberately evil action and (1 non-a) the deliberately good action; the accidental action (2a) and the unintentionally fortunate action (2 non-a); (3 non-a) would be the erroneous good action and (4 non-a) would be the failed action with a fortunate result, (5 non-a) accidental fortune; (6 non-a) the good desire, while (7 non-a) is negative, because it is a failure to take a good action.

   In both ethics and poetics, Aristotle combines three criteria for judging an action: (1) its effect; (2) society's assessment of the action's effect; and (3) the state of mind or intention of the acting person. Typically, the effect of the action is a change in fortune; often, it also results – at least in literature and criminal law – in a reversal from one situation to its opposite. In consequential actions, the reversal (Aristotle's term *peripety*) can be described as a transition from happiness to misery or vice versa, based on a consensus on what happiness and its elements are (see p. 89 above). In Greek tragedy, the suffering hero and the chorus will often be in agreement on what type of transition is at stake, but when ideological and religious views stand in sharp contrast to one another, the consensus on the nature of happiness and unhappiness evaporates. This is the case, for example, in medieval legends of martyrs and their heroic feats. To suffer a gruesome death at the hands of the pagans instead of honouring their idols seems like folly to the hero's heathen friends, because it is purposely self-inflicted misfortune. But to the martyr himself, it is the choice for true happiness and true life; therefore, the martyr's death becomes a transition between misery in this world and happiness in the hereafter.

The judgements of the action's effect and the state of mind of the actor are principally independent from one another, as allowed by the differentiation between *deliberate action, failure* and *attempted action*. We are also inclined to feel sorry for someone who accidentally causes damage to others; on the other hand, attempted murder is also a criminal offence. Yet there is a tendency for the judgement of an effect of an action to influence the judgement of the state of mind during the action. Thus the Roman governor, a frequent character in martyrological stories, considers the martyr's religious ideas to be a dangerous form of civil disobedience that must be exterminated in order to prevent it from spreading any further. The governor often adds to this judgement of the effect that the martyr's behaviour – his or her actions – has that it must also be the product of a corrupt and evil mind.

In opposition to this inclination toward an automatically presupposed agreement between effect and state of mind, it is Aristotle's point that the tragic effect is achieved through a tension between the action and the state of the mind of the actor. An evil person who meets misfortune because of his own crime is, according to Aristotle, not tragic (though it worked to great effect in Shakespeare's *Macbeth*). Instead, the tragic hero should be

> the sort of man who is not pre-eminently virtuous and just, and yet it is through no badness or villainy of his own at he falls into the misfortune, but rather through some flaw of him, he being one of those who are in high station and good fortune, like Oedipus and Thyestes and the famous men of such families as those.
>
> (Aristotle 1932: 47)

The nature of this tragic flaw (Greek *hamartia*) – which may lead to the man's fatal misstep, a mistaken act – has been the subject of much debate: earlier research interpreted it as a moral failure, while in our day it is also seen as an intellectual mistake. If we accept the latter interpretation, then, according to Aristotle's *Poetics*, the tragic action is the voluntary action resulting from a lack of insight into the proper relation between things. In the consummate tragedy, the reversal of fortune will be a consequence of the hero's recognition (Greek *anagnoresis*) of a relative in a person whom he had killed some time before, believing him or her to be a stranger or enemy (e.g. Oedipus). This was Aristotle's preferred type of narrative, and corresponds to his erroneous action (type 3a) followed by discovery and insight. Of course, this is merely one narrative sequence – though a particularly effective one – among many; others can be equally effective, e.g. the collision between two interpretations of law and duty, like the family's and state's in Sophocles's *Antigone*, or the forcibly executed action, e.g. the duty to sacrifice a family member to a god (Agamemnon's sacrifice of Iphigeneia).

Early on in this chapter, the narrative action was described as the transition from one state to another through a deliberate action taken by the main actor, or protagonist. It was also stated that this transition from one state to another applies not only to narrative genres. And we sought evidence that even though the voluntary, conscious, well-informed and competently executed action stands as the prototype for action, ethics, law and narratology acknowledge the existence of attempted, erroneous and accidental actions.

However, if we consider action at a highly abstract level, as a transition from one state to its opposite (epitomized by the transition from happiness to disaster in Greek tragedy), we can appreciate Aristotle's formal definition of it as the narrative action that is 'whole and complete and of a certain magnitude' (Aristotle 1932: 31). Such a narrative discourse need not be a biography, a whole life story, for a hero can perform many actions during his lifetime (e.g. Heracles's twelve labours). Instead, it is a question of connection between narrative elements, the dramatic incidents:

> A whole is what has a beginning and middle and end. A beginning is that which is not a necessary consequent of anything else but after which something else exists or happens as a natural result. An end on the contrary is that which is inevitably or, as a rule, the natural result of something else but from which nothing else follows; a middle follows something else and something follows from it. Well constructed plots must not therefore begin and end at random, but must embody the formulae we have stated.
>
> (Aristotle 1932: 31)

Even though it would be incorrect to consider *beginning* and *end* as absolute states, it is reasonable to see the beginning as an element of the narrative course, where the project and/or conflict is formed. For example, when two youths in a tragedy suddenly fall madly in love, something has already happened, but not something that necessarily or probably refers to this event. As their families hate each other, the tragedy continues with the two fleeing together. This middle of the narrative probably, though not necessarily, follows from the conflict. They are then overtaken by the young woman's family, the young man is killed, and she commits suicide. Of course (at least in the case of a true story) other events will follow, e.g. the authorities become involved, the families feud for generations, or else the families are reconciled. Nevertheless, the young couple's death can be regarded equally well as a consequence of their flight, and as the decisive event that completes the narrative, which began when they fell in love. On the other side, a wedding is the prototypical conclusion of the comedy and many folktales, with their formula-like ending: 'They were married and lived happily ever after.' This formula recognizes that existence continues, but stresses that the story's narrative trajectory has been brought to a conclusion because the protagonist's project has been completed. The great British novelist E.M. Forster writes –

somewhat cynically – in his book on *Aspects of the Novel* (1927), 'Love, like death, is congenial to a novelist because it ends a book conveniently' (Forster 1962: 62).

The elementary narrative is thus triple-phased, a transition from one state to another by virtue of a process that is executed in order to achieve a particular change. If we differentiate between the initial situation and the final situation on the one hand and a static situational field and a dynamic processual field on the other, the action can be presented diagrammatically, thus:

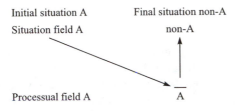

Initial situation A   Final situation non-A

Situation field A   non-A

Processual field A   A

By naming the initial and final situation A and non-A, respectively, we have already (in accordance with Aristotle and A.J. Greimas) interpreted beginning and end as opposites, e.g. as happiness and misery, and Ā as the reversal (Aristotle's *peripety*) through which the transition takes place. Obviously, the transition can also be the reverse, from misery to happiness, so that the diagram can point in either direction; however, we will have to abandon the designations 'initial situation' and 'final situation' and relabel them 'situation A and situation non-A'.

The full diagram intertwines two such triangular processes and consists of four entities united in different oppositions which, still according to A.J. Greimas, constitute the basic driving force of any narrative sequence. In the abstract this is formalized as follows. If a given situation is called A, its opposite is called non-A. Each of them can be negated or contradicted through the narrative process in various ways, which are marked with a horizontal dash directly above the A and the non-A.

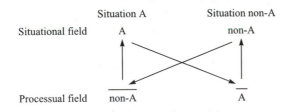

Situation A   Situation non-A

Situational field   A   non-A

Processual field   non-A   A

For this model, which has enjoyed considerable success within narratology, we are indebted to French semiotician A.J. Greimas. It was presented in a slightly modified form in his article, 'Eléments d'une grammaire narrative' (1969). In subsequent years, up to the present time, Greimas's model has been interpreted and applied in a number of different ways. Here, we will focus on the elementary form, with the following prototypical thematic structure:

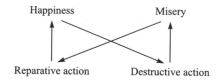

Happiness   Misery

Reparative action   Destructive action

One of its points is that, in the course of a concrete story, the positions (A, $\overline{A}$, non-A, and $\overline{\text{non-A}}$) can be run through several times, since, to paraphrase Aristotle, a number of reversals between happiness and misery may occur, partly because some actions may have a preparatory character, such as the mastering of three individual modalities. By the same token, folktales characteristically present the *test* in its three discursive modalities: (1) the *qualifying test*, in which the protagonist gains the necessary qualifications; (2) the *decisive test* (the fight or trick), by which the protagonist defeats the antagonist and conquers the value object; and (3) the so-called *glorifying test*, in which the protagonist is recognized as a hero who has performed feats and is rewarded (while the false hero is punished).

It is meaningful to speak of a story's 'grammar' because the presentation, in narrative form, of human acts and other events, whether it be a historical or fictional account, generates a number of patterns, i.e. certain types of elements take certain places in the story's chain of events, just as the elements of a sentence follow after one another in a particular order. Propp found that the narrative structure of Russian folktales could be described as an ordered sequence of 31 functions, beginning with (a family member's) (1) *absence*, (2) *prohibition* (of certain act of acts), (3) *violation of prohibition*, and ending with (31) *wedding*. This is a figurative and temporal succession, in which a kind of presumptive relation often exists between the different functions. If we take Propp's first three functions, for instance, it is obvious that (3) *violation of prohibition* presumes (2) *prohibition*, while (1) *absence* is not a required presumption for *transgression*. As the absence here involves a person whose presence could have prevented the transgression, the absence renders the transgression probable, though the person's absence is not a requirement for it.

Necessity and probability – logic and convention

When Aristotle states that 'a poet's object is not to tell what actually happened but what could and would happen either probably or inevitably' (Aristotle 1932: 35), one is led to think of 'realism', i.e. the agreement of action as represented in literary discourse, with our (or rather, the present time's) understanding of how people act in reality. This understanding of the concept 'realism' can find support with Aristotle himself, as he differentiates between the historical and the fictional writer, thus:

> The real difference [between a historian and a poet] is this, that one tells what happened and the other what might happen. For this reason poetry is something more scientific and serious than history, because poetry tends to give general truths while history gives particular facts.

And Aristotle immediately explains this as follows:

> By a 'general truth' I mean the sort of thing that a certain type of man will do or say either probably or necessarily. This is what poetry aims at in giving names to the characters.
>
> (Aristotle 1932: 35)

Here, poetry becomes a model of human behaviour by presenting typical behavioural patterns, i.e. its alleged agreement with general motives and reasons for acting become its hallmark. Following this train of thought, the cognitive and didactic becomes an important feature of literary presentation of action, and this means that we can learn something about human society and ourselves through literature. For Aristotle and, we will venture, the contemporary reader, the presentation of reality in literature, its so-called mimetic function, is indeed crucial. Poetry is a representation of a narrative course of action, which either has occurred but is presented with poetic liberties, or is entirely fictitious, but still analogous (i.e. like or similar) to human behaviour, thereby preserving its credibility.

It would be absurd to deny that fictional narrative discourse fascinates us because of its apparent *agreement with reality* – or rather, the reader's experience of reality. However, this is only half the story, because fictional narrative can very well *disagree with reality*, as Aristotle remarks on two separate occasions in his *Poetics*. First, he notes (1932: 57–8) that tragedy presents people who are better (i.e. nobler and more virtuous) than they are in reality, while comedy presents people who are worse (i.e. ridiculous and inferior) than ourselves, or people who are like ourselves. He compares this to realistic portrait painting, with the idealistic on the one hand and the caricaturistic on the other. Second, he states:

> Since the poet represents life, as a painter does or any other makes of likenesses, he must always represent one of three things – either things as they were or are; or things as they are said and seem to be; or things as they should be.
>
> (Aristotle 1932: 101)

This quotation shows that Aristotle dismisses a narrow interpretation of poetic representation. No doubt the third possibility, that the poet can present things as they would or should be, opens the way for different forms of poetic idealization, the presentation of moral, intellectual, physical and social perfection. It also allows for another type of breach of realistic presentation, such as is found in folktales, in which the hero uses magic to slay the dragon, winning the hand of the princess and half the kingdom.

In the latter case, all necessity and probability seem to have vanished, are even ignored. The fairytale's narrative hardly belongs to what is commonly called 'reality'. In this case, Aristotle offers a little help, because he states that it is erroneous for a poet to present the impossible: 'But it is all right if the poet thus achieves the object of poetry – what that is has already been stated – and makes that part of the poem more striking' (Aristotle 1932: 103). According to Aristotle, tragedy should portray the *marvellous*, while the *inexplicable* is best accommodated in the epic, 'because we do not actually see the persons of the story' (ibid.: 97). For this, he provides this commonsensical argument: 'that the marvellous causes pleasure is shown by the fact that people always tell a piece of news with additions by way of being agreeable' (ibid.: 97–9). This opposition between the *necessary* and *probable* on the one hand and the *impossible* and *improbable* on the other highlights an ambiguity in the presentation of action, both generally and in literature specifically.

On the one hand, the presentation of action is thus a question of truth, credibility, and motivated relations. When we try to discover *what actually happened*, we are attempting to gather reliable information, verify the veracity of the testimony, and comprehend the background, motives and reasons behind the narrative course; why did the events go in a certain direction and not in another? We attempt to find the grounds behind every narrative element and every other factor that appears to affect the narrative. This reasoning can be categorized into three groups: (1) physical or biological explanation; (2) socially motivated action/behavioural disposition; and (3) psychological motivation and intention. When the actions do not conflict with our notions of the nature of the material universe, our notions of social behaviour, and our notions of human motives and intentions, we regard them as sufficiently motivated, because they are in agreement with *what people do most often* and are *as they should be*.

Transgressions of our presentations of physically possible, socially adequate, and properly motivated action require a more demanding interpretation, however. The interpretation of fictitious actions in literature follows our interpretation of real action because we experience and construct the fictitious world as a parallel world that is analogous, as much as possible, to our own. In other words, our starting-point is the assumption that the fictitious world deviates as little as possible from reality. This principle of *minimal departure* (cf. Ryan 1991: 48–60) from the interpretative patterns that determine our perception of reality can be easily challenged by literary fiction. In fact, we can often only understand texts when we acknowledge that the possible world which they depict *deviates maximally* from the laws and customs considered to be valid in our own life world. This holds true of literary genres such as folktales and the artistic tale, where the physical regularities of our world are suspended; while science fiction describes what might be possible in the future.

It is reasonable to assume that the same material regularities are valid anywhere in the world, but this is of course not the case for social customs and norms. Nevertheless, one can distinguish tales which present behaviour within a social organization that is radically different from the contemporary social reality and posits an alternative society. For instance, this holds true for the so-called utopian and dystopian novels.

When we examine human motivations and intentions for action, it becomes more problematic to distinguish action that is clearly counterfactual, for it is here that reality often supersedes fiction. Yet narrative action (*mythos*) also implies a placing and evaluation of the individual action within the framework of the world in which it occurs. And it is here that Aristotle's division between the action's basis in personal characteristics as 'better', 'worse', or the same as ourselves becomes particularly meaningful.

In contrast to the world in which we live, a parallel and fictitious world may distinguish itself by the valour of all its male inhabitants, and the virtue of its women, or every action may appear ridiculous compared to our standards. Thus a text may contain its own norm according to which each individual action is evaluated.

Heracles and Antaios

On his way to get the Hesperides' golden apples, as one of his twelve labours, Heracles crosses Libya, the domain of King Antaios. Antaios has the bad habit of challenging all strangers to a wrestling match, invariably resulting in the stranger's death. As a son of Gaia, the Earth goddess, Antaios is able to renew his power simply by being in physical contact with the Earth. Even as Heracles is about to bite the dust, he realizes the extent of Antaios's special power and defeats him by lifting him up in the air and subsequently strangling him.

This story rests on Antaios's highly unusual supply of energy. The forces of the universe deviate completely from those in our own world, but we as readers choose to accept the impossibility as a conventional feature of the mythical universe. Having accepted this, we are able to worry *whether* and imagine *how* Heracles will get out of this scrap, and we accept his solution to the problem as logical because it cuts off his foe from his energy supply (to throw him in the water would probably have been ineffective, as Antaios's other parent is the ocean god Poseidon).

In this episode, we find again, albeit in concentrated form, the elements and structures we have described in the above. First, we have a universe where certain relationships are *possible, necessary, impossible,* or *contingent,* i.e.

the system that defines what is truth, and characterizes a given universe. This is often referred to as the text's *alethic system* (Greek *aletheia*: truth). Alternative worlds, be they mythological or the universe of an individual literary text, are characterized by the forces and regularities which they contain. What is impossible in one world may well be possible in another, and may be necessary in a third.

Second, the narrative universe is characterized by containing laws and behavioural norms for that which is *prohibited, prescribed, permitted*, or *optional*. This is the text's so-called *deontic* system, i.e. the system concerning morality as duty (Greek *deon*: the necessary, the appropriate). Antaios transgresses, among other things, the moral obligation, or prescription, to protect strangers. To kill strangers is to rob them of their lives, something on which they presumably place high value. Also existing in this mythical world are, third, *values*, arranged either as oppositions or as hierarchies of *goodness, badness* and *indifference* (cf. Aristotle's description of the elements of happiness). Such a system is known as an *axiologic* system (Greek *axios*: value). Finally, Heracles must know what to do in order to kill Antaios. Thus, a text's world is also, fourth, organized into an *epistemic* system concerning knowledge, ignorance and belief (Greek *epistème*: knowledge, belief), i.e. that which *can be known*, that which *cannot be known*, and that which one *presumes* to be the case, that which one *believes* as opposed to that which one doubts (for a short presentation of these four systems, see Dolezel 1976).

As the representation of action is always, either directly or indirectly, related to these four (modal) systems, it is no surprise that it plays a fundamental role in every culture (there are no cultures without tales, myths and historical accounts; see p. 14). After all, narrative is not connected to any particular world. Newspapers, legal records and history books, which contain accounts of human action, strive to be objective and truthful and present themselves as such. But reports, judgements and historical presentations are much more than mere attempts at recording the actual events; they present a culture's way of viewing reality, thus shaping our actual behaviour as well as being shaped by it.

The story of Heracles and Antaios may have once been considered as a historical account of the deeds of an actual hero and a demigod, but for the past several millennia, it has been seen as an entertaining story about one of classical mythology's best-loved heroes. Its continuing popularity may be due to two features: first, a part of the world ruled by chaos and the forces of death is swept clean of the criminal, the agent of death, through the victory of the culture hero. And second, Heracles not only uses his legendary strength – after all, Antaios proves to be stronger – but defeats his opponent by accepting the required presumption. Heracles solves a seemingly unsolvable problem by thinking, by producing knowledge himself.

Myths and fictitious presentations of human behaviour have a different function and set of presumptions than do historical accounts of human action. While the historian strives (or should strive) to record something factually correct, the author of fiction strives (or should strive) to communicate something that instructs, amuses, or moves us, because it tells of conditions or actions that we fear or desire. According to Aristotle, the narrative presentation in fiction can be seen as a way to clarify – and play with – our existential condition, as well as acquaint us with our historical world.

No matter whether the presentation aims to depict fact or fiction, the basic elements and relations on which the narrative rests remain the same. And our presentations of action are also accounts of what we believe – fear or desire – to be possible, necessary, or impossible; what we assume to know; and what apparently cannot be known. The presentation of human action is so important because, through it, we define ourselves and, to a certain degree, determine the limits of our own capabilities.

6 Text

From element-structure to dialogue-structure

What do they mean, these soft-pressed hands, these glances?
What's really said by kisses, fond embraces?
Only the heart for such, sweet girl, has phrases:
My foolish one, what head can grasp such fancies?

But when I find my kisses shunned, forbidden,
My eyes, my arms by you so oft eluded,
Mine is the tiresome task, all else excluded,
Of letting wisdom flow from lips unbidden.

Know then: in part a voice may be disarming
And by poetic heart-felt force win over.
Yet that which is most sweet it ne'er advances.

Therefore let lips and arms, with bosom, glances,
– How shall I say it? – melt into each other
To form a single tongue, as mute as charming.

(Aarestrup 1962 [1826])

This posthumous poem by the Danish writer Emil Aarestrup – we can all surely agree – is a text – indeed, almost the prototype of a text. It contains a completed chain of linguistic utterances, it has a sender and a receiver, it is in addition even dated, thereby underlining – as is the case with texts – that we are dealing with an utterance that can be located in time and space. Furthermore, it belongs to a particular type of discourse (literature), a particular major genre (poetry), and a particular poetic form (the sonnet).

The poem can thus serve as a prototype, an unproblematic example of what we intend to investigate in this chapter. And even though a number of the insights and claims of semiotics concerning texts and the concept of text contradict our intuitive understanding of what is characteristic of a text, there is in the final analysis no contradiction between the everyday and the semiotic concept of a text – the semiotic simply goes further. To underline this relationship we will continue in the following to refer to Aarestrup's poem.

Text and sign

The definitions of and differences between the concepts *text* and *sign* depend on the area and tradition of research that forms the point of departure for the semiotic determination of them. While linguistics as a rule distinguishes between them, philosophical sign-analysis (e.g. the tradition from C.S. Peirce and phenomenology) is not particularly interested in this distinction.

The reason why linguistics distinguishes is obvious enough, since at any rate structural linguistics analyses language texts as a hierarchy of inventories, with each inventory consisting of a number of elements and their combinatory rules. A language text, according to this way of thinking, can be subdivided as follows:

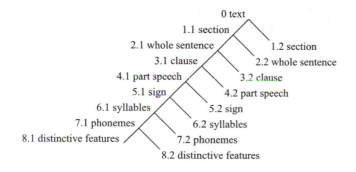

So a text consists of sections, which consist of whole sentences, which consist of clauses, which consist of parts of speech, which consist of signs. When we move down the hierarchy, we also move from inventories with an astronomical number of elements – for the number of texts is of course the same as the product of all permissible possibilities of combining sections, which in turn is the product of all the permissible possibilities of combining whole sentences, etc. When we come to the natural languages' inventory of signs, which also means their entire vocabulary, we still have a very large number of elements (and morphemes have to be added to all the words), since the number of words in natural languages varies from several thousand to several hundred thousand. Added to this, a living language is constantly generating new words, while others, either for a while or permanently, go out of use. Signs, though, cannot be combined in any way whatsoever in a language; even so, the large number of signs and the not very restrictive rules for their combination mean that a living language is constantly able to generate new, previously unseen texts.

An analysis of Aarestrup's poem according to these principles would consist of a segmentation (subdivision) that would begin by dividing it into sections, in this case agreeing with the four stanzas:

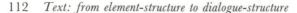

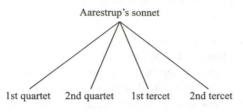

After that the 1st quartet, for example, would remain undivided as a whole sentence, while at a clause level it would be divided into four clauses:

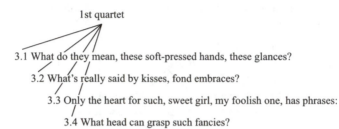

3.1 What do they mean, these soft-pressed hands, these glances?

3.2 What's really said by kisses, fond embraces?

3.3 Only the heart for such, sweet girl, my foolish one, has phrases:

3.4 What head can grasp such fancies?

The analysis can continue by subdividing into parts of speech, signs, etc.; but let us return to the general considerations concerning the relation between text and sign (re sign, see Chapter 3, especially p. 44).

If we move down beneath the boundary of the linguistic sign, important relations change radically. First, the number of syllables and phonemes of which they consist is extremely limited. Now phonologists (researchers into the sounds of language) are far from agreeing on the criteria for what constitutes an independent sound, but according to certain criteria it is claimed that the Hawaiian language only has 12 phonemes, whereas certain Caucasian languages are said to have more than 70. Nevertheless, even 70 elements is not many compared with the thousands or hundreds of thousands of words that languages contain. Added to this, the rules for their combination are especially restrictive – and they vary from language to language.

For individual language families these phonemes are quite different – so much so that a Dane has to learn a pronunciation that, to begin with, will feel foreign and uncomfortable in his mouth if he tries to learn a South African language, or even a Slavonic language. Louis Hjelmslev points out that this is because, as we grow up, we acquire certain pronunciation habits that are determined by the sound-combinations permitted in a given language. He continues:

> *vlk* and *krk* are impossible words in Danish, but perfectly possible in Czech (they mean 'wolf' and 'neck' respectively); *lgatj* and *vratj* would be inconceivable words in Danish, but are quite possible in Russian

('to lie' and 'to rake'); from Georgian (in the Caucasus) words could be named such as *vhsdsâm* 'I eat', *mtha* 'mountain', *mkbenare* 'biting', *dsqali* 'water' – words which a Dane, on the basis of his pronunciation habits, would believe were physically impossible. Danish combinations are just as unusual and just as difficult for people whose mother tongue has a considerably different construction; words such as *skvat* 'a drop' or *skvulp* 'a ripple' would cause a Finn almost insurmountable problems, as would a word like *skælmsk* 'roguish' a Frenchman. This is because Finnish does not permit clusters of consonants at the beginning of a syllable and French does not do so at the end of a word.

(Hjelmslev 1970: 41–2)

If we go down to the lowest level, the distinctive features (e.g. voiced versus voiceless), Roman Jakobson operates with only 12 minimal pairs (although this is not accepted by all linguists), of which all phonemes are built up. If we go the other way, up through the hierarchy of linguistic inventories, we meet an increasing degree of combinatory freedom:

As regards the combination of linguistic elements there exists an increasing degree of freedom. But when dealing with the combination of distinctive features to phonemes, freedom does not exist for the individual speaker – the code has already established all the possibilities that can be realized in the given language. Freedom to combine phonemes into words is limited, being restricted to the marginal invention of new words. In the formation of clauses from the words the limitations which the speaker has to observe are fewer. Finally, the restrictive rules of syntax cease with the combination of clauses to utterances, and every speaker's freedom increases substantially, even if one should not underestimate the number of stereotype utterances.

(Jakobson and Halle 1956: 74)

On the basis of this approach to language there is every reason to distinguish between linguistic signs and linguistic texts and to define the latter as combinations of the former. According to this approach, the utterance *Peter's hat* is a text made up of three linguistic signs: the proper noun *Peter*, the appellative noun *hat* and the morpheme (inflectional element) *'s*, which indicates the genitive. Admittedly, the same element can appear in inventories at different levels. Hjelmslev has, for example, pointed out that in a particular context *i* can be a period which consists of one clause, which consists of one word, which consists of one syllable (which consists of one phoneme), i.e. the Latin imperative of *ire*, with *i* meaning *Go!* But this does not present any real problem; it simply means that what are items from different levels from the point of view of analysis are represented by one and the same element of expression in the text.

If we shift from a linguistic to a philosophical analysis of the sign and text concepts and the relationship between them, the perspective alters drastically, however. Peirce writes:

> Sign in general [is] a class which includes pictures, symptoms, words, sentences, books, libraries, signals, orders of command, microcsopes, legislative representatives, musical concertos, performances of these.
>
> (Peirce, manuscript no. 634, 1909: 18)

If we go to other places in Peirce's writings, we can expand this list with lawyers, who represent their clients in front of a judge and jury, and weathercocks. We are also told that both the word *it* and the whole of Shakespeare's tragedy *Hamlet* is a sign. Peirce, then, would have considered Aarestrup's poem a single sign. Peirce unconcernedly uses the word sign for phenomena that a structuralist linguist would divide up into signs and texts. There are two interrelated reasons for this: first, the amount and variety of the items that are considered signs, and second – and as a consequence – the impossibility of undertaking a similarly rigorous analysis based on segmentation and the setting up of inventories as is possible for language texts. According to Peirce, signs generally have no prototypical characteristics that distinguish them from other phenomena (as we also pointed out in Chapter 3). Instead they are characterized *functionally* and *positionally* by virtue of their *representational relationship*, the fact that they represent an object for an interpretant or, to put it another way: they *mediate* between them. We can therefore add to the characteristics of the sign that it is a *dynamic* item. The consequence of such a conception is that any object can function as a sign or text. And general semiotics also draws this conclusion by defining itself as the study of the general conditions for production, transfer and interpretation of meaning.

Apparently, a formalistic and a functional or dynamic conception of semiotics are diametrically opposed to each other: a semiotics whose point of departure is in the system behind the sequence, which according to Saussure and Hjelmslev it was the task of linguistics and semiotics to discover; and a semiotics whose point of departure is the sign-sequence or sign-process, i.e. the signs that are actually present, no matter whether they form a nice chain as in a linguistic text or appear as a large complex sign as in a photograph or painting, that is, a semiotics of sign-systems as opposed to a text-semiotics.

Even though the title of this book, which is a slight adaptation of a Peirce quotation, 'signs are only signs *in actu*' (5.570),[1] reveals our sympathy with the latter point of view, there are nevertheless good reasons for conciliation. Supporters of both views have made necessary concessions to

---

1 Concerning the reference to Peirce, see page 25, note 1.

those of the opposite persuasion. In a central passage of *Prolegomena to a Theory of Language* Hjelmslev, for example, talks about the importance of the context:

> every item, and thus every single sign, is relatively not absolutely defined – and solely defined by its position in the context. From this point of view it is meaningless to distinguish between meanings which only arise in the context and meanings which could be assumed to have an existence independently of it, or – to use the terms of the old Chinese grammarians – between 'empty' and 'full' words. The so-called lexical meanings of certain signs are nothing more than artificially isolated contextual meanings, or artificial paraphrases of such. No sign has any meaning if completely isolated; every sign-meaning arises in a context, since we here mean a situational context or an explicit context – there is no difference between them, since we can in an unlimited or productive text (a living language) always transform a situational context into an explicit one.
>
> (Hjelmslev 1961: 41)

Hjelmslev's position also appears to contain a necessary concession to the importance of the sequence for the formation of sign-meaning. Scientific dictionaries are based on collections of quotations, where the use of the words in a number of contexts is noted, and it is on the basis of the concrete uses that the dictionary defines the sign's meaning. Just as Hjelmslev wrote, then: word-meanings are artificially isolated contextual meanings. If we push this line of thought even further, one could be tempted to claim that system-semiotics was a totally artificial product created by researchers with an obsessive sense of order – although, if we reflect for just a moment, we realize that this cannot be the case. We only need to consider what takes place when we want to say something, or listen to others. Verbal communications are produced through a selection of signs, i.e. a choice between various signs, and a combination of them into a text (see Chapter 2 on code). But why do we choose one word or a morpheme and not some other (see p. 69f.)? There are many reasons for this, reasons which are good and convincing, and which will be the focus of much of this chapter. Here we are only talking about the meaning of words. In Lewis Carroll's *Through the Looking Glass* the relation between the meanings of words and the speaker is the subject of a conversation between Alice and Humpty Dumpty:

> 'When I use a word,' Humpty Dumpty said, in rather a scornful tone, 'it means just what I choose it to mean – neither more nor less.'
> 'The question is,' said Alice, 'whether you *can* make words mean so many different things.'
> 'The question is,' said Humpty Dumpty, 'which is to be master – that's all.'

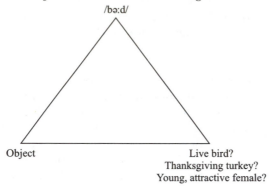

Figure 6.1 Relationship of sign, object and interpretants.

Alice was too much puzzled to say anything; so after a minute Humpty Dumpty began again. 'They've a temper, some of them – particularly verbs: they're the proudest – adjectives you can do anything with, but not verbs – however, *I* can manage the whole lot of them!'

(Carroll 1965: 269)

Even though it later transpires that Humpty Dumpty pays the words every Saturday for working for him, he is nevertheless, strictly speaking, suffering from megalomania, as the power of the individual to change the meaning of linguistic signs is in fact extremely limited (cf. also the quotation from Jakobson, p. 113). For the signs have a history, are linked to each other and have reference and meaning.

Peirce – who otherwise emphasizes semiosis (the sign-process) – has by means of the concept of the sign's *immediate interpretant*, i.e. its interpretability or the *potential meaning* which it possesses before being used in a concrete communication, taken account of this basic relationship. The immediate interpretant is, as mentioned, the sign's *meaning-potential*, while the dynamic interpretant is the interpretation or translation actually undertaken. The difference between the two types of interpretant becomes clear when we are dealing with *homonyms*, i.e. words that have the same expression, but different meanings. Thus, if we take the sentence:

That bird's a pretty sight

we are at a loss to know which meaning /bə:d/ has in the sentence, since it has three widely differing immediate interpretants: a *live bird*, a *Thanksgiving turkey* and a *young, attractive female*. We could illustrate the relationship as in Figure 6.1.

Until the moment when the sign /bə:d/ is interpreted/translated into another sign (i.e. a dynamic interpretant is added), the object of the text (both the immediate and the dynamic) remained indefinite. The choice here is one between the three immediate interpretants – but how do we choose? Well, normally the choice is decided unproblematically by the explicit or situational context. The explicit context means the context that is evident from the other signs in the text – we will refer to this as the *co-text*. In this case, not all that much is required:

> That bird's a pretty sight – she's quite mouthwatering.

The choice in the next part of the sentence of the personal pronoun *she* instead of *it* is enough to choose the solution *young, attractive female* and for the meaning-potential *live bird* and *Thanksgiving turkey* to be deselected, despite the fact that, apart from the pronoun, we could retain the ambiguity for a little while yet:

> That bird's a pretty sight – she's/it's quite mouthwatering. I can hardly wait.

If we exclude most correct speech, the *she* could probably still refer to the *Thanksgiving turkey*. If the co-text does not resolve the polysemy (many meanings), then the situational context – or, as we prefer to call it, the *context* – probably does so. If the conversation is taking place round the dinner table on Thanksgiving day, then it would be reasonable to assume that they are talking about a turkey; if two young males are talking on a street corner, their interest is probably not in a family reunion. And if we are taking part in or listening to the conversation, we can follow the speaker's gaze and pointing finger, i.e. the deictic elements of the utterance that refer to shared surroundings (see Chapter 3, p. 35, and Chapter 4, p. 59f.).

In the above we have seen how it is not possible to provide definitions which on the basis of formal criteria allow us to distinguish between sign and text. As far as linguistic texts are concerned, it is often true that texts are made up of a number of signs. Not always, however. Neither the Latin *i* nor the English *go* consists of more than one sign, though it is possible to argue that we ought to distinguish between *i* and *go* as elements in the conjugation of the verb, for example:

	Imperative	Active		Passive
Present	2nd pers. sing.	*i*		*ir*
	2nd pers. plur.	*ite*		*i-mini*
Future	2nd and 3rd pers. sing.	*ito*		*i-tor*
	2nd pers. plur.	*itote*		
	3rd pers. plur.	*e-unto*	*e-untor*	
			(the passive forms are extremely rare)	

and with 'i!' and 'Go!' as utterances in a communication situation. We agree on this. The addition of quotation marks and an exclamation mark indicates an altered analytical perspective. For by adding them we are indicating that we are dealing with signs in use, not just signs that are elements of a paradigm. The difference corresponds to that between making an inventory of traffic signs and traffic signs placed at the side of the road. This can also be illustrated by the following two signs:

They are mentioned on this page of the book, but not used. Hardly anyone would put out his or her cigarette on catching sight of them. That would also be illogical, since if they had really been used here, the combination would result in a meaningless sign-act that simultaneously permitted and prohibited: 'Smoking here is allowed/prohibited', with *here* in addition indicating wherever a copy of this book has been opened at this particular page.

If one wishes to maintain a distinction between *sign* and *text* and not refer to both simply as *sign*, one could let *sign* indicate that the given meaning-conveying object was considered as a virtual (Latin *virtualis*: present as possibility) and possibly systematic item, whilst *text* could indicate the sign's use at a given point in time. In principle, a text can be dated and located – it has an origin (cf. the Aarestrup sonnet), even though this can be anonymous or collective as well as deriving from a particular individual. This also means that some person(s) can take responsibility for it, or be made responsible for it, although it would probably be difficult to make anyone responsible for the linguistic signs *to*, *it*, or even *owing to the fact that*. In short, a *text* is a part or result of an act, whereas *signs* are potential conveyors of meaning which can be actualized (activated) in a text or as a text. Texts are not simply locatable results of acts; they have material existence – even if only sound frequencies – and they can therefore be perceived in their distinctiveness and variety in relation to other phenomena and to other texts, or as individual copies of the same text. And they can be perceived by a single or practically unlimited number of receivers.

When it comes to natural languages, one can say that the linguistic signs, the smallest units that convey meaning, have a certain type of abstract reality, since, together with their combinatory rules (a dictionary and a grammar), they make up the normative and traditional part of language. They are memory and models, or control programmes that, to a certain extent, are stored in the heads of language users as common property; this is the object of detailed investigation in research and pedagogy. Linguistic texts, on the other hand, are the result of the concrete use of the entire control programme, of which the signs are an important part; but linguistic texts are also the result of something else – a purpose in communicating in a concrete context (the lyrical I in the Aarestrup sonnet is up to something, of which more later on p. 140).

On the basis of this proposed distinction it is perfectly possible to have texts without signs. This is the case when the text is constructed by virtue of analog codes (see p. 17). A portrait or a landscape painting are examples of texts that are not made up of signs in the strict sense of the word, since it is not possible to find anything that corresponds to the first and second articulation of language (cf. Chapter 3, p. 44). This does not of course mean that art cannot be analysed with great precision; but it occurs because art is also a craft with a whole series of traditions of a technical, iconographical and motif-related nature. For this reason, the elements and combinations of pictures can perfectly well be recognized and described from a semiotic point of view, even though the relationship between parts and whole is of a different kind than in the case of language.

Texts also exist that are composed of elements from various different semiotic systems. In an opera, for example, there is a libretto – a linguistic text – which is sung or recited and which is linked to the musical text. In addition, there are the facial and bodily expressions of the singers, as well as costumes, scenery, lights, etc., all of them units of meaning which the producer, conductor, scenographer, singers and musicians – and possibly dancers – seek to bring into a meaningful relationship with each other. Performances of operas or plays pretend, on the basis of certain perspectives and conventions, to be – heavily stylized – presentations of human emotions, speech and action; and if we did not perceive them as such, a very important dimension of them would be lost.

What opera and drama seeks to present – our speech and behaviour – can also be considered – indeed, must be considered – as texts produced with the aid of more or less strict codes and conventions. This is obvious if one thinks of reception ceremonies at royal courts in former times, where the roles were precisely fixed and movements were choreographed. For a present-day reader such an example is, however, merely an illustration of the conventional nature of that behaviour; but all behaviour relates to conventions and seeks to realize aims which are more or less stereotypical (see also Chapter 5). This is why behaviour can be studied as (complex) texts, by means of which individuals and groups communicate with each other.

Text and object

It has been mentioned (p. 114) that any object can function as a text, i.e. be included as a conveyor of meaning in a sign-process, a semiosis. This view is indisputable, something that the activities of, for example, the hunter, the detective and the pathologist bear out. So everything can be semiotized in given circumstances and for a given purpose. When the wise lady-in-waiting cuts a hole in the bag which the sleeping princess has on her when the dog carries her to the soldier, she creates a trail of grains of rice that can lead others to the malefactor's house. When the old, always weatherbeaten, old salt glances at a perfectly cloudless sky and says: 'There'll be rain before nightfall', the sky is being read for signs of something that is on its way. And in our sonnet the lyrical I is engaged in explaining that kisses, glances, etc. are signs in the language of love.

The question should therefore rather be: 'Does anything else than texts exist?' The answer is in the negative and runs as follows: 'No, nothing else than signs exists – at least for us human beings, since our relation to the world around us is one of representation, resting on the interpretation of signs, i.e. the perception of the outer world as it is processed in our sensory apparatus and central nervous system and presents itself to our consciousness.' The argument is naturally far more elaborate, not only involving our perception of the outer world but also of our own body and psyche – a perception that is also seen as being a representation relationship. What we know about ourselves we know by dint of signs, no matter whether we are dealing with mental images or bodily impressions. Many semioticians from both the Continent, such as Hjelmslev and Greimas, and from the Anglo-Saxon world, such as Peirce, seem to agree on this point. Peirce expresses it as follows:

> It is easy to see that the object of sign, that to which it virtually at least professes to be applicable, can itself only be a sign. For example, the object of an ordinary proposition is a generalization from a group of perceptual facts. It represents those facts. These perceptual facts are themselves abstract representatives, through which we know not precisely what intermediaries, of the percepts themselves, and these are themselves viewed, and are – if the judgement has any truth – representations, primarily of impressions of sense, ultimately of a dark underlying something, which cannot be specified without its manifesting itself as as sign of something below. There is, we think, and reasonably think, a limit to this, an ultimate reality, like a zero of temperature. But in the nature of things, it can only be approached; it can only be represented. The immediate object which the sign seeks to represent is itself a sign.
>
> (Peirce, manuscript no. 599, 1902: 35–6)

In one sense the argument is indisputable. Naturally, we only have access to the world around us through and by virtue of our sensory apparatus and central nervous system, but with the important addition that we as humans are able to artificially sharpen and expand our senses through instruments (see p. 31ff.). Every sensing of the outer world is therefore the final point of a complex process that rests on both a species-specific processing of the impulses and on learned habits of interpretation (see Chapter 6). This fact has also led to a rapprochement between semiotics and biology, as it is certain that meaning and interpretation start before we are aware of the fact and before we can control the process, i.e. in our bodies (see the biologist Jakob von Uexküll's theorem of the outer world, and the work of the Danish biologists Claus Emmeche and Jesper Hoffmeyer).

Even so, there are good reasons for not relinquishing any distinction between text and object, since we need this distinction when we want to describe our interpretation of and behaviour in our surrounding world. In practice, we are very well able to distinguish between them. We normally do not experience or interact with sense-impressions, perceptions or signs; instead we perceive objects and persons. This does not, of course, make the investigation of biologists, neurologists and psychologists into the nature and development of the perception–interpretation process any less interesting; but it does mean that in order to understand human use of signs and behaviour one has to assume that we constantly relate to our surrounding world in two complementary (mutually exclusive, but also supplementary) ways. On the one hand, we relate to the phenomena of our surrounding world as objects, living creatures and persons that are familiar to us and which we do not scan for new items of information. Instead we rub shoulders with them unsuspectingly; we use, possibly misuse, enjoy and consume them, or are enjoyed and consumed by them. Naturally, talk of use and consumption implies that the living creatures of our surrounding world can represent a danger to us (as we for them); but in both cases they are opaque bodies which offer resistance by virtue of their inscrutable materiality. A complement to this, however, is that we relate to the phenomena of the surrounding world, i.e. to the very same phenomena which have just been mentioned as objects, persons, etc. – as signs which we use to tell us something about something else (*aliquid stat pro aliquo*), or which reveal to us that which we do not wish to know.

We may exemplify the representational logic of the sign with reference to a country's intelligence service. Let us imagine that the service reads a political pamphlet that describes the country's leadership as dictatorial and corrupt, inciting revolt. At the first reading of the pamphlet the chain of linguistic signs is understood as conventional conveyors of meaning (symbolic signs, in Peirce's terminology). Shaken by the revolutionary content of the folder, the head of intelligence orders the authors to be traced. The symbolic signs, the black letters on the paper, whose material was only perceived as a meaningless substratum for the message, are now perceived as tracks, i.e. as indexical signs, where the rounding of the corners, possible indentations and the precise distance between the various letters become clues that will help the revolutionaries to be tracked down.

The printed political pamphlet has naturally always possessed the tracks which have now attracted the attention of the intelligence service. This link is a causal one: the printing press applies the ink to the paper in a particular way. Despite this, the link between the text and the object is not realized, semiotically speaking, until the moment it is interpreted as a representation of the object, i.e. the moment the object and the sign are linked via an interpretant:

> It is equally essential to the function of a sign that it should determine an *Interpretant*, or a second correlate related to the object of the sign as the

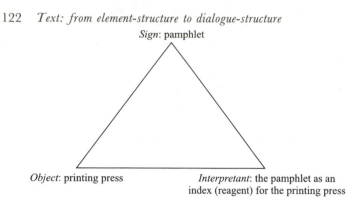

Figure 6.2 Interpretant as mediator between sign and object.

sign itself is related to that object; and this interpretant may be regarded as the sign represents it to be, as it is in its pure secondness to the object and as it is in its firstness.

(Peirce, unpublished manuscript no. 914, 1904: 3)

The investigation by the intelligence service produces just such an interpretant, who relates to the object in the same way as the sign does. Before the interpretation there was only a dyadic (two-sided) relationship:

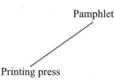

Through the interpretation process, the semiosis, a triadic (three-sided) relationship is established; see Figure 6.2.

In this case the interpretant mediates between sign and object by uncovering the link between them. The interpretant is here a language utterance which says: 'The pamphlet is an index, a reagent, of the printing press.' The interpretant does not, however, need to be an utterance – it can also be realized in action.

The magnificent plumage of the male bird is an index, a symptom, of its masculinity – and the reaction of the female bird, its readiness to mate, is the *energetic interpretant* (as Peirce calls it) of the sign of masculinity. Jesper Hoffmeyer likewise interprets ontogenesis (the biological development of the individual from egg to adult) as a sign-process, since 'a piece of one-dimensional "DNA-writing", which . . . contains "a coded version" of the parents, is transformed into a three-dimensional organism of "flesh and blood"' (Hoffmeyer 1996: 30). If one regards the communicative processes by means of which information is transmitted between the various parts of an organism (endosemiotic processes) as sign-processes, then life, from the most primitive organisms to *Homo sapiens*, will depend on semiosis, on the transference of meaning.

We do not intend to deal with the philosophical implications of Peirce's semiotic – in particular his theory of categories. It should, however, be mentioned that everything that is available to consciousness, according to Peirce, is so either as a *Firstness*, i.e. as it is of itself without any relation to anything else, such as qualities and feeling, or as a *Secondness*, i.e. in relation to something else, such as force and action and reaction, or as a *Thirdness*, i.e. as a mediation between Firstness and Secondness, such as habit, regularity, or meaning.

Semiosis, the sign-process, is a *Thirdness* that mediates between a *Firstness* (the sign considered as itself as a quality/collection of qualities) and a *Secondness* (the sign in relation to the object) in such a way that the first is brought into contact with the second. According to this view, semiosis is a *Thirdness* where the sign-vehicle is a quality/collection of qualities, the object is something else (an otherness) that acts as a force on the sign-vehicle, and the interpretant is the objective result or content of the semiosis.

If we imagine a piece of meat that is hidden but that emits a smell, and a hungry dog that, on account of the smell, begins to salivate, then we have a semiosis as a process that emanates from an *object*, i.e. the *meat*, which emits a *sign* (an index), a quality that can be picked up by the senses, the *smell*, and which provokes an *interpretant*, the *saliva*, in the *interpreter*, *the dog*. (It should be stressed that interpreter and interpretant are two different things; see Figure 6.4 on p. 130).

We can, however, also imagine a *dog-owner*, a *sender*, who utters a *text, 'food'*, which causes the *owner's dog*, the *receiver*, to produce an *interpretant, the saliva*, because the text 'food' has become associated with the *object, dog-food* in the consciousness of the dog. We can illustrate the relationship as in Figure 6.3.

This shows how signs can be substituted for each other, as here where a symbolic sign acts in the same way as an indexical (in this case the two signs illustrate the difference between a conditioned and an unconditioned reflex).

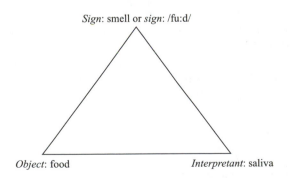

Sign: smell or *sign*: /fuːd/

Object: food   *Interpretant*: saliva

Figure 6.3 Signs as substitutes for each other.

In both the instances mentioned above the two signs are precisely representations of something else. The smell represents the food indexically, here synecdochically (Greek *synecdoche*: part for whole), as a *pars pro toto*, while the word 'food' is a symbolic sign that is associated with the object through habit. If the dog can and is allowed to, it will eat the food to which the sign has led it. The eating is a process through which energy is converted. It is quite possible to continue to consider the digestion processes, or parts of them, as semiotic, since substances in the food activate particular substances and processes in the digestive system (just as the smell activates the saliva). It is, however, reasonable to claim that at a certain level the sign-process is complete, since it has led to a discovery, understanding and use of the object. For the hungry individual, dog or human being, the food does not represent a new object, but is the actual object. Admittedly, it is perfectly possible to say that the food represents an expectation of pleasurable activity and the satisfaction of a need; but these also have the food as object.

The example also shows that sign and object can be one and the same phenomenon, or parts of it in two different functions. The smell is a property of the food, not separate from it, as the word 'food' is. And even if man is characterized by creating a series of symbolic sign-systems on the basis of natural languages that are precisely linked by habit to his surrounding world, the natural languages themselves (and thereby the artificial ones as well) assume that the predominantly symbolic linguistic signs are linked to signs that are predominantly iconic and indexical (see p. 51ff.).

This constant shift between considering a phenomenon as an object and perceiving it as a text is characteristic of human existence. We alternate between seeing the world around us as a collection of traditionally linked stereotypes and a collection of enigmatic texts that are to be deciphered. If this were not the case, we would either fossilize in a completely law-abiding and predictable behaviour in relation to an outer world full of stereotypes (including other human beings), or we would be destroyed in an endless and ultimately distracting attempt to interpret all the phenomena of the outer world as texts – texts that were continually changing meaning.

Thus the boundary between texts and objects cannot be drawn between two types of phenomena, for the same phenomena can be the one or the other. Every object is a potential text, and every text is also an object, because it has a material substratum. That does not mean – at least not necessarily – a semiotic imperialism, for the onus of proof lies of course with the person who believes he has uncovered the textuality of a phenomenon (for a more detailed discussion of these issues, see Johansen 1993b).

Text and intertextuality: the text as expanding syntagm

Both the distinction between sign and text and that between text and object are – as the above has shown – the result of functions, not of specific characteristics. But are not the text or the texts definable units? Are we able to say with certainty when a given text stops and a new one begins? If the requirement is criteria that with absolute certainty can enable us to determine where the boundaries of a text are to be found, then the answer is: 'No!' In the world of meanings drawing boundaries is a question of relative independence and of appropriateness and reasons. Even types of text that traditionally insist on and are invested with marked boundaries – such as, for example, poetry – end up raising a host of questions when it comes to drawing boundaries. Is the individual poem or the collection of poems the unit that it is meaningful to consider as the relevant unit? The question cannot be answered generally, only concretely. Collections of poems can be compilations of poems that have been written independently and as an expression of widely differing forms of inspiration. On the other hand, we may be dealing with a sonnet in a cycle of sonnets, i.e. a poem which formally and thematically is extremely closely linked to the other poems of the collection and which therefore can scarcely be considered as an independent text.

The above does not mean that good reasons cannot be found for drawing boundaries – far from it. Even so, it would probably be more productive to begin with a completely different point of view, one that – even though it disagrees with the conventional perception of texts as clearly separable units – provides an interesting perspective on the text as a production of meaning and not simply as a product (Johansen 1988a).

The linguist Hjelmslev defines the text as a chain of signs or as a semiotic process; and within a living language this process is considered as one, continuous and constantly expanding syntagm. Such a point of view means, for example, that all Danish texts, i.e. texts formed in accordance with the Danish language-system, are seen as one text which is constantly being enlarged by the texts that are being produced every minute of the day and night. Even if this point of view seems to run contrary to intuition, it is at any rate in line with the aim of linguistics, since the description of a natural language has to rest on material that exceeds any number of texts. Indeed, in principle a description of language has to be valid for all texts that simply are possible in the given language, for otherwise it cannot have described the language-system correctly.

In Hjelmslev the aim is the linguistic description of the system; but the philosopher and logician Peirce comes to a similar view by combining the concept of the sign with the idea of thought as a constantly expanding argument:

> *There is a science of semiotics whose results no more afford room for differences of opinion than do those of mathematics,* and one of its theorems increases the aptness of that simile. It is that if any signs are connected, no matter how, the resulting system constitutes one sign; so that, most connections resulting from successive pairings, a sign frequently interprets a second in so far as this is 'married' to a third.

Thus, the conclusion of a syllogism is the interpretation of either premises as married to the other, and of this sort are all the principal translation-processes of thought. In the light of the above theorem, we see that the *entire thought-life of any person is a sign*; and a considerable part of its interpretation will result from marriages with the thought of other persons. *So the thought-life of a social group is a sign; and the entire body of all thoughts is a sign,* supposing all thought to be more or less connected.

(Peirce, unpublished manuscript no. 1476, *c*. 1904: 38)

Others view the relationship in a similar way. This applies, for example, to the German hermeneutic philosopher H.-G. Gadamer, who sees the single text as a moment in the tradition of thought or art. Every text is part of what he refers to as the dialectic between question and answer, because texts are attempts to understand something, the universe, the outer world, history or the subject himself, and because this attempt at understanding takes place in a dialogue with attempts made by others (cf. Gadamer 1960).

Let us now return to our Aarestrup sonnet. The form of the sonnet can be considered as closed, self-centred, as it were. The two four-line and two three-line stanzas apparently form a self-sufficient unit. But let us listen once more to the opening of the sonnet:

What do they mean, these soft-pressed hands, these glances?

The sonnet pretends to be part of, or is part of, a dialogue. It pretends to be, or actually is, an answer to a question that a (young) woman puts to the lyrical I. The text opens out on to a communication situation by presenting itself as a line in a dialogue.

In the light of the above, it is not strange that literary researchers (and researchers into art and music, for that matter) also speak of an intertextuality between the literary texts. Broadly speaking, this means that the texts refer to each other, quote each other, that there are allusions in the text to other texts. Such an influence can, for example, take the form of adopting the conventions, material, action or themes of other texts. Finally, there is also a more active form of intertextuality, when a given text establishes a dialogue-type relationship to another text or to other texts.

For example, a text can seek legitimacy in another sacrosanct and/or authoritative text, as when Dante's *Divine Comedy* finds its basis of belief in the Bible and in the Catholic tradition from the Fathers of the Church to Thomas Aquinas. A text can, however, also contain a critical and subversive dialogue with another text. A well-known example is Jean Rhys's *Wide Sargasso Sea*, which seeks to undermine Charlotte Brontë's *Jane Eyre* as part of a post-colonial literary strategy turning British classics upside down by rewriting them from the perspective of the peripheries of the empire, in this case the Caribbean.

Intertextuality is thus able to comprise a sharing of (1) *codes and conventions* of varying degrees of generality – from simply belonging to the same semiotics (e.g. that the texts are paintings) or the same natural languages to a close sharing of specific conventions (the texts can, for example, all be twelve-tone music or Greek tragedies).

Furthermore, intertextuality can consist in a sharing of (2) *a real or possible world*. This kind of intertextuality alludes to the co-referentiality of the texts, i.e. that a number of individual texts refer to a common discursive universe, no matter whether the presented world is historical, fictional, ideal, or the like. In our everyday conversations with each other this co-referentiality is often taken for granted (and is often quite unproblematic), because we refer to a common surrounding world which we localize and relate to in the same way. A number of texts can also share a fictional or mythical universe. Homer, Hesiod and the classical tragedians share a mythical universe that comprises the Greek pantheon (the total world of the gods); and practically all the authors of Greek antiquity produce new stories or new versions of old stories about the heroes and the gods. As far back as antiquity the so-called mythographers (those who wrote down myths) were collecting, summarizing and systematizing stories from the various sources and presenting general outlines. Even though such works are normally only of cultural, literary or religious interest, one ought to remember that one of the biggest and most merited successes of European literature, Ovid's *Metamorphoses* (2 BC to AD 9), also is a compilation of myths.

Finally, there may be a sharing of a (3) *communicative and intersubjective nature*. Rhys's undermining of Brontë has already been mentioned. Here we are dealing with a consciously emphasized disagreement. Texts can, however, also express a shared conception of the outer world and the self, without consciously entering into a dialogue with each other. It is not necessary for that reason for them to refer to a common universe, for every fictional text, for example, nearly always refers to its own particular universe. This also applies in a single authorship; for there are strictly speaking no shared references for Camus's *Caligula* (1938) and *The Stranger* (*L'Étranger*, 1942), just as the fictional world of this novel is different from that of Sartre's *Nausea* (*La nausée*, 1938). Despite this, there is something which not only Camus's play and his novel share, but which these works also share with Sartre's novel. That a single author's texts possess a shared quality seems natural to us, as we perceive the individual texts as an expression of the same understanding of the outer world and the same subjectivity. We do not wish to dispute the reasonableness of letting such an assumption form the point of departure for a closer examination of the text; but the hypothesis definitely needs to be *put to the test*.

Human beings change more or less radically, which means that the texts they have produced at a certain point in their development can in some respects bear a closer resemblance to those of other contemporary authors than their own later works. The reason for these changes within one and the same individual and, conversely, the degree of concord between different individuals are formulated by Peirce as follows:

> a person is not absolutely an individual. His thoughts are what he is 'saying to himself,' that is, is saying to that other self that is just coming into life in the flow of time. When one reasons, it is that critical self that one is trying to persuade; and all thought whatsoever is a sign, and is mostly of the nature of language. . . . man's circle of society (however widely or narrowly this phrase may be understood) is a sort of loosely compacted person, in some respects of higher rank than the person of an individual organism.
>
> (5.421)

This point of view is important, because it draws boundaries untraditionally and because the reason for doing so is taken from the idea that the production of meaning is always a dialogic venture, no matter whether we are dealing with an inner dialogue that is (consciously or subconsciously) always taking place in us, or the dialogue that is always taking place within given social groups, often without many of its members being aware of the fact. This point of view also means that the single individual is perceived as a highly complex unit: on the one hand, it is itself made up (i.e. is precisely not indivisible) of positions in a dialogue and, on the other hand, it is – as far as the production of meaning is concerned – itself only a moment in the constantly flowing stream of collective thought – an instrument in an uncountable orchestra. Perhaps it is one that has an important voice that can clearly be heard and whose themes are taken up by other instruments, or perhaps one that can scarcely be differentiated from those of other instruments. This point of view is also in accordance with psychoanalysis's conception of the formation of identity as a long-drawn-out process that comprises such mechanisms as introjection (the incorporation of elements from outside into the psyche), projection (the ascribing of the psyche's own elements to external objects) and identification.

Even if we are – or think we are – often interested in the individual text or in a particular group of texts, in order to understand it or them we have tacitly to accept that a whole series of prerequisites have been fulfilled. The love-letter we receive we include, without thinking about it, as one letter among several, of which we have written some and received others. These letters are a part of a relationship between two people, in which a steady stream of texts is exchanged, most of them verbal. So the letter becomes an intersection among others in a continuing dialogue that has the behaviour and interaction of both parties as the closest meaning-creating *context*. This means that interpretation always involves a contextualization, and that it is by virtue of this that the boundaries of the text are drawn.

The point of departure is naturally the text that is materially present; but only through interpretation will we become able to decide whether the existing text constitutes a relatively independent and relatively demarcated unit of meaning (see p. 147). What we call a fragment is precisely a single text that lacks the closure in terms of expression and/or meaning that we expect. Apart from the ravages of time, which have made what has survived fragmentary – the *Venus de Milo* has missing arms – or death or abandonment, which have left the text incomplete, the fragment can also be a consciously chosen art-form. The Romantic poets consciously wrote fragments, and sculptors often prefer portraying the torso to the entire body. Added to this, every text – from a semiotic point of view – is in a sense fragmentary, both because it is a link in a sign-process and because we have to place it in a meaningful context in order to be able to understand it. Aarestrup's sonnet is a case in point. It is an example of a text that carefully indicates its context: the young woman's question. Intertextuality – the intended dialogue of the texts with each other or their shared characteristics with other texts and shared context – is therefore not a superficial phenomenon. It is fundamental to their potential to generate and afford meaning.

Text as semiosis: the semiotic pyramid

If the text is a point of intersection that leads outwards in several directions, then it is the task of semiotics to map out and present the paths leading to and from it. The triadic conception of the sign, according to which the sign is a unity of sign (sign-vehicle), object and interpretant, has been presented both here and in Chapter 3. We have further proposed distinguishing between the sign as a virtual (possible) unit that is actualized as text in a process of signification through which it is also inserted in a co-text and a context. Normally this process has a *sender* (or at least a *source*) and a *receiver*, where the text can be seen as an act by virtue of which the former refers to, or affects, the latter. So a text can be defined as a sign-act by means of which someone refers to someone else about something with the aid of one or several semiotics that can be more or less coded. The definition of a text can be represented as in Figure 6.4.

Semiosis is portrayed here as a pyramid with five poles, one at its tip and four in its ground plan. Each of these poles has an internal and an external aspect and – we will argue – it is the relationship and constant backward-and-forward flow between them that makes meaning possible (for an extended description of the pyramid see Johansen 1999).

The text as token (replica) and type (representamen)

The two concepts replica and representamen, or *token* and *type* as Peirce (and the Anglo-Saxons) also call them, need to be distinguished (in the model of the pyramid we have put copy for token and text for type because these terms

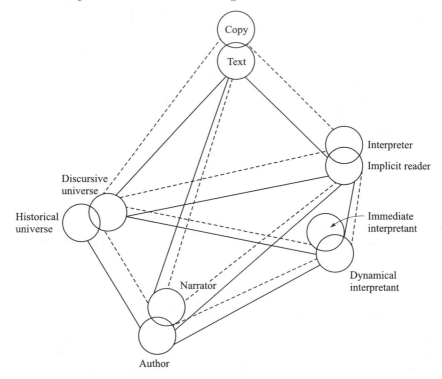

Figure 6.4 The definition of a text: the semiotic pyramid.

are familiar). We have already met the distinction between them in Chapter 3, although there they were named differently:

B   **B**
₁   ₂

B_1 B_2

If we use the alphabet as the basis for description, we have two different *tokens* (replicas) of the same *type* (*representamen* or letter: *type*). The difference between them is in fact not of the kind that we would conceive them as tokens of two different types. In other instances, however, we may be in doubt, as the following example – also borrowed from Nelson Goodman (1968: 139) – shows:

b
a d a
d

Here we are really unsure about how we are to interpret the horizontal series of letters. If they spell ADD, they could mean the verb *add*. If they spell AAD, which gives no meaning horizontally, then the vertical column reads BAD, i.e. *bad*, while BDD is meaningless. If we were to meet a potential partner whom we become interested in, it would be important for us to be able to distinguish between his/her saying 'You're adorable' and 'You're deplorable'; but since we do not really like to ask, we try on the basis of the co-text and the situational context to work out which is the more likely of these two possibilities. If (s)he had said: 'You're spineless, and characterless – you're . . . ', we would probably pick 'deplorable', whereas the text 'You're so sweet, you're . . . ' would probably induce us to choose 'adorable'.

When philologists publish so-called critical editions, they attempt to establish a text that is free of chance lapses of the pen or misunderstandings. The text they (re)construct has never existed before, because it is built on a collation of manuscripts and editions, where the manuscript, first edition and final reviewed edition of the author(s) are especially important.

The aim is to establish a text, the individual parts of which are assumed to be in accordance with its overall context of meaning, with the author's intention (even authors make slips of the pen), and with what seems to be in accordance with the state of knowledge and understanding at the time. Textual criticism rests on linguistic and cultural intimacy with the period when the text was written. It is also a craft where certain rules of thumb apply; but in addition it is a question of weighing the probability of the various interpretations in relation to all poles and aspects of the semiotic pyramid.

It is often quite clear what a token is, although the concept of type creates a number of problems. We never hold a type, only a token, in our hands. At the same time, we compare the token with a type that, to a certain extent, is nonexistent. However, the type can be considered as a norm or rule that prescribes what the token must or ought to look like. A US dollar bill has to be printed on a certain type of paper produced at a particular location, and the imprint has to come from particular plates of a particular billprinting press at a certain time under proper control. Apart from the serial number, the dollar bills are in principle identical – you could say they are tokens of each other. But this is not enough: just as for children to be legitimate one has to know their father and mother and the time of birth; therefore the bills are also reagents, indexical signs, for their own production process.

In the above examples there is no privileged bill of which the others are tokens. Instead there is a plate from which all of them are printed; but this plate is not itself a banknote. The same applies to graphic printing. The individual graphic sheets are printed from the same plate, which means that they are tokens or tracks of the same object. In principle, though not in practice, the artist who has made the engraving or plate can print an unlimited number of tokens, all of which are equal and of equal worth.

When it comes to paintings one talks of originals and copies rather than types and tokens. Apparently, the distinction is clear enough. Let us for the time being ignore fakes and think instead of a portrait painter at a royal court. He is paid at different rates for an original portrait and a number of copies (for use at legations or as gifts to royalty and nobility). He paints the original himself, while the copies are painted under his supervision by apprentices in his studio. One of his apprentices falls ill and, to complete the order, he paints one of the copies himself. Although the copies are less carefully painted than the original, the touch and conscientiousness of the master are immediately recognizable, so the question as to what is original and what is a copy cannot be answered (there is a series of ingenious examples concerning the relationship between original and copy in Eco's article 'Fakes and Forgeries' in Eco 1990: 174–202).

If one is to decide whether a painting has been painted by a particular painter, a whole series of criteria will be used – from the type and nature of the materials to letters and documents that seem to confirm or disprove its validity. An important criterion will be a study of the brushstrokes that make up the details of the picture. Just as a graphologist is sometimes able to reveal that a signature has been imitated (forgery), art historians can prove that the painting technique differs so strikingly from that found in paintings that are undoubtedly genuine that the picture cannot be attributed to the given painter.

The important distinction from a semiotic point of view between *type* and *original* is that the type is not itself a text but a norm, while an original is itself a unique text. Music and written manuscripts can be valuable on account of the corrections they perhaps contain, and that say something about the production of the work, about the choices that have been made and, by means of this, perhaps something about its meaning. Apart from this, any reliable edition is just as good to read or play from. In painting and sculpture the work of art is itself a text which in principle cannot be imitated, since it is not made up of pre-existing elements and combinatory rules, and because the very material forming of the tangible surface and/or spatiality is crucial for its aesthetic and communicative effect. Because the painter's code is normally both analog (see Chapter 2) and individual, it is – in principle, at any rate – impossible to deny that the original possesses other characteristics than copies and reproductions of it, and characteristics that are relevant for its aesthetic effect and meaning (a magnaprint edition of a literary work also differs from a normal edition, but this difference is only relevant as regards its legibility).

This short presentation shows that the relation between type and token of the text-pole cannot be isolated from the relation of the text to the other poles of the pyramid. Just the establishing of a reliable text shows the necessity of linking the text to its object, interpretant, sender/speaker and receiver/interpreter, since the study of documents and monuments, the historical–philological consideration of texts in the broad sense of the term, is a process of co-textualization and contextualization.

The text and the immediate intepretant: codes, conventions and knowledge

We have earlier (p. 29) defined the immediate interpretant as the potential meaning of the sign, as the number of potential translations which signs contain. This also means that the interpretant is a controlling force for the use of the sign. A symbolic sign is used, for example, because it is the traditional designation of a given object, a given state, process or behaviour, because it is formed in accordance with the structuring principles of the given semiotics (including its syntax), and because the speaker chooses it as a suitable element in an attempt to affect the receiver, or because he comes to use it for reasons unknown to himself.

The immediate interpretant thus covers the sum of the genetically coded, socially valid or individually created links that the individual text contains. What a text's immediate interpretant contains depends therefore on what semiotics or what text we are dealing with. It may involve various degrees of complexity, right from the rather simple but extremely strong and virtually unambiguous coding of a traffic-light (cf. Johansen 1993a: 311–42) to the overwhelming complexity of such creative works as James Joyce's *Ulysses* (1922), to give just one example.

In the same way that there are varying degrees of complexity, there are also varying degrees of control. We recall Jakobson's idea about the increasing degree of combinatory freedom, from the total lack of freedom as regards the combination of phonemes to the considerable freedom as regards the combination of sections into texts (see p. 113). A linguistic text is thus characterized by the simultaneous presence of structuring principles which both apply to various text levels and possess various degrees of controlling force.

Broadly speaking, one can characterize the immediate interpretant of a text as the total set of *interpretation habits* that make it meaningful. The concept *habit*, which plays such a large role in Peirce, has the advantage of being able to be used about all types of processes, from the tendency of a book always to open to the page where the binding has split to the current of a river, the mating-dance of birds and the use of formulas in popular literature. The concept *habit* also has the advantage of indicating that there is something which is formed and which can be ended: habits can be acquired and they can also be broken.

It is probably appropriate in the case of habits to distinguish between those that occur as regular, unbreakable rules on the one hand – let us call them *codes* – and *tendencies or conventions* on the other hand, i.e. textual and behavioural patterns that are usual but not inevitable or compulsory (see p. 194). The problem is, however, that since habits are dynamic, the individual principles of structuring and interpretation can, in the course of time, change status from tendencies or conventions to codes, and maybe from the latter to the former – perhaps even finally disappearing.

This underlies the fact that the capacity of codes and conventions to be interpreted is a question of the extension of a common semiotic competence. The decoding by various species of animals of their surroundings is precisely species-specific; what is immediately interpretable for one species cannot be sensed by another at all. Every species of animal that survives, however, has to be able to identify and react adequately to (in accordance with) survival-relevant signs in its surroundings. This means that the surroundings must possess a minimal amount of interpretability, so that they are linked as a text, for the given species, to a number of immediate interpretants that the species is coded to be able to understand. Added to this there is also, as far as the higher species are concerned, a varying learning capacity (as in our dog's reaction to the utterance 'food', p. 123).

If we assume that any phenomenon, a sign, can furnish *n* items of information about another phenomenon, its object, as long as their interconnection is established or discovered, then the number of a text's interpretants is in principle unlimited. For most species of animal – we assume – the number of signs from the surroundings and the interpretants linked to them are limited, but for man, who seeks to make the entire universe his surroundings, and whose semiotic competence allows him to create alternative, possible worlds, the number is probably unlimited. This is due to the double view we have of both our surrounding world and the possible worlds. We perceive them as being at one and the same time stable and closed in relation to established habits of interpretation, and labile and open to renewed interpretation.

The immediate interpretants occur in two ways: as larger or smaller systems of similarities and differences, and as descriptions and accounts (or, as Eco formulates it, as *dictionary* and as *encyclopedia*; see Eco 1984: 46–86). If we come across the word *bachelor* in a text, we can translate it by the synonym *unmarried male adult*, i.e. we can indicate the semantic features that are part of the systematic relations of difference from other features, i.e. their opposites: *unmarried* versus *married*, *male* versus *female*, and *adult* versus *child*. But we can also undertake a description such as: *in a society, X, the sexual relationship between man and woman, and especially the propagation of the species, is sought to be limited to sexual intercourse between married persons. Marriage is compulsory for free men from the age of . . . , and bachelors are made to pay an extra tax and are the object of derision* (this description actually fits the status of a bachelor in periods of Greek antiquity). Eco – as well as most contemporary semioticians – considers the two types of interpretants (definitions and descriptions) to be complementary. And this means that the encyclopedia cannot be reduced to a dictionary or, in other words, that descriptions and accounts cannot be reduced to paradigms. Therefore the codes and conventions of texts are ultimately parts of areas of knowledge that are also descriptively and narratively organized. Structure-codes and process-codes are inseparable in semiotics (p. 9ff.).

A sign or a text without an immediate interpretant would be unintelligible. Researchers are perfectly familiar with such texts within various disciplines, e.g. archaeologists and linguists are in no doubt that a number of inscriptions on stones, potsherds, etc. are linguistic texts, because the visual picture of the text resembles that of already interpreted languages. Even so, they are at a certain point unable to link the signs to syntactic and semantic values and to pragmatic rules of usage. Until this has been done, the text remains illegible.

The text and the objects

The object of a text is what it is used for and/or what it refers to. It follows from the possibility of using texts to refer to fictive and other possible worlds that their immediate objects are neutral as regards their mode of being (they can just as well be fictive as real). A painting can represent Aphrodite born out of the spray of the sea as it can Madonna (the pop star) bathing in the nude; but it is in no way possible to get a photograph of Aphrodite, whereas we can get a photograph of Madonna posing as the spray-born Aphrodite. And we also suspect that the artists who have represented Aphrodite made use of living models. In the language usage of semiotics the *object* has, then, a wider meaning than in everyday language:

> The Objects – for a Sign may have any number of them – may each be a single known existing thing or thing believed formerly to have existed or expected to exist, or a collection of such things, or a known quality or relation or fact, which single Object may be a collection, or whole of parts, or it may have some other mode of being, such as some act permitted whose being does not prevent its negation from being equally permitted, or something of a general nature desired, required, or invariably found under certain general circumstances.
>
> (2.232)

The object of the utterance 'Go!' is the demand that the person addressed realizes in the immediate future an act designated by the speaker. 'I am happy' has as its object an emotional state in the speaker; and 'The sum of the angles of a triangle is always 180°' is a (true) claim that any member of the class of triangles, acute, obtuse and right-angled, possesses certain relations, while the lyrical I in Aarestrup's sonnet *talks about* the language of eroticism to his female addressee. The erotic relationship between a man and a woman is thus the object of the text. In this instance the object is the actual relationship between the partners in the dialogue (more of this later, p. 138ff.); but it is even so possible to distinguish between speaker, object and addressee.

In a fictive linguistic text such as Aarestrup's sonnet, distinguishing between the text and the object presents no problems, for even if the represented world is possible, not real, and even though it is dependent on the text for its 'existence', there is a clear distinction between the chain of signs and the fictive world that is being referred to. It becomes more difficult when we are dealing with non-figurative art and music. What does Max Bruch's violin concerto refer to? Peirce was in no doubt about the answer: musical texts communicate emotional states from composer to listener. Harmonies and melody, the syntactic links between notes and orchestration, articulate qualities which affect our mood in a particular way because they both resemble and release certain emotions.

This view is supported by the fact that we very often characterize music by words for emotional states, such as *joyful, painful, glad, melancholy*. Indeed, the reference to the emotive has even gained a foothold in the composer's 'stage directions', his indication of how a particular movement or piece is to be played: *allegro* means in a quick and lively manner, *andante* means at a walking pace, *furioso* means ardently, wildly – even furiously. Let us just add some other indications, preceded by *con*: *con abbadono*: with dignity, *con affizione*: sadly, *con brio*: with spirit, *con grandezza*: grandly, *con passione*: passionately. Small wonder that the reflections on and evaluation of music in antiquity take place in psychological and ethical terms. Both Plato and Aristotle talk of ethical and unethical music, and the latter of the cleansing influence of music on the soul.

Nevertheless, this characterization of music has at least to be supplemented by a structural one. Music is also a highly complex series of ordered sound; and this means that the individual parts of a musical opus mirror and represent each other. For this reason, it is in a certain sense also correct to answer the question 'what does music represent/what does music refer to?' by 'itself'. *Self-representation*, or *self-reflection*, as it is sometimes called, is an important characteristic of all complex texts. Self-reflection has a double function: first, it links the individual parts of the text to each other (one could think in this connection of the role of relative pronouns in a linguistic text); and second, the text's own textuality is displayed.

Aarestrup's poem teaches an entire semiotics of erotic flirting by presenting its silent gestures and body language. The poem, however, does something else as well – it displays itself as a poetic text that also says, or takes for granted: 'I am a sonnet.' The relationship is even more complicated, because the representation of the object – here that of the catechism of erotic love – is also dependent on the text's self-representation (one can test this by para-phrasing in prose).

This is not only evident from the external organization of the poem into stanzas: two quartets, followed by two tercets. It is also evident from the rhetorical form and content of the poem, in the way the quartets and tercets are linked. The classical sonnet form requires the two quartets to present a concrete situation, or possibly the premises for a given argument. The following two tercets are then to extract the general lesson of the presented premises, or to 'act' on the basis of the presented situation. The transition from the quartets to the tercets is called *la volta*, i.e. the turning-point, because either a shift to another level of thought or another situation takes place. Aarestrup's poem thus realizes precisely what is characteristic for this poetic genre in the transition from quartets to tercets. With the first tercet's 'Know then' the lyrical I takes the matter into his own hands and tries to unravel the true nature of the matter and to persuade the resisting young woman. In our context the poem, however, also does something else at this juncture: it demonstrates that it is a legitimate sonnet. For the person who is familiar with the code, it says precisely this: 'Just look at me! Don't you think I'm a mighty fine sonnet?'

According to the above, a text can both represent an object, no matter its mode of being, and it is – at least as far as complex texts are concerned – also self-representative. So the question is how the immediate objects, which the text always presents, are linked to the dynamical objects, i.e. the objects that influence or determine semiosis from the outside.

With the aid of signs, individuals and collective groups are able to produce their own worlds to which no existing objects in our surroundings correspond (as in the painting of Aphrodite, but the photograph of Madonna as Aphrodite). For these parallel worlds to be intelligible, however, iconic and indexical signs must, possibly via a number of links, be able to connect them to the experience of our own surroundings and ourselves. As regards the fictive worlds of literature, this linking to the world of experience is often unproblematic, even though self-representation naturally plays an important role in such texts. Problems often occur, however, when imperceptible conditions in the universe or relations in, for example, the ideal world of pure mathematics are sought to be translated into our horizon of experience, because rendering intelligible – i.e. the attachment of known iconic and indexical signs – is often unable either to transfer all the items of information of the artificial language to the natural language or to explain the conditions by means of the chosen everyday analogies.

Apart from demonstrating the problems involved in translating from artificial to natural languages, the example also shows that the object constantly 'challenges' the sign, because aspects of the object that have been made semiotically accessible, i.e. the immediate object, contain unintelligible aspects and seem to be part of relationships that are concealed from our gaze. In practical dealings the immediate object is the cornerstone and boundary of the meaning; in our attempt to explore a given world it is the place where the boundary between the known and the unknown is constantly being moved. This moving of boundaries can either be the result of an accumulation of knowledge, because through collective and extended research we have come to know more about the object, or it can be the result of a changed perspective which brings about a rejection of previous assumptions and the putting forward of new hypotheses about the nature of the object.

The changes in the perception of the object also affect the signs (which after all comprise the object and the interpretant), leading to a revision of texts. This state of affairs causes Peirce to claim that

> every symbol is a living thing, in a very strict sense that is no mere figure of speech. The body of the symbol changes slowly, but its meaning inevitably grows, incorporates new elements and throws off old ones.
>
> (2.222)

Peirce's own example is the word *electricity*, which in his age, he says, means much more than it did in Benjamin Franklin's lifetime. The sign *electricity*, by appearing as a text-element in a number of scientific texts, becomes

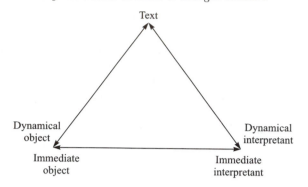

Figure 6.5 The information plan of the text.

'enriched'; its application, i.e. the objects it can be used about, acquires precision, and its meaning, its immediate interpretant, grows. The dynamics of the sign-process consists in the fact that the three instances in the sign or text, when meaning and reference are problematized, begin to move in relation to each other and to affect each other; see Figure 6.5.

This part of the semiotic pyramid we refer to as the information-plan of the text, although it is a good idea to add two more poles, as shown in Figure 6.4: a sender-pole and an interpreter-pole (see p. 130).

Text, sender (author) and speaker (narrator)

At one point Umberto Eco remarks that semiotics is the study of why and how it is possible to lie. We have already seen that texts can very well refer to possible worlds without lying. Whether a text is lying and whether its statements are true or false concerning a given world are two different things. To lie involves the sender having the aim of misleading the receiver of a piece of information about certain relationships by making false statements. This assumes that the mendacious text has a sender who is responsible for communicating it. For while the truth or falsity of a statement can be decided without referring to the sender, its sincerity cannot. The split between the sender, who has produced the text, and the speaker, the person who is represented by the I, voice or narrative structure of the text, has been thoroughly dealt with in the theory of literature as the difference between the author, the person who writes the book, and the narrator, the person who stands as the producer of the story. Scott Fitzgerald's *The Great Gatsby* is narrated by a first-person narrator, Nick. Even though Fitzgerald is of course responsible for the narration – who else could possibly be? – Nick is not necessarily Fitzgerald's representative in the universe of the text. On the contrary, there is a marked difference between the author and the somewhat naïve Nick from the Midwest; and the fact that Fitzgerald is responsible for the text does not mean that he shares, or ought to share, Nick's opinions – rather, that he is responsible for letting Nick have his own opinions.

The fact that the theory of literature has busied itself so much with the narrative structure of texts is due to two things. First, literature as an institution allows the otherwise close link between sender/author and speaker/narrator to be relaxed. Second, this relaxation has led to a long series of experiments with narrative structure, voices and points of view (Johansen 1986b, 1990, and 1998a).

Literary texts are naturally not the only instances where the distance between the sender and speaker is both unproblematic and presumed. Similar instances are the jest, the witticism, and role-play in playful conversation, where the sender – in accordance with an implicit mutual agreement – is not responsible for the speaker's tomfoolery. Together with literature, these examples are the opposite of the completely bound, institutionalized speech acts where the sender – in principle – has no choice, but is ritually obliged to fulfil a speaker-role that has been rigorously fixed in advance. This applies to the minister's (and congregation's) role and speech during a church's morning service. Apart from the sermon, everything which he or she says is determined in advance. When pronouncements are made *in an official capacity*, or *ex officio*, as it is sometimes called, it is unimportant whether the pronouncement is also *ex animo* (sincere, from the soul). Indeed, the institution can in a precisely fixed situation make the sender an infallible speaker, as when the Pope speaks *ex cathedra*, i.e. makes an official pronouncement from the papal throne on behalf of the Roman Catholic Church on matters of belief. The opposites of jest and seriousness, and play and authority, share the characteristic that the commitment and trustworthiness of the individual sender are unimportant in relation to the filling (and execution) of the speaker-role.

Apart from the instances where nobody expects or is concerned about the coincidence between sender and speaker, such a lack of agreement is dangerous; indeed, it can end up in a court of law. The reason for this is that to say something is to act, to enter into an obligation as regards others. This aspect has been studied within language utterances over the past three decades by linguists and philosophers (see, for example, Austin 1962, Searle 1969 and 1979, and Habermas 1981); and it has also been studied from a slightly different angle by classical rhetoric. In connection with discourse analysis (see Chapter 4) we have linked the analysis of the speech act more closely to the role the subjective intention plays. Here we are looking more broadly at how mutual obligation in the dialogue through the speech act becomes part of the text.

The American philosopher John R. Searle (Searle 1979: 1–29) has classified linguistic utterances as (1) *assertives*, (2) *directives*, (3) *commissives*, (4) *expressives*, and (5) *declarations*. The speech-act theory has always been hotly debated and there are alternative classifications of speech acts. Let us, though, stick to Searle's classification, since it at any rate reveals the fact that the speaker modalizes his utterance and thereby brings it into certain relations with the dialogue partner and with the world that is being talked about. The five categories can be exemplified and linked in the following way:

(1) **Assertives**
(a) The ball hit the top of the net
(b) They are married
(c) I assume that Peter had his fingers in the till
(d) I swear that Paul is out of work

(5) **Declarations**
(a) Fault!
(b) I hereby declare you man and wife
(c) The court finds the accused Peter Smith guilty . . .
(d) You are fired!

Assertives involve the speaker claiming with varying degrees of intensity (assume versus swear), and thereby committing himself to the fact that something is the case. The speaker wishes and believes that his utterance is in accordance with a case in point. Assertives, and preferably true assertives, are of immense importance, because our actions, among other things, are based on them. We act in such and such a way, because we assume that this or that is the case. From gossip to witnessing under oath, assertives can deal with anything at all, from what has merely aroused our interest to what is of existential significance for us, a fundamental role in our existence.

When the witnesses have been heard, a sentence still has to be pronounced, i.e. a binding declaration has to be made about what are to be *deemed valid* as true assertives about a course of events that is concluded by virtue of sentence being pronounced. And sentences have consequences: Peter Smith receives written proof that he is an absconding cashier and is sent to serve a sentence in a prison. Declarations are therefore one of the most important ways by which we regulate human behaviour and interaction – and thereby alter realities. By means of the marriage ceremony the vicar alters the reality of the bridal couple, since they assume institutionalized obligations toward each other in a different way than formerly (maybe in a religious way, at any rate in a legal and social way). 'You are fired!' is also a declaration that will often have dire consequences for the person involved. While a marriage means entering into a contractual relationship, losing one's job marks the revoking of such a relationship. Typical of declarations is that they are (only) valid when the speaker possesses sufficient authority and/or power to ensure that the declaration *de facto* alters reality:

(2) **Directives**
(a) Would you be so kind as to . . .
(b) I implore you on my knees to . . .
(c) The assignment is to be handed in on Monday morning
(d) Are you coming tomorrow?
(e) What does 'semiosis' mean?

(3) **Commissives**
(a) I think I'll do it later
(b) I promise to . . .
(c) By my signature I pledge myself to . . .
(d) OK, I'll come tomorrow

Directives and commissives are speech acts by means of which we commit ourselves – the partner in the conversation and/or ourselves – to future acts, to alter reality to a lesser or greater degree. These two types of speech acts are important because – to a certain extent – they allow us to plan our actions and to assume or delegate responsibility. Requests and orders on the one hand and promises and recognition of commitments on the other are necessary for social interaction; if they were not actually respected in our everyday life to a great extent, our world would be completely chaotic. From a semiotic point of view it seems reasonable that Searle counts questions as being directive speech acts, since the person who questions is trying to commit the person answering to transfer knowledge.

(4) **Expressives**
(a) Congratulations on your birthday
(b) Thank you for the present
(c) I'm sorry to be such a nuisance
(d) I'm so sorry for you, you poor thing
(e) I'm so happy for you
(f) My condolences

Expressives are something of an odd-man-out among speech acts. They are closest to assertives; but instead of talking of surrounding conditions, they express – principally – a psychological state in the speaker *vis-à-vis* the receiver. This state is most often a form of sympathy, and expressives often have something of the formula about them, like the above polite phrases; although 'May you have an accident, you lousy creep!' is just as much an expressive speech act that expresses the speaker's aversion. It would be a serious mistake to underestimate the importance of expressives, for even though they do not speak about the nature of the world or try to alter it, they establish and influence the psychological climate between those taking part in a conversation, creating alliances and hostilities just as much as assertives and declarations.

The crucial insight that speech-act theory adheres to and studies is that sending a text is a complex act which, apart from asserting something about the world, also seeks to define the mutual relationship between the sender and the receiver and to influence this and/or the object of the text by means of the text itself. This shows the kinship between speech-act theory and rhetoric. The art of persuasion is precisely an attempt to act and to influence action through utterances – verbal and non-verbal. This kinship is also underlined by the distinction made in speech-act theory between the *locutionary* (the utterance, Latin *locutio*: speech), the *illocutionary* (the text as a [speech] act, Latin *in + locutio*: speech or speaking to [someone]) and the *perlocutionary*, the specific intention and effect of an utterance (Latin *per + locutio*: through speech). For every utterance contains a *statement*, which is modalized into a specific type of speech act that is uttered by a given speaker/speakers to another person/persons at a given point in time with the intention of attaining a given effect.

The Aarestrup sonnet is an obvious example of a text as an act. It is (professes to be) an answer/question not only in a conversation, but in a course of events between the lyrical I and the young woman. The I has an intention with his presentation of the language of erotic love. It is not just a piece of instruction; it is an attempt to overcome her rejection and resistance. This is why the I professes that her lack of compliance is the result of ignorance. So he pretends to be instructing her ('My foolish one' and 'Know then'), it being implied that when ignorance is replaced by knowledge, insight will lead to an abandonment of resistance. The lyrical I transposes an issue that is first and foremost a moral one (should a young girl engage in erotic play?) and an emotional one (is the young girl sufficiently attracted by the poem's I figure?) to a question of education, the dissemination of knowledge. Using Austin's terminology we could say that the illocutionary aspect of the text is the dissemination of knowledge in the form of a series of assertives, while its intended perlocutionary effect is a directive, i.e. an attempt to persuade and seduce.

Linked to the above aspects of the utterance is the question of whom the speaker is actually addressing. In a basic sense the answer naturally has to be: the speaker is talking to the person(s) being addressed. Just as the object of the text is split into the immediate and the dynamical object and the person speaking into sender and speaker, the receiver pole is split into *addressee* (within literary theory *the explicit and implicit reader*) and *interpreter*. The sender is in many cases speaking to a present dialogue partner of flesh and blood, whom he is trying to convince about something or other. But, strictly speaking, his speech is controlled by his picture of the other person, i.e. of the way in which he, more or less well-foundedly, perceives the addressee. This is why we are always speaking in a dialogue to the addressee and to ourself at one and the same time – the same naturally applies to our partner in the dialogue. Precisely the dialogue makes it possible, however, to 'negotiate' the pictures of the other person and ourself, because we gain an opportunity in the dialogue's (implicit) exchange of question and answer of correcting and stabilizing the speaker and the addressee. The interpreter, the real dialogue partner, always appears as the unknown factor in the dialogue, and since we ourselves become interpreters in the dialogue's exchange, a dialogue is like an equation with two unknowns, whose value or importance is sought to be determined on the basis of what seem to be relatively sure interpretations of the flow of the text. Two unknown people, because even if we – mistakenly – believe that we know ourselves, we cannot determine ourselves as speakers or the effect we have on the interpreter; even though we very often, perhaps always, form ourselves according to the picture we assume the other person has of us.

Added to these complications is often – and always in literature – the fact that speech is addressed to more than one person at the same time. In Aarestrup's poem the addressee is a young girl; but is the poem not rather addressed to a reader, to someone who can admire the poet's talent and wit?

Despite this, communication is successful amazingly often. So let us – to give some reasons for this theoretically almost impossible success – return to

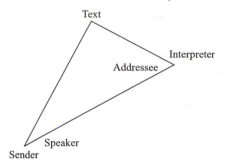

Figure 6.6 The text's communication plane.

the diagram of the semiotic pyramid (Figure 6.4, p. 130). The diagram
depicts a dialogue. The unbroken lines indicate the sender's (in the model
the author's) perspective on semiosis, while the broken line represents the
interpreter's perspective. In a face-to-face language dialogue the signs will
be perceived as tokens, but in order to be able to understand them, the
interpreter must identify them as tokens of types; and this involves an interpretative activity, in which they are linked with interpretants and objects and
with the speaker and the interpreter him- or herself. If the understanding
between the dialogue partners is optimal, at least as far as the purpose of the
conversation is concerned – and meaning and opinion include, according to
Peirce, a reference to the purpose of the conversation (cf. 5.175) – the sender
and interpreter will both identify the tokens as manifestations of the same
types. The immediate objects will, for the purpose of the dialogue, be sufficiently like each other in the sender's and interpreter's perception. Among the
possibilities that the immediate interpretants of the signs contain, the interpreter will choose those that the sender has intended. And both of them will
understand and recognize their respective roles within semiosis – and as persons they will accept these roles and assume them. Moreover, communication
by dialogue can be corrected via further metalinguistic explanation, via clarifying reference to a common outer world (e.g. through ostensive (displaying)
definition, i.e. the object is pointed out), via the presentation of intentions and
purposes and via continued question and answer, by virtue of which a situa-
tive context is made explicit – to use Hjelmslev's formulation.

The plane which is marked off by the poles sender–text–interpreter we
refer to as the text's communication plane; see Figure 6.6.

It is the linking of this plane with the information plane that gives rise to
meaning. One should not, however, believe that it is possible to point to a
particular spot within the semiotic pyramid as the cradle of meaning.
Admittedly, we have, in accordance with Peirce, talked about the immediate
interpretants as the potential meaning of the text, but precisely as something
not actualized – and the actualization of certain meanings rather than others
is precisely due to the relationship between all poles of the pyramid.

The dynamical and the final interpretant

The dynamical interpretant is the objective content of the interpretation of the text (i.e. neither the interpreter nor the act of interpretation), which means that it is an actualization of a part of the meaning-potential of the text. According to Peirce there are four ways in which a sign or a text can be interpreted or translated: to (1) a totality of feeling or quality; to (2) an energetic reaction or action; to (3) another text or another sign; or finally to (4) habitual behaviour. The first possibility, the *emotional interpretant*, we all know from, for example, our reaction to a piece of music that often makes us happy or sad without our analysing it. The *energetic interpretant* can be simply coded into our body, as when we pull our hand away from a live wire because we, or our body, interpret the pain as being linked to an outer object that one can get away from. The *logical interpretant* is the translation of a text or a sign to another text or sign.

Here one could mention Roman Jakobson's distinction between *intralinguistic* translation (translation within the same language), *interlinguistic* translation (translation between two languages) and *intersemiotic* translation (translation between different types of semiotics). The English sign *cat* can illustrate this simply; see Figure 6.7.

The relation between the intralinguistic and semiotic translation is a crucial prerequisite for languages to have meaning. In other words: if iconic and indexical signs could not be linked to symbolic ones, natural languages would lose their anchorage in human activity and the natural and cultural surrounding world – and thereby their potential for meaning. The various semiotics are each other's mutual prerequisites, e.g. speech presupposes images and a structured surrounding world, just as images and a surrounding world presuppose speech to be able to mean anything (it is in fact possible to make sense and communicate without possessing a language, but the possibilities of understanding without language are more restricted). The intersemiotic translation is a process through which the senses are formed culturally, and sensing is transformed into experience.

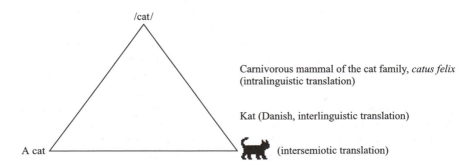

Figure 6.7 Three types of translation for *cat*.

The so-called logical interpretant, the translation of one sign into another sign, is, however, in principle infinite, because the new sign itself has a dynamical (logical) interpretant, and so on. This is why Peirce speaks of an *ultimate logical interpretant*, which is not a translation into a new sign but into a *habit*, i.e. a given sign or a given text will always lead to the same interpretation. Peirce also talks of the *final interpretant* as being different in category from the dynamical. A final intepretant is not, however, a new kind of interpretant; it is the dynamical interpretant that has changed (categorical) status, because it is compelled to appear by the sign and designates the final interpretation based on a knowledge that does not change or increase any more, because an infinite body of research accepts it as the correct and inevitable interpretation.

Peirce uses the concept of the final interpretant in two ways. He uses it in an epistemological sense, where the final interpretant would be the remainderless description of reality, and would resolve the distinction between a dynamical and an immediate object, so that object, sign and interpretant would constitute a remainderless totality: the universe as a self-explanatory semiosis. In this sense the concept occurs as a regulatory principle for research, as something one hopes to approach. Peirce talks in this connection about a *principle of hope* as a guiding principle for research.

However, he also uses the term *final interpretant* about a habitual interpretation of a given text that concludes semiosis, the sign-process. When we always stop at the red light and drive on when it is green, this interpretation is a habitual act that ends the sign-process. Such instinctive or learned interpretants are of course absolutely essential for all types of societies, no matter whether they regulate the lives of bees in the hive or those of humans in an industrialized society. Often freedom, spontaneity and creativity are set up on the one hand against regularity, predictability and stereotypical behaviour on the other – with the former being assessed positively and the latter negatively. Apart from the fact, for example, that the unpredictable expressiveness that we admire in a musician, singer or dancer – or the improvisations of a football player or a chess player that can change the course of a match – come into existence on the basis of the learning of interpretative rules which have become automatic as the result of much blood, sweat and tears, this negative attitude towards habitual behaviour is ill considered. For habitual behaviour is predictable, and predictability is the *sine qua non* for coordination. Cooperation rests on instinctive or learned coordination of not only behaviour but also expectations of behaviour. When we drive on when the lights turn green at an intersection, we expect that traffic from the right and left will be facing red, and we also expect that light to be respected. Indeed, our interaction with others is controlled by what we expect they will do, rather than by what they are actually doing at the moment we act. Quite simply, we project their behaviour, acting in relation to the reaction we expect. The trapeze artiste and the catcher subconsciously predict each other's positions seconds or fractions of seconds before they actually find themselves at the calculated spot. It sometimes happens, however, that they misjudge – and the trapeze artiste falls. Even habitual interpretations are fallible, with altered conditions necessitating altered habits of interpretation. Only in a universe in the interpretation of which chance can be completely eliminated would we have infallible final interpretants in the first sense of the concept.

The boundaries of the text

In this chapter we have mainly looked at the text as a process, as an expanding syntagm through dialogue. We feel that it is important not to view texts as isolated, but as parts of a continuous ongoing production of meaning. Each one of us is continuously involved in a long series of dialogues; some of them are unique in our lives, others continue until divorce, retirement or death put an end to them. Even here the boundary is not absolute – we can, for example, see our children continue parts of our dialogues. These texts, dialogues and processes of interpretation are at one and the same time both fleeting and stable – fleeting since no one can recall precisely how they went, stable since they usually form patterns: the compulsive neurotic dreams the same dreams and has the same fantasies time after time without knowing their interpretants. In a company or institution the employees may interact almost according to a script or choreography. And in the family fixed roles and predictable sequences of actions arise.

A human society has, for many reasons, however, a use for texts that have permanence, or that can be repeated in a structurally identical form. Apart from the fact that texts that were to travel – apart from the oral texts of messengers – had to be fixed in some fairly durable material, the reason for preserving them has been that they were found to be important and worth remembering. Five different functions in particular have encouraged this preservation: (1) the text as contract and document; (2) the text as history and monument; (3) the text as manual; (4) the text as liturgy and mythical account in connection with a cult; and (5) the token text which both imitates other texts and is self-reflexive – i.e. the artistic text.

The first group comprises the texts of administration, the legislature and commerce, as handed down from the earliest Middle Eastern writing cultures. These texts have a tendency towards standardization: the special relationship between the parties in a contract is inserted as specific conditions; the same applies to administration and the legislature – obligations to pay taxes and actual sentences are written down in a (more or less) standardized form that is characteristic for given cultures.

While the writing down of the first group of texts favours systems of letters and numbers, the second text function encourages linguistic, visual, architectural and musical expression. The sung or recited account of what is considered history is supplemented by monuments, which remind people of a king or a great man (barrows or pyramids), and historical painting, which down through the centuries has been considered the finest genre of European painting. Added to this is the unity of word, music and dance in the celebration of, for example, the Olympic winner.

The manual is an attempt to preserve and pass on another type of knowledge that is also considered important – theoretical and practical. From treatises on astronomy to medical documents and cookery books, people have sought in words and pictures to systematize and disseminate knowledge to later generations. The academic dissertation and the textbook are prototypes of this textual function.

A whole range of texts is linked to religious practices, manifesting one or more semiotics. The cult site, the temple, the statue, song, dance, the hymn and the myth show that most human senses and their semiotics are involved (add incense and the shared meal), so that the sacred place, the ritual and the myth make up some sort of *Gesamtkunstwerk* which claims to represent all aspects of human existence.

The artistic textual function can imitate the four others (see cooking recipes in Tolstoy and courtroom dramas in Dostoevsky), but it is especially linked to the religious and historical textual functions. As there, the artistic textual function is linked to all the senses and their semiotics, and, as with them, the celebration and preservation of the memory of the exploit, ecstasy or epiphany would appear to be central. But these functions are often fictionalized in artistic texts; and even if the artistic texts portray historical or religious material, it becomes linked to the self-reflecting function that is characteristic of artistic texts. Painting is just as taken up with colours, light and composition as with the birth of Aphrodite or the sacrifice of Isaac by Abraham. The key, harmonies and melodies concern the sonata just as much as joy or pain. The ballet presents the death of the poor swan, but it is also deeply involved in the structure and effect of the steps. Even imaginative writing, in which reality and history always adhere to the words, is very much interested in displaying itself as formal structure and as sound.

The semiotician Jurij M. Lotman, who was particularly interested in the semiotics of culture and literature (see p. 169ff.), has drawn attention in his book *Die Struktur literarischer Texte* to four categories in regard to literary texts that characterize the individual text: *visibility, demarcation, structuring* and *hierarchization*, although the last category only appears in Lotman as a consequence of *demarcation* and *structuring* respectively. Let us add a fifth category to Lotman's four, one which is also implicit in his writing (see below), namely *functional focusing*, and begin with this last category.

Continuously ongoing dialogue activity, such as conversation with others, is – fortunately – characterized by being functionally diffuse. An evening spent with good friends seldom has a set theme on the agenda; instead, the conversation moves from one subject to another. Texts that are produced with an eye to permanence are very often functionally focused. This does not mean that the text only fulfils one function, even though that could perfectly well be the case. A cookery book conveys a particular form of practical knowledge, as do timetables. Very often, however, texts are multi-functional, i.e. they fulfil a number of functions at one and the same time. Indeed, some texts are simply – to use the formulation of the Canadian literary researcher Northrop Frye – *encyclopedias* (Frye 1957), i.e. they gather together the relevant knowledge of a society at a given point in time as, for example, the Bible, which contains revelations, prophecies, codes of statutes, chronicles, genealogical tables and tales of families, songs of praise, erotic poetry, proverbs, anecdotes and novellas, parables, etc. Nevertheless, each single part of the Bible is specifically focused, and, taken as a whole, the relationship of human beings to God and their history, from the time of Creation until the Last Judgement, gives it an overall focus.

The *visibility* of the text means, according to Lotman, that it can be identified as a string of signs or – we would like to add – as a complex sign (an analog text). According to this perception, the text is a material manifestation of various semiotics and possibly of subsystems of these. The *demarcation* of the text is twofold. On the one hand, a boundary is drawn between the elements that belong to the text and elements that belong to other texts. This demarcation is known, for example, from the frame of a painting, within which everything belongs to the picture, while everything outside it is irrelevant (see also the raising and lowering of the stage curtain at theatres). The other demarcation is in relation to the non-demarcated, constantly expanding texts (in Hjelmslev's and Peirce's sense). Regarding linguistic texts, Lotman underlines their analogy with the word and the sentence, which are demarcated linguistic units, because the individual text, at any rate in a certain sense, can be perceived as an irreducible and minimal sign for a cultural function (a document, a paean, a prayer, a holy robe, a statue, etc.). And this double demarcation in conjunction with its functional focusing makes it a totality of meaning. The demarcation not only exists in relation to other visible and constantly expanding texts; internally, texts are also intersected by boundaries such as foreground, middle distance and background in painting, spatial divisions in architecture, movements in music, *exordium* (introduction), *narratio* (point of view), *partitio* (division), *confirmatio* (argumentation) and *conclusio* (conclusion) in the courts of antiquity. A consequence of this inner demarcation in the visible texts is their *hierarchization*. They will, to a greater or lesser extent, be constructed and able to be analysed as the hierarchy we presented at the beginning of this chapter.

The *structuring* of the text, i.e. construction by virtue of structural codes, is evident both from the internal demarcations – a hierarchy is in itself a structuring – and possibly from the combination of several semiotics in the concrete text. An operatic performance involves, for example, the coordination of many semiotics and (it is hoped) their mutual enrichment. Visible and lasting or repeatable texts can be seen as manifestations of systems and/or traditions, though also, it should be noted, as their sequential organization, which can be both specific and original. Single texts are thus often perceived as more or less developed systems of relations between elements that find themselves on different levels and of the relation between these different sets of relations (Aarestrup's sonnet illustrates clearly such relations and relations of relations).

These five characteristics – *functional focusing, visibility, demarcation, structuring* and *hierarchization* – are useful for the determining and analysis of visible and lasting or repeatable texts, no matter whether it is a question of a standard contract for purchasing and selling, South American patterns for basketweaving or the above-mentioned sonnet. Certain reservations and clarifications are, however, important.

First, there is naturally a difference in the degree of standardization, both between various types of text and between various texts of the same type (the requirement of originality within the artistic genres is, for example, fairly recent).

Second, the single text will most often have characteristics that are specific to it, from the mere filling in of empty spaces (the buyer's and seller's name and the date) to the unique work of art, where the very brushstrokes are meaningful and exceptional. Complex texts will, however, at any rate contain elements that cannot immediately – or maybe not at all – be referred to a structural principle.

Third, the individual structures of the text will not comply with each other smoothly. There may very well be tensions set up between them; they may even undermine (irony) or contradict each other. Texts are therefore more often polyphonic rather than homophonic.

Fourth, the autonomy that the five criteria indicate is extremely relative. It is of course only by virtue of its affiliation to other texts and to cultural codes and traditions that the single text acquires its meaning. An example of this is that an element can be absent from a text, and precisely its absence is the decisive factor for an understanding of its meaning, because it is required or expected in that cultural context and actually occurs in other texts of the same type (it is also highly significant if one *omits* to greet someone). In this way the single text is always linked to, and always nourished by and dependent on, the eternal, but fleeting dialogue, which it sums up, corrects and fixes – and thereby gives structure and durability.

7 Nature and culture

From object to sign

What is cultural semiotics?

Nature is a crucial element in all cultures, but it does not occupy the same position in the cultural semantics of different cultures. In a globalized and mass-media-dominated western culture such as ours an important conception of nature is nature as landscape, i.e. the surface that is immediately observable, and which is attractive and soothing, perhaps exciting and a bit frightening, with mountains, ice plains or deserts – an aesthetic scenery whether intimate or panoramic. Nature is also, and to an increasing degree, identified with environment, i.e. the physical surroundings containing the resources and the waste from the material production of our culture, an appendage to industry and technology, agriculture included. From this perspective, nature is more connected to humans in functional and ethical categories like duty and responsibility in the exploitation of nature, than with the predominantly aesthetic experience of which the landscape is a part. As scenery or resource, nature indicates the boundary of different types of cultural control (Larsen 1993b, 1994b).

Nature, then, is not only an object, order, gathering force, or locality that can be placed, as landscape or environment, within or beyond the limits of a given culture. It is also, and more importantly, the border for what a culture can agree to understand and potentially control and, therefore, a border that shifts as the culture's horizon of understanding and control over the surrounding world shifts. Thus, it is the difference that makes both nature and culture into sign-complexes that we use to orient ourselves and to formulate our actions. Such a sign-complex can be a comprehensive plan for water filtration that contains interpretations of chemical and physical processes and practical instructions; or it can be an unexpected tornado with signs for direction and strength that we must interpret correctly in order to survive. The process of marking the border between nature and culture exists in both these cases, and is a semiotic process that gives simultaneous meaning to both nature and culture (cf. Larsen 1996, 1997d).

However, humans are not the only organisms that create signs, communicate, and exchange information so that particular domains are thereby outlined. Cells send signals to one other, electronic networks exchange information, and bees communicate. In other words, semiotic processes operate beyond our own cultural domains. Nevertheless, such processes also involve humans, for we too are built up of cells. We are also biological phenomena whose neural networks follow the same basic principles as those of other organisms, and whose behaviour to a certain extent can be simulated and replaced by electronic processes.

Therefore, although everything studied in cultural semiotics is placed in relation to human life, this study may extend beyond the area of human activity to grasp the preconditions for this activity. Cultural semiotics does not claim that all human activity is culture and that it is clearly separated from nature. And it certainly does not hold that culture is a thin membrane of signs and symbolic structures that is stretched over independent and solid material processes in society, the body and our physical surroundings. Cultural semiotics tries to provide for a gradual transition, semiotically and otherwise, between humans and other sign-using creatures, holding that cultural processes are intertwined with their natural foundations, and that sign-processes are material phenomena anchored in a concrete reality.

However, cultural semiotics also claims that humans, beyond the semiotic talents shared with all other life forms, have a semiotic competence that belongs to our biologically specific and therefore natural equipment, regardless of its origins. What cultural semiotics seeks to discover, as it focuses on or moves beyond the borders of human culture, are the conditions determining this competence and its functionality. Therefore, this semiotic competence not only functions in isolation within the area for human culture, but is the manifestation of the very border between human culture and the foundation on which it rests. Humans exist on nature's conditions, but the border is marked by culture's semiotic systems (Emmeche and Hoffmeyer 1991).

The centre of these semiotic systems is human language, the so-called *natural language*. This is as self-evident to us as is the ocean, blood cells, and the starry sky. Language is, of course, not the only semiotic system that we use, and must use, in order to construct and maintain the human culture. Yet the particular semiotic competence that forms the basis for our human culture is created only when all other semiotic systems cooperate with language.

One of the most peculiar properties of natural language is its ability to be used to construct entirely imaginary worlds, fictitious universes, alternatives to the world familiar to us. In and by language, we can plan vacations to destinations we have never visited, paid for by personal loans that even the most foolish bank manager wouldn't approve, or with the main prize in the lottery that we only have a microscopic chance of winning. We can simulate what it is like to walk on the moon before sending anyone there, just as we can invent contraptions that we find practical uses for much later, thereby letting the sign for practicality come before actual practicality. In other words: while we live determined by language, we not only *adapt* ourselves to the border between what we call culture and what we call nature, but can also *move* the limits of our cultural scope, thereby modifying both our natural foundations and our cultural understanding of ourselves. Sometimes we do this to dramatic effect, as with genetic manipulation or radioactive leaks that bring about irreversible natural processes; at other times, we do this to symbolic effect, e.g. by purchasing a lottery ticket to challenge the natural randomness of our lives.

To us, then, culture and nature are phenomena that are mutually dependent. The ocean waves form the coastline and create some naturally conditioned cultural possibilities and problems, which again change as dikes are constructed to hold back the waves and reclaim the land from the ocean. Pollution of the Baltic Sea puts some chemical processes into motion that in themselves are no less than the force of the waves, even though the pollution is caused by industrial production and big cities. Though produced by human activity, it is just as much a natural condition as are the ocean waves and tides, which are produced by lunar gravity. We cannot draw a clear line between nature and culture; nor can we, alternatively, consider the existence of two natures and two cultures – one set being mutually exclusive and autonomous and the other set blended together; rather, both nature and culture are but two different ways of drawing the line between nature and culture that characterize our culture.

Therefore, we cannot see nature *independently of* culture; rather, nature receives meaning *within* the culture as a necessary condition for our relationship to it. Regardless of whether this meaning is formed by science or popular beliefs, or is embedded in our everyday practical routines, it is the differentiation we make between nature and culture that simultaneously gives meaning to both phenomena: a culture's understanding of itself exists within its practical and conceptual relation to nature, and a culture's understanding of nature exists within its understanding of its own potentials (about the past, see Glacken 1967; about the present, Merchant 1990).

It is often taken for granted that cultural semiotics deals primarily, or perhaps exclusively, with cultural objects and their meanings and interconnections. Most visitors to a museum of cultural history will see a multitude of objects that are explained as signs of cultural habits, actions, norms, values, etc. This is the basis on which most of cultural semiotics rests: it investigates the codes of, e.g., bar and café life, Jewish marriage rituals, body language in Brazil, and so on. However, such a way of seeing things can easily lead to the misunderstanding that the very difference between nature and culture is a given, and that culture is an autonomous area of objects, signs and meanings. Rather, it should be stressed that cultural semiotics is primarily concerned with the process that creates or constructs culture in relation to a natural basis, with a demarcation line that allows objects to become signs and to be connected to one another in a cultural whole. Cultural semiotics investigates not only how reality is constructed where humans live, but also how the border is drawn in relation to what is excluded from this domain.

The focus of cultural semiotics is the interrelation of three interconnected fields of investigation:

1 The *borders* of a culture in relation to its natural foundation, aided by the semiotic systems controlled by humans. This relates to the *creation of culture*.
2 The *conditional requirements* set for these borders to allow them to create culture that can be differentiated as different human cultures. In this chapter, we will present and define three such requirements: for (a) *time and space*; (b) *body and subject*; and (c) *action and action model*.
3 The *codes and structures* that identify a (sub)culture as such and regulate the relations between its elements.

We place most weight on the first two items. Here, we see the culture's foundation: how do objects become signs that construct a space for a body equipped with senses, and which conditions must be fulfilled for this whole to become culturally relevant? Later in this chapter, we will also concern our-selves with the third item, which is covered by most existing cultural semiotic analyses. In our discussion of this item, we will focus primarily on the basic codes that hold a culture together; in addition, we will analyse a limited cultural text in a particular culture – the urban park.

The borders of culture

Surroundings and surrounding world

Since Jacob von Uexküll (1980, 1982) we know that human culture is not the only one that draws borders, while other creatures – and often also so-called 'primitive' cultures – are supposed to be 'closer to nature' and therefore to have more fluid borders. But each organism sets its borders, although differ-ently, depending on its particular semiotic abilities.

Every organism has *surroundings*, but only some of its surroundings belong to its *surrounding world* – or *Umwelt*, in Uexküll's terminology. This part of the surroundings consists of all that the organism can apprehend with its sensory apparatus, identify and use to orient itself, based on four functional require-ments. It must be able to:

1 distinguish food from other objects;
2 distinguish members of its own species from members of other species – a necessary requirement for reproduction;
3 distinguish life-threatening phenomena from harmless ones;
4 distinguish pathways from impediments to sensory and bodily movements.

Thus a surrounding world is constructed, with four functional areas: food, sex, enemies and movement. These can overlap one another from one species to the next. Humans and dogs, for instance, can be said to share some of their surrounding world: dogs seldom refrain from snatching a steak from the dinner table, when the master isn't looking. But dogs are certainly not humans. To orient themselves dogs use smells and sounds we are unable to perceive. And when we run angrily after the dog that has stolen a piece of meat, we often act clumsily, and easily get stuck in narrow places where the dog runs through without problems.

The surrounding world is therefore a common, intersubjective sphere for organisms belonging to the same species. To some degree, organisms can teach themselves how the surrounding world of another species is put together and adjust themselves accordingly, but only if there are factors in that species' surroundings and behaviour that also belong to their own surrounding world. To be successful, this is what a predatory animal, hunter, lion tamer, or behavioural biologist must do.

When surroundings become the surrounding world, a semiotic process takes place. The surroundings' sensory impulses are translated via the organism's sensory apparatus and nervous system into a sign for an object, and take on a particular identity in relation to the organism receiving the impulse; the sense-perception is made referential. A space to which the organisms belong is created, and these sign-forming registrations make up one representation of the surrounding world – an 'inner world', as Uexküll has it – that is projected on to the surroundings as a horizon for possible actions. The organism and its *Umwelt* are mutually connected, based on semiotic conditions.

Every organism stretches out toward its surroundings with two arms: perception and operation. When the surroundings become sign, they form a particular surrounding world, where perception and operation are unified in one process. This is not a simple or mechanical action/reaction process; the decisive turning-point is not that the organism registers sensory impulses and subsequently takes action, but that it masters the interpretation of each impulse so that it refers to a phenomenon with a particular identity in the organism's surrounding world, i.e. becomes a sign with a coded reference to some object. If the organism fails to master this semiotic process, it is duped. And that can be dangerous: decoys, for instance, can make easy prey for hunters of ducks and other animals. Even though no creature can apprehend what lies beyond its surrounding world, it can very well penetrate into the border zone of that world.

The human construction of our surrounding world as the construction of culture presumes and builds upon these common features for organisms' construction of their surrounding world. The fundamental culture-forming process lies in this transition from mere perception to sign, emphasizing each species' particular semiotic competence. In his *Die Krise der Psychologie* (1927), Karl Bühler places human language in relation to the sign-systems of other organisms. This occurs in three stages, with *semantics* as the code word (Bühler 1978: ch. II).

1 *Contact and contactual universe*: For organisms to build a community in which they adapt their perceptions and actions to one another, they must have certain guiding tools. These are signs (the surrounding world's and the organism's own smell, sounds, colours, light, etc.). All organisms are supposed to interpret these signs – or signals, in Bühler's terminology – as the same signs for the same phenomena in relation to the community's functions: food, enemies, reproduction, division of labour, abode, etc. The signals refer to the core of a semantic corpus that does not belong to any single organism, but instead is a structure that constitutes the community as a whole. The individual organism can use this structure to guide itself and thereby take its place in a labour-divided whole, e.g. as a worker bee in a swarm of bees. Thus an individual organism's place in the community enables it to orient itself meaningfully in its surrounding world.

In this situation, Bühler states, there is *contact*. What we want to call a *contactual universe* is present when three elements exist simultaneously in the same physical space: the sign (e.g. smell); the object to which it refers (e.g. food); and the perceiving *organism*, which through different channels (wind, touch, neurological apparatus, etc.) connects sign and object to decide whether the object is edible or not. The organisms interpreting the signs understand the relation as a coded one, directing them towards the food. Insecticide does not always directly kill the pest, but instead distorts or blocks the signals and signal apparatus, thereby blocking the semiotic ability, so that contact cannot be made. This method is equally effective.

2 *Common semantics*: If the signals refer to something that is not present simultaneously with the signals themselves, higher-level guiding tools are needed, according to Bühler. The stomach growls with hunger, but there is no food around. It is here that the common *semantics* receives its decisive guiding function. To survive, all organisms must 'stretch out' after something that cannot immediately be found. This is why all organisms must be able to convey this sign-bound common semantics, this 'knowledge', to others, and use it themselves to check the perceived signs' identity whenever something appears that resembles food. Like humans, the individual organism cannot be satisfied with its private semantics if it is to verify that it has properly registered something as being edible or not. It has to be able to obtain access to an accumulated common experience for the proper interpretation of signs, by which the perceived signs' validity is delimited. If the organism is unable to do this, it will die.

The organism can also go wrong even if it knows the common semantics, but violates it. All males cannot get the female at which they each are ready to throw themselves. A sign must first be created: the strongest male. It tells the other males and females that he is, in fact, the 'right' male. Thus the female 'knows' with whom to mate, and with another sign, the other males acknowledge their respect (they vanish, let themselves be killed, bend their heads, crawl along the ground, move their ears or tails in a particular way, and so on). The sign for 'strength' belongs to the superior common semantics which constitutes the group as a functional whole, and in this semantics belongs together with corresponding signs for, e.g., 'submission' and 'rut'. If a defeated or inferior male nevertheless gives in to his lust, it will prove fatal. Through the sign-process, and only through this sign-process, are the agents present as members of the same community in different positions.

3   *Language*: Even though the mating is still a future event and therefore not yet part of the contactual universe, the sign and its object are inextricably connected to one another. Lions, after all, cannot use one sign for strength one year and another sign the next year; they cannot decide to stop battling for the females and hold a lottery instead, with the best female as the main prize. Honeybees are not free to use any sign to indicate they have found honey. Animals cannot choose the sign, interpretant, or object.

However, through human *language* – Bühler's third level – we have developed an enormous degree of freedom in relation to sign and object. Language characterizes the collective semiotic register of our human society, and without causing confusion; instead, it grants us a special way of understanding the world surrounding us. This sign-process does not have to be connected to a particular material behaviour: with language, we can unite different gestures, sounds, images, etc., so that they in practice express 'the same': this occurs, e.g., in a theatre play. And the object can have more than one status in relation to the same object, dependent on the connection: the horse to which the word 'horse' refers can be real, fictional, a photographic image, part of a dream, and so on. Finally, the code that connects sign to object can change: when the word 'horse' is said, it can be an order to get a horse, a warning not to get run over by a horse, a description of someone as a horse, etc.

But the expression 'horse' can also have a more specific function. The word can be used in a school spelling test, it can be a repetition for a slow-witted receiver, it can refer to a dictionary entry for 'horse', or it can function as an example of a noun in grammar class. The word 'horse' can, in other words, also refer to the linguistic sign-system or the sign-process itself. Language is a sign-system which can constantly be made *reflexive*.

The males battling for the females, on the other hand, cannot sit down by the camp fire to evaluate reflexively their most recent duel and discuss alternative fighting techniques; nor can they set up fighting schools and training camps where the battle as sign-system and technique can be mastered and improved. Only in combination with language can other sign-systems – either non-reflexive or reflexive to a limited degree – enter an extended reflexive connection: a game of soccer is not made of kicking feet and a particular movement of bodies; to be played, refereed, evaluated and to be an object of betting it needs to be framed by verbalized rules and discursive processes.

Through language, we can also create one or more metalevels and thus take a position regarding the sign-systems' own nature and elements, their effects and limits, and our way of dealing with them. We can invent new signs, new codes, and new worlds that thereby become alternative *discursive universes* (see Chapter 4). Jurij Lotman (Lotman and Uspensky 1978) remarks that, with language at its centre, any culture can create, and cannot help creating, models of itself, i.e. its surrounding world and its limits. The culture's definition of itself – of its nature and scope – is itself an active contribution to cultural change.

Even though verbal language thus has a specific function, Bühler maintains that all three layers which he has revealed are constantly active in our culture-forming semiotic process. Culture consists of the sign-processes that inextricably intertwine these levels. Language is therefore highly useful for *inventing* all sorts of new signs, codes and worlds, but we cannot *live* in all of them and certainly not agree on all of them. The reflexive *language* is certainly a phenomenal tool, but must be embedded in a material universe in which there is *contact* between signs, objects and sign users, and which we can mutually identify as a common universe by way of a common semantic core, or else the language will fail to build reality. A culture delimits signworlds so that we may inhabit them together.

We have previously mentioned the three presumptive requirements for the culture's drawing of the border between nature and culture. The *first requirement*, dealing with the relationship between time and space, can be formulated as follows: the border must be drawn so that *culture's sign-systems enable us to localize phenomena in time and space where contact exists.* Things are therefore never simply presented to our senses, but always embedded in a cultural sign-process. This means that even the physical space, which for most of us is a given, independent of cultural differences, is in fact delimited differently in different cultures. Some cultures incorporate phenomena like evil spirits in their contactual universe, where they are as concrete as rocks and tools, while other cultures reject such phenomena as mere superstition, placing them within culture but outside the contactual universe. No single culture can exist without the ability to delimit its contactual universe, but each culture does this differently and does not integrate all phenomena that prompt meaning. Therefore, the signs that satisfy this requirement for embedment in a culture function simultaneously as signs for the way in which the culture perceives its own limits. Such signs are the *designator elements* that make the discursive universes' *designator functions* concrete (see Chapter 4):

1   With the designator elements we use to perform the *real designator function*, we delimit a shared material universe made up of signs, their objects, and the sign users – this is a contactual universe. This process takes place

through glances, pointing, bites, touching, road signs, etc. It delimits what exists for us in time and space.

2   With the designator elements we use to perform the *discursive designator function*, we delimit a shared recognizable and identifiable universe, so that this universe is experienced not only as existing but also as 'ours'. It delimits what we can recognize in relation to earlier experience, i.e. something that has already become a sign during an earlier contact – e.g. smelling something that tells us Christmas is on its way, describing a habit, seeing a national emblem, and so on.

3   With the designator elements we use to perform the *ideal designator function*, we delimit alternative or supplemental universes that function side by side and at the same time. With a blink of an eye, we indicate to the receiver that we are speaking with irony, yet simultaneously we know that we exist in a real universe where the blink is simply a movement of the eye and can be physically recognized. With a drawing or other model of a house, we can speak of a future residence while we are out on the streets without a roof over our heads. With words like 'maybe', 'if', or 'I promise', we can indicate alternative possibilities for a reality we are familiar with and in which we are actually standing and speaking. With particular intonations, we can express that something we say actually means the opposite. With the word 'not', we can speak of something, such as superstition, that does not belong to the given discursive universe, or maybe does not exist at all.

Perception and meaning

In all perceptions, the biologically conditional ability for sensory registration is linked with a culturally formed focus on the limited segment that we are able to recall. Bühler states briefly that there is no perception without meaning. We cannot avoid observing and ignoring simultaneously, and can therefore lie and forget in good faith. The border between nature and culture cuts directly through these two intertwined sorting mechanisms, which reduce sensory impressions to identifiable wholes. This occurs every time we observe something – in other words, all the time. We reduce a mixed bombardment of influences to objects with meanings, which therefore refer both to the sensed and to the sensor. It is a basic culture-forming semiotic process.

According to Bühler, it follows the principle of *abstractive relevance*, which primarily relates to the perception of distinctive features in phonology (Bühler 1990). We hold on to the relevant sensory observations and forget or fail to register others. Relevant observations are those that enable us to unite a muddle of individual sensory impressions into a whole that can be identified as something particular in a certain context (for instance, when we catch a fragment of a sound from our mother tongue at a busy station in a foreign country, this recognizable linguistically relevant sound makes us forget other sounds and allows us to place the sound in the context of an entire language). The relevant remains, and we infer the rest in order to build a coded hierarchy of sensory impresssions (see Chapter 2, p. 11). This process is partially determined by our sensory-motoric and mental equipment, but also by the combinations made in and by the sign-systems we are familiar with: we may encounter sounds that fool us; we overlook or misread traffic signs in foreign countries because we use the traffic signs in our own country as our code; certain feelings of hope or fear can guide our attention.

We are, however, not always left to random impulses from the surrounding world, nor to purely subjective moods. We can also define a context in which the abstractive relevance happens with a particular purpose. If we want to hear the news broadcast on television, we abstract from the sex of the news reader, from the studio's hopeless colour scheme, or from the occasional interruptions to the broadcast. If the purpose is to consider the news broadcast as genre and to compare NBC to CNN, we make another selection. If the aim is to compare news readers, we make yet another selection. This is why human culture becomes dynamic: it can to a certain degree choose what is integrated and what is omitted, i.e. select codes and contexts for the hierarchical arrangement of perceptions. This is because it possesses a sign-system as language, which is reflexive and allows the construction of metalevels so that the culture can relate to its own borders. The culture's dynamics are intimately connected to its semiotic character.

Bühler's characterization of this abstractive relevance can make us wonder what he means by *contact*. Is it possible to speak of real objects in a universe which rests on the integration of selected and interpreted sensory impulses? James Gibson, for one, does not believe that the notion of object is particularly suited to understanding the real space which we sense (Gibson 1979). Even though he recognizes that the surroundings range quantitively from atoms to asteroids, they do not belong to the surrounding world which we inhabit. We inhabit a space where body and surrounding world are mutually dependent, in which we are observers of the world and active participants in it. This space is most important: the proportions of both molecules and the Milky Way must be translated into the dimensions and realities of our living space before we can relate to them, e.g. with tools such as microscopes, with iconic signs like three-dimensional molecular models, or with linguistic metaphors (the Milky Way) and diagrams. Gibson calls this contact universe the 'ecological space', which he defines in relation to the living creatures' vision and movement, i.e. their physical presence. In this he also takes the contactual universe to be the basis of this theory.

The contactual universe is built up of three components: *medium, substance* and *surface*. A medium – such as air or water – is an aspect of the surrounding world in which sensing or movement is channelled. Everything that hinders movement or undisturbed passage of sensory impulses is a substance. It indicates discontinuous features of the surrounding world, and neither medium nor substance is identical for all organisms. The transition between medium and substance, e.g. a horizontal line or a lamp-post we run into, is a substance. What meets the body are not objects but surfaces, reagents to the existence of the surrounding world (Larsen 1991b).

However, we rarely exclaim, 'Look, there's the façade of a house', but rather, 'Look, there's a house!' We sense a border, the surface, but we experience an object. It is our semiotic competence that enables us to translate surfaces into objects, according to philosopher Alfred Schütz (Schütz 1955). His account fine-tunes Bühler's more general interpretation of abstractive relevance. The sensing process activates a series of *processual codes* (see Chapter 2), which Schütz calls *schemes*, that connect consciousness and the surrounding world. The basic processual code for all schemata is *pairing*. We recognize something by association: whether one wants to or not, and independent of the context, the sound of a drill brings to mind a visit to the dentist, even when the dentist's instruments are at safe distance. According to Schütz, this pairing is also involved when we face phenomena less concrete than visits to the dentist. Inspired by phenomenologist Edmund Husserl, he operates with four schemes for pairing. They all rest on the sign-relations that involve abstractive relevance to build the surrounding world's objects:

1   The most elementary pairing is an *apperceptual scheme*. It operates even when we receive an entirely disconnected, singular sense-perception, e.g. an indeterminate observation in heavy fog or something we have never seen before, because we always inevitably pair it with the *type phenomenon* or the category to which we believe it to belong. 'I wonder if this muddled visual impression shouldn't be some kind of stone – or perhaps it is just a hallucination.'

2   If the sense-perception is thus interpreted as a kind of object, it will invariably be paired with something that we cannot apperceive. We test the *spatial character* of the surface we have encountered. We can reject the observation as imaginary, i.e. non-spatial, or determine that, 'Aha, the brick surface is a façade.' The collection of bricks is paired with a new category, 'building', even though we cannot see all the way around the three-dimensional phenomenon. This is what Schütz calls an *appresentational scheme*.

3   Based on the link between the surface and its spatial character, we give the phenomenon an identity – 'But it's a house!' We have linked the spatial to the semantic. This is what Schütz calls a *referential scheme*.

4   We cannot decide to refrain from using the schemes; without them, there is no surrounding world. This also holds true for the last scheme, the *contextual or interpretational scheme*. Here, the objects that have been established by using the other schemes are given a precise meaning. We have linked them to a context that is defined in relation to *human presence* – 'It looks as if it's inhabited', or, 'It resembles an animal's lair', or, 'It looks empty and deserted.'

Marlow can give us an example of this. He appears in Joseph Conrad's *Heart of Darkness* (1902), travelling up the River Thames aboard the *Nellie*, where he relates his expedition to the darkest heart of Africa to meet the mythical ivory hunter Kurtz. With a group of whites and Africans, Marlow has penetrated into unknown country by way of a stream. Near Kurtz's station, they encounter the remains of a cabin and discover a note advising them to turn back. They set up camp for the night:

> The reach was narrow, straight, with high sides like a railway cutting. The dusk came gliding into it long before the sun had set. The current ran smooth and swift, but a dumb immobility sat in the banks. The living trees, lashed together by the creepers and every living bush of the undergrowth, might have been changed into stone, even to the slenderest twig, to the lightest leaf. It was not sleep – it seemed unnatural, like a state of trance. Not the faintest sound of any kind could be heard. You looked on amazed, and began to suspect yourself of being deaf – then the night came suddenly, and struck you blind as well. About three in the morning some large fish leaped, the loud splash made me jump as though a gun had been fired. When the sun rose there was a white fog, very warm and clammy, and more blinding than the night. It did not shift or drive; it was just there, stranding all round you like something solid. At eight or nine, perhaps, it lifted as a shutter lifts. We had a glimpse of the jungle, with the blazing little ball of the sun hanging over it – all perfectly still – and then the white shutter came down again, smoothly, as if sliding in greased grooves. I ordered the chain, which we had begun to heave in, to be paid out again. Before it stopped running with a muffled rattle, a cry, a very loud cry, as of infinite desolation, soared slowly in the opaque air. It ceased. A complaining clamour, modulated in savage discords, filled our ears. The sheer unexpectedness of it made my hair stir under my cap. . . . It culminated in a hurried outbreak of almost intolerably excessive shrieking. . . . What we could see was just the steamer we were on, her outlines blurred . . . and a misty strip of water, perhaps two feet broad, around her – and that was all. The rest of the world was nowhere, as far as our eyes and ears were concerned. Just nowhere. Gone, disappeared; swept off without leaving a whisper or a shadow behind.
>
> (Conrad 1987: 65f.)

Schütz's schemes do not necessarily indicate the perceptions chronologically; rather, they are ordered logically as a series of levels that alternate simultaneously. The quotation describes Marlow's encounter with the fearsome unknown that comes to dominate the river's easily recognizable surroundings. The unknown takes possession of the whole, so that the known categories of perception are immobilized and the very process of perception and identification needs to be constructed again and again. In this process, Schütz's schemes are activated. Marlow's first apprehensions follow the *interpretational or contextual* scheme: the width of the river is interpreted in relation to human presence and activity, and is compared to a 'railway cutting.' But the surroundings' indeterminability rapidly gains prominence, and the contextual scheme only allows itself to be applied negatively: 'It was not sleep.' The apprehensions are difficult to identify ('the dusk came gliding in', 'it seemed unnatural', 'amazed', 'being deaf', 'blinding', 'opaque air', 'outlines blurred', etc.). From time to time, the senses are disconnected entirely. The sense-perceptions are isolated, unique and unconnected ('glimpse'); they have barely any characteristics of an object ('unnatural', 'a state of trance'). The basic *apperceptual* scheme now appears to the effect that the perceptions receive object-like features and are connected to abstract categories ('immobility', 'sheer unexpectedness', 'infinite desolation') or to metaphors and comparisons (e.g. 'stone', 'as though a gun had been fired', 'like something solid', 'savage discords').

Following the *appresentational* scheme, the apprehensions are also connected to an indisputable three-dimensional physical surrounding world oriented perpendicularly and horizontally ('high sides', 'sun above' versus 'undergrowth', 'shutter down'), with a marked difference between proximity and remoteness, between breadth and narrowness, between large and small dimensions – the surrounding world resembles a 'state of trance', but is not. The fog 'was just there like something solid'. The overwhelming visual and auditory sensory impressions define the space and its limits and provide a new application of the schemes and new orientation in the surrounding world. Furthermore, in a relatively nuanced semantics, the spatial objects obtain an identity following the *referential* scheme as a near-claustrophobic jungle landscape – the visible space is only 'two feet broad': individual elements and their properties are specified (e.g. 'trees', 'creepers', 'twig', 'leaf', 'blazing little ball of the sun', 'loud splash', 'strip of water').

In conclusion, Marlow attempts to comprehend what is apprehended in relation to human presence, following the *contextual* scheme, but with a negative result: the world is lifeless and barren ('the rest of the world was nowhere') or filled with sensory perceptions, i.e. that follow the apperceptual scheme and the appresentational scheme, but simultaneously transcend any sensory identification and specification, i.e. that preclude the application of the referential scheme ('intolerably excessive shrieking') and the contextual scheme. And yet, it is the violent sensations that delimit a human universe with sound, vision, anchor cable and ship. Using metaphors and comparisons building on sensory perceptions and human activity, Marlow finally attempts – in vain – to define 'nowhere' following the contextual scheme, to transform it into 'something' or 'somewhere'. Thus the objects appear following the contextual scheme's attempt to localize a human presence as an ambiguous sign for the very border between a world of human experience and a world beyond, between a human and a non-human universe, a natural and an unnatural space.

Regardless of whether we encounter a house or a complex unknown object like a jungle landscape, we always simultaneously interpret objects and our own presence in relation to them, even when our attempt has a negative result. This is how Bühler defines contact; it is the prerequisite for our ability to use designator functions to anchor objects and relate to them discursively. Even something as simple as to see a house is to *supplement a sensory perception by our presence*. Only in this way does something occur as a house in a contactual universe. This is what happens when we fulfil the first requirement for cul- ture-forming delimitation: localization of phenomena in time and space in relation to our own presence. First then, and first therefore, can we begin to choose, act, plan, correct mistakes, discuss issues with one another, and so on.

But what about the body whose presence is required? Does it also qualify as an object? We cannot see an entire house at one time, but will have to use Schütz's appresentational scheme. The same goes for the body. However, the house allows us to walk its circumference in order to check that we correctly employed the referential scheme and verify that it is indeed a house, and not just a theatre prop. Others can do the same with our body, and we can do the same with theirs. But we cannot circle our own body. Therefore we cannot, without outside help, make our own body into an object with a socially accepted meaning. For the body to obtain the character of a whole, there must be other bodies around it, as well as objects in which it can be mirrored, i.e. phenomena that react to our presence in such a way that they enable us to understand our body as a whole, and become signs for our physical presence. The body seen as a whole is therefore a semiotic sign, a bodily image that is part of a semiotic process to become a sign because of the relationships we have to other objects and bodies (Larsen 1994a, 1994c). Phenomenologists like Maurice Merleau-Ponty and psychoanalysts like Jacques Lacan (Merleau-Ponty 1945 and Lacan 1966) return to this theme constantly.

When we successfully hit in a nail with a hammer, these objects confirm that our coordinated motoric effort is a collective whole; they verify that the body is one and affirm the validity of our bodily image. We could not per- ceive the body as a whole without an object universe, nor without other bodies: when a father addresses his fourteen-day-old son, who does not yet understand a single word, as 'you' or 'Peter' instead of calling him 'the loose collection of skin, hair, and pink sensory impressions', it is a form of address that is gradually internalized by the child, thereby incorporating into the child's experience that it has one whole body, and that it also *is* one whole body. And as this happens using verbal discourse, this body does not become a whole simply as one object among others, but as a subjective whole – not just a body, but *my* body rather than *your* body.

James Gibson emphasizes this relation by pointing out that the body is in motion. Motion is our way of being present among objects and other bodies. Here, we join surfaces and substances that we use to guide our movements in the medium that allows sensory perceptions and motion to pass through. Therefore, it is not merely our semiotic genius, but also the surfaces' layout, that allows them to become a possible surrounding world for us. Carrying in it several *possibilities* for motion and expansion, this layout appeals to *our* body, as it is there. The surrounding world 'affords' itself, as Gibson states. He ties this appeal primarily to light and vision. The light arranges the surface in relation to a point of view from which the surrounding world is used by subjects to orient themselves. But the body and the eyes constantly change direction and focus, because we use the schemes' processual codes to follow the appeals which come from certain directions and not from others. The surrounding world exemplifies such a semiotically formed appeal to motion, as it is interpreted by a body in motion among other objects and bodies.

Hereby we reach the *second prerequisite* for the culture-forming border delimitation of our natural foundation. In addition to the temporal and spatial localization in a contactual universe, *bodies* must be formed that *can be present as subjects among others*. The signs that enable this to take place – touch, registration of bodily distance, dress, bodily decoration, perceived comfort, construction of homes and furniture, tests of strength, naming customs, forms of address, modesty, etc. – also belong to the signs that a culture employs to mark its borders. We must therefore expand our earlier formulation of seeing a house: even something as simple as seeing a house adds something to the sensory perception through our presence *on intersubjective conditions*. This means that even individual perceptions, like those experienced by Marlow on the African river, or simply observing a house, cannot be viewed as individual processes. If the body and its senses are not developed so that they can enter differentiated intersubjective semiotic processes of a socially shared character, both these processes and the individual body will fall apart. This applies, for instance, to pathological conditions like schizophrenia, which causes time, space and subjects to become unstable and the body to be experienced as a series of fragments, and which disables stable perception (Bateson 1972; Rosenbaum and Sonne 1979).

Perception and socialization

Senses *can* develop differently, and the sensory apparatus is not entirely natural. Individuals can lose their sight as well as their other senses. Also, different cultures modulate the sense-perception in particular ways in socialization processes and through the various objects which they produce or to which they give prominence, just as the likes and dislikes of individual and socially determined operational structures guide the sensory apparatus. Even something as simple as a spontaneous experience of *comfort* or *pleasure* is culturally an enormously differentiated and varied process – a pleasant sound, a nice smell, a comfortable body position, a gentle touch, etc. – and can be embodied in almost diametrically opposite things when we move from one culture or subculture to another. Delicacies like snakes and snails are today considered mouth-watering in western gourmet circles, but can instead evoke other reagents in other areas. The senses therefore present a process that is not only culture-forming but also culture-formed – that is, a socialization process.

In his cognitive psychology, Jean Piaget points to a basic semiotic development of the sensory apparatus that must be included in the human cognitive development, regardless of which senses or sign systems are activated (Piaget and Inhelder 1969). In Piaget's theory of psychological development, cognitive process and semiotic process are joined in the construction of the surrounding world (see Chapter 3).

Following Piaget, in the first fourteen years of its life, a child passes through a triple-phased development that determines how the child constructs reality. In the first, *senso-motor*, phase, the development is tied to the perception of objects in a contactual universe where they are concretely present together with the child. In the next, *symbolic*, phase, the child can also relate to objects without needing them to be present simultaneously, e.g. the child can pretend to be a dog and invent signs that refer, to a greater or lesser degree, to a dog, regardless of whether the animal is in the vicinity or not. And the infant can attain an even greater degree of freedom in relation to itself, the sign, and the object by withdrawing or constructing replacement objects that can become signs for absent objects or for one another: the breast is replaced by the rubber nipple, which is again replaced by the security blanket, and so on. It is a game with limits set for similarity between sign and object, and thus provides indispensable practice of semiotic competence in relation to a surrounding world under construction.

Verbal language is placed in the symbolic phase, and its primarily arbitrary character is a prerequisite for the child's ability, in the final *conceptual* phase, to structure the surrounding world into systematic and abstract classifications through logical and strictly formal operations, e.g. spelling or counting. This phase concludes a cognitive process in which the surrounding world is constructed through increased abstraction. Not only do the phases follow one another, but – as Piaget emphasizes – each phase integrates and modifies the preceding one, so they can ultimately combine and affect one another.

The construction of *space* illustrates this ongoing integration process. In the first phase, space is organized around the physically present subject and the objects perceived by the subject, and constructed of simple binary oppositions such as 'near/close', 'away from/next to', 'my place/others' places'. A classroom with assigned seats for all the pupils is organized is such a way: this is known as the *topological* space. In the second phase, the *imagined* space is developed. Within this horizon, space is organized according to positions where one can imagine a subject to be present. If John and Jane are standing face to face, John will have to imagine being in Jane's place in order to know what is on her right-hand side. And when John tells Jane that he is standing at the bottom of the stairs, he is imagining her positioned at the top of the stairs and not next to him. This does not hold true for the topological space: if John is close to Jane, she is also close to him; if he is far away from her, she is also far away from him. In the imagined space, we thus encounter relative spatial designations such as 'left/right', 'up/down', 'surface/depth', and so on.

We also refer to imagined space when we give road directions, aided by a network of subjective positions: 'See that large tower? [topological space] When you stand on that intersection over there with your back to the tower, turn to your right and take the second road on your left after you pass the traffic lights [imagined space].' If we add that, 'It is two miles from here, so the walk will take about half an hour', we have entered the third type of space, *Euclidian* space (from Euclid, the patriarch of geometry), which is related to the conceptual phase. Here, space is quantified using varying yardsticks, entirely independent of objects and subjective positions. Units for time ('half an hour') and length ('two miles') are logically related ('so') with an impersonal subject ('the walk', implying an average person, and easily replaceable by 'you'). In the imagined space, on the other hand, 'you' is not replaceable by 'it' though it can, on occasion, be replaced by 'one'.

Anthropologist Rik Pinxten (Pinxten 1976) has examined whether such spatial constructions are developed similarly in different cultures. He concluded that all cultures constitute a topological space organized with the physical presence at its centre. According to Piaget's theory, all cultures thus satisfy the first two requirements for basic culture-forming delimitation of time and space, body and subject. On the other hand, some cultures lack (or have a very poorly represented) Euclidian space, and some cultures have a de-emphasized imagined space. If we state that the walk will take half an hour instead of saying that the distance is two miles, we de-emphasize the Euclidian space and emphasize the imagined space (one imagines the body walking). And if we direct someone to go straight ahead until they can walk no further, or tell someone that the ticket booth is two steps away from the entrance, we give higher priority to the topological space. This is reflected in old yardsticks like feet and inches, and in more vernacular yardsticks like 'an arm's length' or 'spitting distance'.

Static cosmologies and societal models, familiar from European feudalism and absolutism to modern-day parliamentary democracies and non-industrialized cultures, perceive society with the topological space as model. In this hierarchy, each person and each phenomenon has its place. When the king throws a dinner party, the guests' distance to where he is seated represents the social space and their place in it. Space, including the social space, is often perceived by analogy with the body – the head represents the king and the limbs his loyal subjects. On the other hand, in a modern industrialized society, modelled on the American system, mobility (relating to employment, residence, etc.) is assigned a much higher priority. The American dream about the road upward from rags to riches, a story in which anyone can imagine himself playing the lead, and the Wild West as the setting in which anyone can imagine himself as a strong and energetic subject, forms the society with imagined space as its basic model.

Therefore the abstraction process described by Piaget is not a constant, but is instead a culture-forming and culture-formed development. Bühler considers abstractive relevance to be necessary, while Gibson views the perceived combination of medium, substance and surface as obligatory, and Schütz believes the four schemes are unavoidable. In all three cases, the inevitability is rooted in a culturally formed development and learning process.

The semiotic aspect of this process allows for its flexibility. In Piaget's view, the semiotic turning-point is not the first but the second (symbolic) phase. It presumes a pre-symbolic, senso-motor phase in which *representational skills* are established (meaning that the senses refer to objects), and extended in a post-symbolic conceptual phase allowing for *formal constructions* (meaning that objects can be freely combined). While in Piaget's doctrine the development of symbolic skills, in the second phase, takes centre stage, he views the entire cognitive process semiotically, as a representational as well as a constructive process in which the human person constructs his/her own environment. This is what we have earlier called an *intentional,* that is a conscious, process, focusing on things without being a priori determined by definite senses or sign systems (see Chapter 4, p. 72ff.). Piaget's three-phased theory shows first and foremost the fundamental intentional semiotic *functions*, different from Bühler's sign elements, verbal and otherwise, and also different from Gibson's privileged senses, such as the visual sense, which is particularly developed in humans.

In the pre-symbolic but not pre-semiotic phase, the surrounding world is constructed through combinations of sensory data. Through a so-called representational schema (analogous to Schütz's four schemes), sensory impressions are interpreted as objects sharing the same space as the body, the space where (in Bühler's vocabulary) there is contact. A child hears a footstep and perceives the presence of its mother; the child sees a bottle and perceives a possible and longed-for sequence of possible actions. The perceived indexes and signals – Piaget employs both terms indiscriminately – are intentionally oriented towards an object.

In the central symbolic phase, as language emerges, mental images or material objects appear as symbols. They refer to an object that can be absent, or even excluded from reaching the vicinity of the subject, except as symbols (e.g. imaginary animals or made-up scenes as they occur in children's games and play). For both Piaget and Bühler, what is decisive is that symbols presume a representation of phenomena that exist independently of these symbols. This requires a contactual universe in which the construction of phenomena follows the representational schemes of the senso-motor phase, which we use to process the indexes and signals of the objectual world.

This means that the symbolic surrounding world is constructed by absorbing the representation of the senso-motor surrounding world – that is, by imitation. This grants the symbol an iconic dimension, as Peirce calls it, or motivated dimension, as Saussure has it. For Piaget, the way in which symbolic functions process and develop indexical experience, with imitation as its primary driving force, is particularly evident in children's drawings. Piaget's train of thought is close to Peirce's (the symbol corresponds to his iconic sign), but his terminology is more germane to Saussure, whose work Piaget read at an early age.

The symbol not only builds on the pre-established indexes or signals, but with its constructive freedom also points to the arbitrary signs that emerge in the conceptual phase. The arbitrary signs (which Peirce calls symbolic signs) refer to objects exclusively through socially agreed conventions, but also necessarily build upon the two sign-functions and incorporate both representation and imitation. Piaget stresses that all three sign-functions are engaged in interaction, though in different configurations and with different weight, in the construction and control of the surrounding world, both individually and socially. The common denominator is that the processing of indexes in the senso-motoric phase is ubiquitous.

The codes of culture

Culture as model

In the preceding section, we have given greater prominence to culture as a delimiting process than as a delimited field inhabited by objects, signs and codes. Therefore, we have until now examined the transition from perception to meaning as a semiotic process that enables objects to become *signs in use*. And we have insisted that this culture-forming process not only develops in directly social situations, but is also active every time we sense, every time we individually localize an object, every time we move our body, every time we act, and every time we react to and affect one another. Furthermore, we all experience the sense of belonging to a culture, which is perceived as a relatively independent and coherent area that is instrumental in granting us a particular identity, both in relation to other cultures and to the non-human part of our surroundings. Such an area is upheld by common codes and sign-systems that allow information collection, communication, socialization and transmission of knowledge, experience and other social actions. Cultures as delimited wholes, the structures that specify them, and the elements out of which they are constructed, are therefore also part of the area covered by cultural semiotics.

The definitions of culture as a delimited whole have changed throughout cultural history, and have themselves helped construct this history (one comprehensive catalogue of definitions is Kroeber and Kluckhohn 1952). By such changing definitions of culture generally or of a (series of) subculture(s), a culture continually produces models of itself, which it can use to observe its own contents and borders. Such a self-reflexive mechanism for identification presumes the possibility for introspection offered by natural language and penetrating all activities of the culture. This forms the nucleus of the semiotics developed by Jurij Lotman, the first to focus on a collective cultural semiotics. It was formed in the School of Tartu (in Moscow and Tartu from the early 1960s onwards). Although its starting-point was information theory (machine translation, mathematical linguistics, formalist structuralism, etc.), its studies of literature and folklore in particular transformed it into cultural semiotics (Lucid 1977; Lotman 1990; Lotman and Uspensky 1978).

The briefest definition of culture given by Lotman and his associates is *collective non-hereditary memory*. Since culture is not hereditary, it must be based on socialization; and since it is collective, the socialization must be based on information exchange, i.e. on signs. Therefore, culture as memory includes not only the *content* of the memory (e.g. a stable set of values concerning the family, nation, education, dress, etc.) but also the *process* in which the memory is constructed out of information gathered, exchanged and stored. Moreover, since culture is a socialization process, it is also subject to change. Memory is therefore primarily connected to signs which can take a self-reflexive stance, both on themselves and on the processes in which they partake, and thus give cause for change. Therefore natural language is at the centre of a culture, and linguistics is the Tartu School's primary starting-point for the study of culture as cultural semiotics. Although it is inspired by a plethora of sign-notions and definitions from both European and American semiotics, the Tartu School is primarily based on the concept of sign as developed in structural linguistics and shaped by Saussure and Hjelmslev (see Chapter 3). But with text and model as basic concepts, Lotman attempts to avoid simply equating culture and language.

Culture as recollected content and process is materialized in *texts* (see Chapter 6). Texts therefore maintain certain constant features in a given culture, cultural *invariants* that are connected to the culture's sign-systems. Cultural semiotics takes these invariants as its subject of study. For Lotman, texts are supersigns consisting of expression and content, i.e. with the same dual form as the binary signs of language of which they are made (Grzybek 1989). But there is one decisive difference from the signs of structural linguistics. In the linguistic tradition, invariants are the elements that are defined only by virtue of the differences between them. Thus they attain a formal status that allows them to function within the semiotic system to which they belong. From a linguistic vantage-point, the linguistic sound /a/ is not something in itself, but simply a linguistic element because it differs from the phonemes /i/, /e/, etc., and vice versa (see Chapter 3).

Cultural constants, on the other hand, are not connected to individual signs, sign-systems, or texts. In relation to cultural invariants, the text's expression plane is therefore not a formally, but primarily a materially, determined entity. It is a material entity that can be perceived and identified within culture as a well-delimited and meaningful phenomenon, i.e. consisting of signs that refer to objects. For instance, street life at an intersection in a major city includes traffic, people, houses, signs, shouts, billboards, smells. Of course, the traffic signs and the words and images on the billboards can have some constant formal features of their own that enable them to be identified as texts employing certain systems of expression. But these features are not identical to cultural invariants, only to the distinctive features of the medium of expression in question, which qualify them as belonging to verbal or pictorial language. Such features allow the culture's objects to appear individually with a certain structural or communicative accessibility, the prerequisite for their ability to obtain cultural meaning (Lotman and Uspensky 1978). After all, the (sub-)elements of the street intersection are not chaotic, but have what James Gibson sees as an intersubjectively shared layout. The intersection is organized according to structural codes and, as stated by Raymond Boudon (see Chapter 2, p. 19), behaves as a systemic object. Thus a linguistic analysis will at the most provide some information about the preconditions for the cultural invariants, but without revealing anything about the invariants themselves.

This is where the notion of *model* becomes relevant. Since the model implies that something is modelled by it, the notion first of all implies a hierarchy of at least two levels. Invariants, then, are the selected elements that remain constant when passing from one level to the next, from model to modelled and vice versa; they are not constant on just one level, like linguistic phonemes. Second, the concept of model implies a code that processes, duplicates, or replaces the object with a model, a processual code that maintains a partial and incomplete similarity between model and object.

The model refers to a text, because all cultural objects are texts. Since texts are semiotic signs, they refer to something else. And since the model also refers to something else, it must also be a text – one that refers to another text while simultaneously containing the codes that allow this reference. Any text in a culture can act as a model in this way, provided that it is embedded in a textual hierarchy. Boudon refers to this textual structure of culture as structures defined within an effective context (see Chapter 2, p. 19). A model is not a particular text but a particular *textual function*.

Lotman believes that such a hierarchy, in which the culture's texts are promoted to potential models, consists of two modelling systems. A *primary modelling system*, such as a verbal or visual text, models our relation to the surrounding world – perception, action and communication. A *secondary modelling system*, on the other hand, reconstructs the primary modelling system's organization of the relation to the surrounding world and the conditions for this relation, through myths, tales, art, science, etc. The characteristics of the secondary modelling system can therefore be found in both systems and become cultural invariants. The instruction book of a driving school is a primary modelling system that allows us to know what to do at a street intersection. Using a series of aesthetic codes, Fritz Lang's film *Metropolis* (1927) turns our contact with moving machinery into a cultural invariant; the film itself becomes a secondary modelling system.

According to Lotman, the constant presence of two such modelling systems rests on a particular precondition: the primary modelling systems must include natural language and thereby a permanent potential for the construction of a secondary level, or metalevel. Effectively, model and object never coincide, just as word and object are never one and the same. The relation between words and objects can always be commented on at a higher level. The battling males and coveted females of an animal group interact on the basis of one-to-one relations between sign and meaning in the signs involved. This differs essentially from sign-mediated interaction in human culture; otherwise, culture would be essentially guided by automatic and invariable reflexes.

Of course, such reflexes are part of a culture too, e.g. in the relation between hunger and food. Yet the central role of natural language means that such reflexes are not *basic* cultural phenomena, simply because they, as reflexes, are considered to be spontaneous and natural. Reflexes only become fundamental in the culture to the extent to which they can be made reflexive through language. When hunger becomes fasting, culinary aesthetics, or table manners, and enters verbal discourse, it has thereby found cultural forms that can be evaluated and altered, and thus be moved towards a secondary modelling system. The intestines' peristaltic muscle reflexes on the passage of food, on the other hand, are not as basic as *cultural* reflexes. They cannot be changed in one direction or another by being talked about. Models are therefore not necessarily always dominated by iconic signs, but by all signs that can be made reflexive by language, i.e. also by indexical and symbolic, or arbitrary, signs. The effect of the model hierarchy is therefore that culture is a continuous complex semiotic process involving indexical, iconic and symbolic signs. Lotman refers to the collective texts functioning in this fashion as the *semiosphere* (Lotman 1990). Unlike the biosphere, which includes the communication between the cells of our intestinal flora and the metabolism of the plants on the windowsill, the semiosphere is, to Lotman, the human surrounding world that can be differentiated in a number of different cultures.

Since the primary and secondary modelling systems are never identical, they are connected to one another by implementing certain processual codes. Hereby, Lotman states, perception becomes text and direct experience becomes culture. He calls the processual codes a *programme* for the continuous collective cultural construction of the surrounding world (Lotman and Uspensky 1978). The programme is executed by culture's actors, who exhibit a particular behaviour or perform particular actions, and is manifested in texts, e.g. the family at the dinner table munching their way from hunger to consumption to satiety. Like any text, these are determined by verbal language, and the process that duplicates them in a secondary modelling system therefore takes the form of *discourse* (see Chapter 4). This discourse is a type of *action*, and it can therefore be represented in a *narrative structure* (see Chapter 5): recipes with directions that *tell* us how to prepare the food; table manners that *tell* us how to behave at the dinner table; information about healthy and unhealthy eating habits that *tell* us the effect of food on our body's processes, etc.

Having discussed the first two presuppositions for culture's way of delimitating its borders – localization in space and time and presence of bodies that can become subjects – we have now reached the third and final presupposition: the border between culture and nature must be marked in such a way that bodies can enter in time and space into *discursively formed actions*. In other words, the way culture marks its borders must be susceptible of being made narrative (see Polkinghorne 1988; Ricœur 1984–88).

Lotman himself does not go that far: that objects are localized *in time and space* is to him simply given as a precultural constant; the actors that execute the programmes that convey the two modelling systems are, on their own, functional roles without necessarily being connected to a *body*, and the programme itself is a series of events that does not necessarily become discourse and thereby *action*, but can just as well be the cycle in a four-stroke engine. In the following section, we will examine more closely the processes that make the programme a border-marking discursive action of a narrative character.

Culture as exchange

Although Lotman is primarily interested in culture as memory, he clearly states that memory rests on the exchange of information. The exchange becomes culture-forming only when the verbal language enters the historical development of the organisms. Then, the participants are no disconnected individual subjects, but act through a common code that they can use to change their role. They themselves become instances in the exchange process, sign and texts defined in and by this process (Lotman 1990). Through the continuous exchange of signs, a culture is continuously testing, through its actors, the validity of its borders and codes, and the validity of the identity it gives its actors. A culture's texts can continue to exist, just as the Latin grammar is still intact, but if they are not exchanged, the culture becomes as dead as the Latin language. The programme introduced by Lotman is activated primarily as exchange.

The two anthropologists Marcel Mauss and his disciple Claude Lévi-Strauss have, in a cross-cultural perspective, studied certain basic forms of exchange in pre-industrial cultures, where borders and identity are questioned and at risk. Mauss, in his 1923–24 article on the gift (Mauss 1950), examined the exchange of gifts and the underlying connection between property right, objects and social power structures. Lévi-Strauss has, in a series of publications, analysed the exchange of women and the connection between body and sexuality, i.e. its biological origins and social organization and, by extension, the myths through which cultures uphold and expand their interpretations of their origins with a cosmological perspective, and the rites that, in their relations to their origins, mark their relationship to nature (Lévi-Strauss 1967).

On first examination, the giving of a gift is a non-committal gesture that bears no relation to the restrictions connected to buying and selling or other contractual and legally binding transactions. One voluntarily relinquishes a piece of property to someone else. But those cases where objects cannot be seen apart from their meaning, and thereby from the unwritten laws that hold a community of cultural meaning together as consistently as do written laws, are not as straightforward. And since objects are always semiotic phenomena, it is never this simple.

In our culture, it can be difficult to regard the giving of gifts as a cultural model, because objects are exchanged primarily as goods with a monetary value, i.e. the exchange takes place in what Piaget calls the Euclidian space. Nevertheless, Mauss attempts to generalize on his observations of certain Pacific and North American societies to include modern societies. When an object becomes a gift, it enters into an exchange process. The meanings it thereby receives and transmits to those partaking in the process are more important than the meanings that the object can have in other connections (food, tools, economic value). The gift becomes what today is known as a status symbol. Gifts become meaningful because the exchange must satisfy three requirements: one must give; one must receive; and one must return a gift with a gift. These requirements thus institutionalize a special form of property right: the right to own and the demand to renounce; the right to give and the demand to receive.

The exchange of gifts is related to certain social situations (arrival, departure, births, weddings, and other festive occasions), and the demands which the persons involved in the exchange must satisfy are related to their respective positions in the given situation – the difference between host and guest, between bridegroom and father, etc. To satisfy the demands, therefore, serves to test and confirm one's position; to have others recognize one's position then becomes a collective confirmation of certain cultural codes for division of property. This implies that one's position in society is not necessarily individual and private; for instance, the host's position incorporates the entire family which he represents *qua* host. The demands can also vary; for example, tribal chiefs and other representatives of power satisfy certain demands in numerous situations. Their gifts – the ones they give, as well as the ones they receive – must always be the largest and most generous. In cultures where the gift exchange is a fundamental cultural process, it is a symbolic act through which cultural identity, power and legitimacy are tested, just as labour – exchanging one's labour capacity with goods and services – is in our culture. One can participate in the exchange and exploit the potential for freedom this has to offer, but one cannot change the fundamental rules of the game: failing to define one's identity in relation to a possible participation will leave one in a cultural void.

We have hereby already indicated the common logic behind the three demands or requirements: when one exchanges gifts, the gifts are not of equal size or importance, or there would be no test of power. To give a large gift shows that one has much to give, and that one is without equal as giver. If the receiver refuses to satisfy the demand to receive the gift, he signals that he fears not being able to return the gift, i.e. he fears not being able to demonstrate his own power to return a gift of at least the same value. When the gift is returned, i.e. when one places oneself in the earlier giver's position or a similar situation, the gift must at least be equal to the gift that was offered initially. The gift-giving thereby becomes a mutual act, a mutual recognition of the involved parties' cultural identity. By giving a gift, one gives oneself, and thereby gives oneself and one's property to others, Mauss concludes.

Thus the exchange of gifts functions not as an exchange of objects, nor even as symbols, but as a demonstration of the strength to dispense with certain objects and still maintain a powerful position. To give back can therefore just as well be to destroy or waste. This act is inherent in the religious act called potlatch by anthropologists: a society's collective exchange of gifts with a divine power, which after all has no need to receive anything, manifested as a collective waste of values, a nearly self-destructive sacrifice that brings the society's members in direct connection with the divine power. In the cultures studied by Mauss, the circulation of objects as gifts is the only possibility for attaining cultural identity in a mutually obligating recognition; this possibility is rooted in the religious character of the objects.

However, Mauss went further, claiming that every culture through exchange establishes its particular form of identity, power and legitimacy. Earlier, we have seen how the body becomes an intersubjective phenomenon. In his essay on the person, self and subject (included in Mauss 1950), Mauss showed how the establishment of a particular identity in a mutual situation-bound exchange process not only forms some fixed social masks, roles, or persons (etymologically, 'person', from Latin *persona*: 'mask'), but also sows the seeds of self-reflection and thus the possibility for identity change. This brings us beyond the exchange of gifts. With self-reflection, Mauss stated, the formation of cultural identity gradually disconnects itself from the actual body and the given situation, and can therefore be seen as rising above the logic of the exchange. Identity is then seen as individual autonomy. According to Mauss, it is this historically developed view of identity that characterizes European culture, and that erroneously elevates the absolute ego to a norm with metaphysical status and universal validity.

On these conditions, identity is related less to situations and physical presence than it is to constant formal structures (individual rights, linguistically bound name-giving, positions determined by linguistic structures such as the *pluralis majestatis* ('*We* are not amused'), derogatory ways of addressing someone ('Can *he* bring my hat as well?'), or by logical arguments like Descartes's famous 'I think, therefore I am'). Here, it is not so much the relation to others that gives the identity, as the relation to oneself by way of formal structures. Self-reflection is more important than reflection by and through others, and is postulated radically differently. However, the prioritizing of I and self as basic categories in the construction of identity, instead of social positions or persons, is still related to symbolic exchanges, albeit now of a more formal character.

Therefore, neither the I nor the self rescinds, despite possible objections, the exchange from which they spring, but assumes different forms through the exchange of signs. This is the basis for Peirce's view of the self (see Singer 1984). We have emphasized earlier that the body can become a whole only through other objects and other bodies, i.e. in virtue of the conclusions I reach about my body on the basis of the signs transmitted by external objects and bodies as reactions to my presence together with theirs (see p. 163f.). The same holds true for self-reflection as the observation of one's internal world, which Peirce called introspection: 'Introspection is wholly a matter of inference. One is immediately conscious of his Feelings, no doubt; but not that they are feelings of an ego. The self is only inferred' (5.462). This inference has no other manifestation than the body in which it occurs, and which may emit some signs. But as an inference, it follows the general principles of the semiotic process, and therefore takes the form of an internal dialogue or exchange of signs between an 'old self' and a 'new self', through which the actual self is established.

If this were not so, a self could not be delimited in relation to others and would therefore fail to constitute a personal identity. The self cannot avoid contact with others because its very physical existence is intersubjective, and cannot avoid contact with others on some shared, social basis. By the same token, language, as this common basis, cannot avoid segregating between I and you and expressing I as a unique and independent phenomenon, an absolute I. An internal dialogue is also connected to an expressive structure (see Chapter 3, p. 35 and Chapter 4, p. 59f.).

Thus there is no discontinuity between internal and external sign-processes, between introspection and other, outer forms of sign-exchange. Both dimensions are sign-processes rooted in the interaction in Piaget's senso-motoric phase. The internal dialogue does not separate man from culture, keeping him in individual isolation, but rather includes man into culture. Peirce calls the cultural community a 'loosely compacted person', with the same effect as semantics, which Bühler designates as the collective's anchoring point:

> [A] person is not absolutely an individual. His thoughts are what he is 'saying to himself', that is, is saving [*sic*] to that other self that is just coming into life in the flow of time. When one reasons, it is that critical self that one is trying to persuade; and all thought whatsoever is a sign, and is mostly of the nature of language. The second thing to remember is that the man's circle of society (however widely or narrowly this phrase may be understood), is a sort of loosely compacted person, in some respects of higher rank than the person of an individual organism.
>
> (5.421)

Peirce emphasizes the formation of the self in agreement with general semiotic principles: the logical inference and the reasoning dialogue. Thus he has stressed the self and its cultural integration not so much as abstract, but rather as subject to change.

The exchange has a fundamental role as gift-giving in the cultures where it is bound to particular objects, and where the meaning of an individual identity is present only in its essence as seed, Mauss emphasizes. But the exchange is changeable and fragmented in cultures like our own: on the individual level it becomes a psychological process not unlike introspection, and on the collective level a more general or abstract process in which objects circulate in an abstract monetary economy. There is not just one type of object, the gift, that can and should be the basis for the entire exchange and the identity, power, and law inherent in it.

When we give gifts, e.g. in the form of tips, particularly abroad, we notice immediately the obtrusiveness of these abstract relations: if we give too much, do we demonstrate that we believe the waiter or taxi driver to be underpaid, or do we simply flaunt our western affluence? If we give too little, do we demonstrate scorn or stinginess, or do we indicate that we consider the receiver to be an independent creature whose subservience we need not appeal to? And if we give nothing, do we demonstrate that we do not recognize the exchange forms of other cultures, and do not care to learn more about them? Or do we show respect for other people, whom we believe should not be treated as beggars in disguise? Our uncertainty on this issue is manifold and usually so uncomfortable that we feel the need to inquire about the local norms. The exchange logic of semiotic processes with their blend of identity, power, law and reason is culturally stable, although the kinds of objects and forms for cultural identity that play a role in the actual exchange may vary (see Larsen 1991c, 1997c).

Culture as mediation

These shifts are the focus of Claude Lévi-Strauss's myth analyses. In his first major work on familial relationship structures, *Les structures élémentaires de la parenté* (1949), he examines how women are exchanged in a South American tribal society. Structure here is a model that consists of formal relations between elements, and that can be tested and used to explain social relations between objects and persons. Lévi-Strauss's structure and Lotman's model are parallel. Lévi-Strauss's structure is therefore defined in and by an effective context, according to Raymond Boudon, who uses it to illustrate the type of structure that has a finite number of distinctive features and can be tested empirically (on Boudon's structural types, see Chapter 2, p. 19ff).

Lévi-Strauss also uses structural linguistics as his starting-point, but he is less interested in the actual construction of a static system of mutually connected elements than he is in the system's active function: it regulates the exchange of meaningful elements in a collectively binding but not necessarily conscious manner. Through this process, a culture constructs and alters its border with nature. It localizes such a border in the exchange of women: with the taboo on incest, a marriage between those whom a particular culture considers to be closely related is impossible. The natural difference between male and female appears in the culture as an absolute and impassable border between closely related men and women.

At the same time, this implies that those who are not closely related make up an area where relations between the sexes are allowed. A culture can organize these relations as marriage rules, through which the border can be specified: what is understood by closely related in a given culture? When access to sexuality is limited, and when one cannot relate arbitrarily to the natural differences between the sexes, and thus to one's human origins, then sexuality, gender differences and origins must be dealt with in another way: as a complex of prohibited and permitted possibilities for social relations, derived from the relationship between the sexes, they become a culturally structuring force. Lévi-Strauss sets up a structure of kinship relations, in which mother, father, uncle, etc. hold culturally specific positions in a system that, like the linguistic system, is based on internal relations regulating the exchange of women. Because the exchange is placed within a system, it can also take place without the women actually being present: in place of women, the exchange can involve gifts that confirm a marriage agreement as efficiently as the women themselves would. The exchange can also involve ritual acts like a handshake between the fathers, incantations, etc. that also serve to confirm the agreement. Thus an exchange process can be performed that radically affects the entire culture.

Such an exchange process consists of the following progressive steps:

1 The border between nature and culture is represented in culture by an impassable border, a taboo on incest, between two elements, male and female.
2 The border between nature and culture thereby simultaneously receives a special meaning: the difference between the genders – which enables the culture to process it.
3 Thereby, other elements can be specified further: certain male and female persons, closely related and less closely related, receive specific meanings related to permission and prohibition, mutual rights and requirements, and can thereby be compared to other persons – in relation to their differences as well as their similarities.
4 Through the system constructed from elements, they are exchanged with one another, following certain rules, and can thus become a part of the culture's collective systems of meaning.
5 Therefore, they can also be exchanged with elements from systems that are not based on differences between the sexes, but in which the relationship between near and distant also constructs meaning: the exchange of women can be translated into symbolic gifts, or can be compared to the relationship between near and distant locations within the society's territory, or translated into tales about exchanges, i.e. into myths.

6   We have moved from (1) the impassable border, through (2) the specific opposition and (3) elements with a specific meaning, to (4) exchange between these elements and to (5) exchange of the culture's elements of meaning between them and others. Such a movement is a *mediation*: it runs from incompatible oppositions to exchangeable oppositions that culture can control and set conditions for, and which therefore can become socially shared activities.

This mediation process sets limits for a culture's social activities. The process and its resulting collective memory of the origins and limits of culture are recorded in and through mythical tales and rituals. The best known of Lévi-Strauss's myth analyses that expounds on this point of view is that of the Oedipus myth (Lévi-Strauss 1958). The myths deal with more than incest: when Oedipus sleeps with his mother and is then confronted with his own origins, and when he solves the Sphinx's riddle of our human origins, he circumvents the culture's necessary chain of mediations and thereby exceeds the culture's border. In this story, the culture thus recreates and transgresses the border that constitutes it.

Lévi-Strauss describes the logic of mediation as follows:

> Let us say . . . that in a tale a 'king' is not only a king and a 'shepherdess' a shepherdess, but that these words and what they signify become tangible means of constructing an intelligible system formed by the oppositions: *male/female* (with regard to *nature*) and *high/low* (with regard to *culture*), as well as all possible permutations among the six terms.
>
> (Lévi-Strauss 1983: 142)

The process propels itself between three pairs of elements: from male/female, through high/low, and to king/shepherdess. The final pair, as it consists of fictitious characters, enables the construction of a story, and allows the process to be communicated and thus made available as a cultural process with validity within society as a whole. As Lévi-Strauss marks in parentheses, one never encounters the opposition between nature and culture, but rather the mediating forms in which the culture processes this opposition. It is a presumed border that appears only in the way in which and to the extent to which it is represented in the culture's sign-systems. Likewise, in our earlier discussion of perception and the meaning-making process, we have observed that the oppositions between object and sign, between object and consciousness, between one's own body and other bodies, can be manifested only in those signs that represent the oppositions.

The basic mechanism of mediation logic is parallel to the *displacement* which Freud observed in the transfer of physical energy (chapter 6 in Freud 1953–54). The investment of meaning or energy in one area can be displaced to another one: e.g. from sexual behaviour to shopping behaviour; from nature's unpredictability to the chance involved in betting. The psychical energy never shows itself directly and unmediated, but is always represented by its particular effect. The connection between the process analysed by Freud and general semiotic developmental processes is therefore not just a superficial analogy, but a genuine relation. The mediation could appear purely as an escape from reality; but since the displacement is based on certain points of similarity between the starting-point and the area to which the meaning is displaced, this displacement area can collect the meanings embedded in the starting-point.

Parts of the original meaning resulting from the displacement are thus presented in *condensed* form: through advertising and other means, shopping is sexualized as lust and pleasure. In this way, the culture can 'live' with that which is beyond its control. In this fashion the result is *overdetermined*, i.e. determined by the meanings borrowed from several elements in the displacement process. Lévi-Strauss therefore emphasizes that mediation does not invalidate the oppositions involved, but enables them to act together. And it is thus that the mediation, by displacing meanings, does not stall the culture but instead becomes an active force in its development and history.

Thus the culture not only recreates and exceeds the border that constitutes it in its mythical narratives, but also in all other actions that can receive a narrative structure. This occurs in every semiotic process if the processual code is a mediation based on displacement and condensation. Mediation thereby closely approaches Gregory Bateson's view of games and play as a fundamental human activity, within as well as beyond the child's universe (Bateson 1972; see the discussion on Piaget above, pp. 151f. and 165ff.). The game presumes that it can be delimited from that which is not a game. It can always be questioned. Hence arises the query: it this for fun or is it serious? The game tests and plays with the border with what is called reality in a culture and comprises a whole range of activities from wilderness sports and professional soccer to *Monopoly*, lotteries and children's play in the back yard. The game has three important characteristics:

1 The game has an *iconic* relation to reality, meaning that it has selected features in common with reality: a puppy's bite refers to a real bite, but not to the real bite's references to anger, hostility, fear, etc. And the child repeats, in its game of hide-and-seek, the relationship between being present in and being away from the real world's identity drama, and thereby learns to master it.

2 In the game, several designator functions are performed that *delimit* its place in time and space in relation to what is not a game: it employs signs for beginning, ending, discontinuation, violation of rules, etc. Here, both humans and animals can take part, and therefore non-verbal designator elements can also be present and functional.

3 Unlike dreams, daydreams, hallucinations, etc., the game allows for the possibility of what Bateson calls *meta-communication*. It is trapped in a

variation on the classical paradox: it is true that I am lying. Who knows in the course of the game that it is true that I am playing, even though I assure you that I am – I could be pretending to play, and simply be playing that I am saying it is true that I am playing. Therefore the game must allow for meta-communication to identify it as such, legitimizing the game and its rules. According to Bateson, the game must have a frame and context which it cannot put in place itself, a level from which we can determine whether it is true that we are playing. With verbal language, we can take a position on these things while playing, without permanently interrupting play. We can simultaneously participate in the game and stay outside it. The game thereby allows for change, which becomes part of the way in which a culture redefines the scope of what it calls reality. This is why the whole panoply of games constitutes valid but variable cultural mediation models.

We can now specify the three requirements for culture's delimitation in relation to its natural basis which we have tried to define on the way (see p. 153). If these conditions remain unsatisfied, a culture can neither be generally developed nor specifically embodied in particular actions and norms, conventions and codes:

1   *Time and space*: The border must be drawn so that the culture's sign-systems can localize phenomena in time and space within a contactual universe in which they can be exchanged (see p. 157).
2   *Body and subject*: The border must be drawn so that bodies become subjects that can engage into discourse on intersubjective conditions (see p. 164).
3   *Action and action model*: The border must be drawn so that bodies are brought into relation with one another and other time/space phenomena, and embodied in actions that take the form of a mediation process, so that the culture's basic models receive a narrative structure (see p. 172).

Nature's tale

From city to park

Up until now we have been focusing on (1) the fundamental culture-forming process in which we, as humans, with our particular semiotic competence, participate incessantly in order to delimit a common human space, and (2) the requirements that must be met in order to enable the construction of specific cultures through the process.

Although we have already dealt with the semiotics of games and play, it remains no easy task to come to terms with cultural semiotics. Let us therefore relax a little and take a stroll through the nearest city park (the following is a generalized analysis based on studies of Prospect Park, Brooklyn – Larsen 1994e, 1997b). The border between street and park is clearly marked – if not a wall, fence, or gate, then at least a sign informing us where the street ends and the park begins, supplemented perhaps with an appeal to general responsible behaviour in what is public property, as well as some rules prescribing what should not be done ('keep off the grass', 'keep dogs on a leash', etc.).

Traffic laws and other formalized and enforced rules, specifically and mandatorily prohibiting or commanding particular actions, apply on the streets beyond the park. While the park is physically clearly delimited, as a social space it is more vaguely organized: children tear away from their parents at the entrance and run around unsupervised. Here, almost everything not specifically prohibited is allowed. Paths run off toward other parts of the park beyond view, and the park's border with the street is less visible from within the park than it is from without, perhaps even completely obscured. Yet signs, rubbish bins, wheel tracks, etc. constantly remind us that the border is still there.

The park is a piece of nature within the city, formed like a landscape. By this token, nature as park or open landscape has provided an alternative in many cultures to the city and human society in general. Such a landscape has had various meanings in different cultural eras: cosmic order and beauty; secular image of paradise; expression of appropriate city planning; safety; royal power and wealth; freedom and lack of borders; privacy within a public space. The park has also had different practical functions: as enclosure for the king's hunting prey; a secluded place for meditation; cultivation of fruits and vegetables; hygiene; cemetery; recreation area; separation between city zones.

However, the park we are currently traversing is of more recent date, and is largely designed along the same principles as those applied in all cities where urban culture took hold in the mid-nineteenth century or earlier still. The open land, or the existing parks that were transformed into modern city parks, could have had varying meanings and functions, but they developed a dominant common character. With the city park, the international urban culture created one of the texts it uses to determine the border with its natural foundation and thereby defines itself as culture (Green 1990; Larsen 1993b; Schmitt 1990; Schuyler 1986).

The hustle and bustle of everyday city life, its constant demands and obligations on us, are not easily escaped, even in the middle of a park. Looking around, we do not see an elegant Arabic garden with splashing fountains, nor a Zen Buddhist garden with four stones and a broken branch. Unlike the traffic rushing past outside the park, there is no visible or audible rhythm that moulds the park's activities into a whole. There are shouts and talking; some people are walking or sitting, alone or in small groups, with no purpose other than to walk or sit; a young girl meets a friend and gets up from a bench; someone takes her place. A group of school children play soccer on a field, while a kindergarten combines an outing with a staff meeting. A group of senior citizens have brought along picnic baskets and thermos flasks. People are lining up in front of a hot-dog stand. A couple of joggers and roller-skaters go by. Fathers are operating model ships by remote control for sons who would prefer to do it themselves.

School children fight, prompting the teacher to take the class back to school. A dog does its business where it should not. A bag lady who apparently spends the night here is searching through the rubbish bins. Some boys are throwing stones at the birds. And wasn't there something in the newspapers recently about city foxes with rabies? And about drug deals, flashers, robberies and a murder? Unless you have a black belt in karate, the unwritten rule is to stay out of the park after dark. As aesthetic and social space, the park is closed at night, even though the trees continue to grow and the benches continue to get wet. But by and large, anyone can delimit his or her own space, anywhere, anytime, and unchallenged, and quickly move the borders again: sit down on a bench or spread your picnic cloth on the grass; the spot is yours as long as you stay there.

Even when the park's designers had a specific higher purpose in mind, it can be very difficult to read the park directly. The culture's signs and codes and manifold activities are compacted into the space of the park, and their particular life consists of fragments sharing a green background. The space is open and uncontrolled, giving the culture's expressions forms that are *ad hoc* and determined individually. As an alternative to the city or not, the park is always part of the city and formed by and for it.

The city park in which we are sitting is the result of urban planning, which is not specific to a particular city like London, Paris, or New York, but developed along with the urbanization that dominates western culture materially, symbolically and socially. From its earliest days, the park had three functions that were determined by the negative side of city life:

1 *Hygienic* – before the discovery of bacteria, disease was thought to spread through the so-called miasmatic air. The epidemics in overcrowded cities, particular in the early nineteenth century, served to strengthen this conviction of the dangers of stuffy air. Parks were added to allow the cities to breathe; dangerous nature, disease, would be fought with good nature, the well-organized landscape. The park's *material* character – an undeveloped area with water, animals and plants – is decisive here.

2 *Aesthetic* – as dynamic centres in the middle of growing industrialization, the major urban centres began to resemble one another in both a positive and negative sense. The growing internationalization of communication on all levels made them comparable. External signs of power, such as fortresses, became inconsequential, while signs of a harmonious relationship with nature now empowered the city with identity and attraction – open space and green to replace conglomeration and dirt. Parks became

attractions, and continue so today. The park as *iconic sign* for a harmonious landscape is decisive here.

3   *Social-psychological* – the city was generally considered as a negative cultural element: the individual disappeared into the crowd, the sensory bombardment induced stress, and the rapid changes proved destructive to a stable human community. The parks were intended to serve as a social-psychological safety valve. During the leisure time which became gradually institutionalized by the city's organization of labour, the parks were to restore the urban dwellers both mentally and morally. Through direct contact with nature, they could harmonize with their own nature: to be responsible members of the family and the labour force. Uplifting and enlightening could go hand in hand: in botanical gardens and, to a lesser degree, zoos, one could also include more exotic nature in the park's orderly precincts. When the city's growth and the poverty of its masses hindered most from coming regularly into contact with nature, both near and far, nature was recreated within the city itself. The park as institutionalized public place with a minimum of restrictions – an *open social space* – is decisive here.

In all three cases, the border between city and nature is redefined as the city's role changes: the city is not merely a particular location, but a structuring factor that constantly changes both itself and its surroundings, thus dominating the entire culture to which it belongs. Its natural basis cannot simply be taken for granted; rather, the city is responsible for it. In a primitive hunting society, one can sacrifice a heart or blood and thus, through a sign, rebuild and re-enter nature's own constant, invariable housekeeping. But in the city, one cannot depend on fixed signs for nature's order, which can be read in the Great Book of Nature; rather, the urban culture itself creates the signs it uses to read nature, based on the nature for which the city can bear responsibility and for which it has use. This is what happens in the park; it is therefore important that the park be situated within the city. This placement has also proved to be the subject of more debate than its naturalness, i.e. the particular way in which it marks the borders with the street, its proportions in relation to the city's overall size, and the economy of its land use.

Like all cultural phenomena, each new park receives its cultural identity through discourse. It must enter into some narrative, dependent on whether it already exists as physical phenomenon or only on the drawing board. Preferably, the narrative should involve the park's origins; otherwise it is no more than an unspecified green spot. It can be a story about a journey to parks in other cities and countries in quest of a suitable model; an inspiring walk through some other park or cultural landscape; or a history of the city's development or of park landscaping – generally focused on special parks whose particular identity should be emphasized. The story never involves the endless march of nature, but rather deals with the way humans have given, or failed to give, cultural meaning to nature: through discourse, the physical surroundings are integrated into the urban culture and elevated from mere material phenomena to being used as signs. This is what French engineer and landscape architect Adolphe Alphand did when laying out Paris's parks and green areas. In a summary presentation of his work (Alphand 1867 – 73), he retrospectively gave, through a history of landscaping, a collective urban identity to Paris's new or reconstructed green areas. On the other side of the Atlantic, the landscape architect Frederick Law Olmsted, a contemporary of Alphand, became the master-builder of a host of still-existing parks in cities all over the USA – Prospect Park, Brooklyn, among them. He based the park's design on the history of the city in which it lay, thus defining a particular American identity for each park (Olmsted 1981).

In the stories which Alphand and Olmsted had the parks tell, they differed somewhat in their emphasis. Alphand primarily accentuated the adaptation to local climatic and other natural conditions, while Olmsted placed more emphasis on the contrast with the surrounding city and urbanized Europe. This is not surprising, as Alphand's main task was to convert existing gardens and parks, often stemming from the seventeenth century, to modern city parks. Olmsted, on the other hand, had to provide sound reasoning for parks in cities which had been envisaged as a grid of streets that allowed no room for green spaces. Of greater importance is the common ground covered by both Alphand and Olmsted: the park had to satisfy the three requirements presented earlier, and thus become a natural *mediation* of the opposition between man and the man-made entity *par excellence*: the city. The park is thus not a harmonization of the relation between nature and culture but, rather, an iconic sign for nature that has already been mediated as idealized landscape. This is why the park can fulfil its role as the city culture's collective semiotic process. Alphand emphasized an aesthetic harmonization of the integrated natural elements, punctuated by monuments and symbolic architecture, while Olmsted stressed the park's social function as a public space in which individuals can freely meet without regard for the city's restrictions and thus experience, in natural surroundings, the foundation of republican democracy. This makes the park a part of the city culture's understanding of itself and its relationship to its natural foundation.

The border between nature and culture shifts accordingly: as the city integrates natural elements previously outside city limits, what remains beyond culture also changes its character. The landscape imitated by the park was prefigured in the perspectivist space of the Renaissance. It is a purely material space, a three-dimensional box, not a religious and definitely not a metaphysical space. Although this space is static and clearly delimited, its centre can shift, following the individual observer. The space is a scene with a perspective that changes as the observer moves around, but remains unchanging and well organized whenever the scene is frozen in relation to this observer. The dynamic of the space is thus dependent on the continuous series of possible positions taken by a human observer, without any actual change at any time in the way in which the space adapts to human dimensions. This series of scenes can be observed and controlled from a distance by the human at the centre. The space is presented again and again in images, buildings, city plans, literary descriptions of landscapes, etc., from the Renaissance on. We encounter it as the imaginary space in Piaget's cognitive theory, and it remains our culture's basic interpretation of the natural space, largely unaffected by modernism and modern physics.

The parks also belong to this space (Cosgrove 1993). The city park's primary model is the English garden as could be found in the grounds of noble and royal residences, from the early eighteenth century onwards. With winding paths and curving shapes, not-so-randomly arranged trees and shrubbery, and apertures that provide a view of the processed cultural landscape, perspective theory is materialized in a semiosis with nature as object. Unlike the formal garden's strict symmetry, the English garden combined perspective with the individual spectator in movement. No one could observe the garden from all perspectives simultaneously, nor from a central point of perspective. Each corner passed offered a new panorama that could be seen only from that specific viewpoint. The individual spectator firmly believed that his or her perspective was never beyond control and never became dangerous and unpredictable. Likewise, there were no visible borders that revealed to the spectator that the number of possible new and unexpected positions that could be taken, the private discoveries that could be made, was actually limited. Any space is supposed to be accessible at any time and place, spontaneously and immediately, as determined by the individual.

The park employs a number of material elements (trees, rocks, cement, iron, etc.) in order to imitate the English garden and its cultural landscape. Thus, as a complex iconic sign the park refers to nature, specifying itself as part of the surrounding world that is not man-made, but can come under spontaneous human control, unencumbered and unconflicting. The park can therefore become a mediating factor in the city, something that the originators of the English garden had, in all probability, never intended.

When the scenic landscape as found in modern urban culture is the highest category of 'nature', then nature's meanings are organized so that nature is, first and foremost, spatial – a delimited object built out of phenomena that are not man-made and have physical extension. This landscape is to be approached and controlled both for our physical survival and our leisure activities with the effect of supporting the construction of our identity as individual and sovereign subjects *vis-à-vis* nature.

But this way of delimiting culture from nature on predominantly cultural grounds is changing under the influence of the problems springing from this strategy of mutual demarcation. An overall perception that is not primarily spatial is reinforced by the ecological debate that revives conceptions from earlier periods in our cultural history and also has an echo in modern physics and biology, which are preoccupied with forces and relations of non-spatial nature that fit into the schemata of causality. Also, it can be seen by the naked eye that the border between culture and nature is on the move. The unspoiled landscape is overrun by tourists, while other untamed natural elements wreak havoc in the form of culturally created natural disasters (holes in the ozone layer, nuclear waste, disease); besides, natural sciences relativize the relationship between the subjective and the objective, and thus the clear differentiation between the subject and the surrounding space has also reached a larger audience through the modern media. Nature as merely a landscape with space as its dominant basic category gradually begins to fade into the background. Thus the culture's history is a continuous negotiation of its border with nature, including the categorization and values underlying it; see Figure 7.1.

At one time, the park held an important function in this historical development, but its social role and relation to nature have gradually changed. During the early days, when the first parks were under construction, the discovery of bacteria changed our understanding of epidemic diseases in our major cities, and the park's hygienic function lost its importance. Means of transport and communications developed rapidly as the cities grew and further penetrated the open landscape that the park had originally been intended to replace. The park's aesthetic value was no longer the only or best imitation of nature: the view from the train or car, life in the suburbs, as well as films, travel, nature reserves, etc. provided equal opportunities to find locations suited for the city dweller's projection of the urban culture's perception of nature. Simultaneously, the park occupied, along with private gardens, lawns and other green areas, a clean niche within the new, ecological understanding of urban nature. The park's physical appearance and extent and its imitation of a harmoniously evolved natural landscape became less important than its social function. Instead, the park became merely one among many areas in the city's organization of public space, and just one of many alternatives for human recreation. It is primarily this function which the park's sign-system reinforces; the park no longer needs to imitate nature.

Semiotic analysis of culture

Despite its historical–descriptive character, this presentation is based on a general notion of the steps in which a semiotic analysis of culture is made, and the nature of the basic problems that are investigated (Posner 1991). In the following summary, we will use the findings in the previous section to concretize more systematically some of the signs that characterize the park as a delimited cultural text at a particular point in time, and we will also outline the course away from imitation of nature that the park takes during a cultural semiotic analysis.

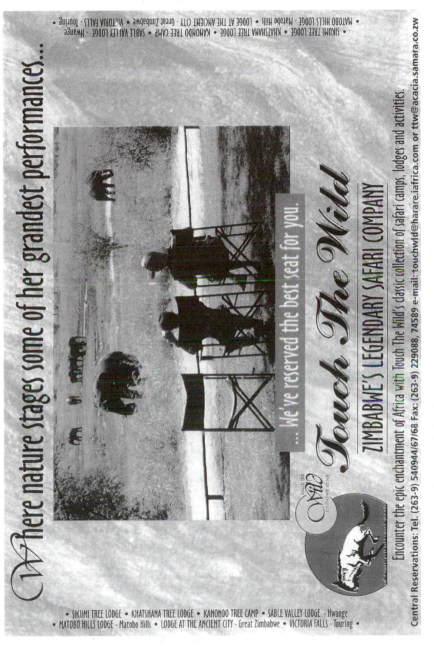

Figure 7.1 An advertisement for a scenic landscape.

The analysis is made in four steps, each of which can be formulated as a question:

1 How is the text *delimited* so that it can be analysed as a specific cultural text?
2 In which *cultural processes* does the text in question draw the border with nature?
3 Which *codes* are involved in these processes?
4 Which are the basic *presumptions* of the coded processes?

Delimitation

As argued above, culture is basically a border we define collectively in relation to nature. It is formed with the help of the particular human semiotic abilities which integrate those facets of the natural foundation that support the construction of a human surrounding world. Human language and other arbitrary sign-systems cause the border to be a shifting entity. To delimit a phenomenon so that it becomes a cultural text is, then, to delimit it so that its role in border-drawing, in the integration process and in subsequent changes can be understood.

The delimitation can therefore not be determined empirically on the basis of the text's medium of expression (verbal, visual, etc.) or its physical limits in space (walls, drains, streets, etc.). Although we can easily determine that we are dealing with a spatial phenomenon, this does not reveal anything about the cultural *process*. As the object is itself part of the culture, its placing in the culture's discourses (images, reports, film, literature, political arguments, etc.) is as important as its physical appearance in determining its delimitation (see Chapter 4). It is on the basis of its discursive and material manifestation that we make a global delimitation of the city park as a European or European-inspired phenomenon and a diachronic delimitation from *c.* 1800 to *c.* 1925, the age of industrialism, during which cities developed at a break-neck pace. And it is through this that we can consider the city park synchronically and place it in relation to other culturally meaningful areas (work areas, private areas, interior areas, non-urban areas, etc.). But only rarely can we use the same delimitations to cover all aspects of a phenomenon's cultural semiotic role.

Where do we find the criteria to determine which features of the object and its discursive network are relevant to its delimitation as text? Since the text must satisfy our three previously formulated necessary conditions for the culture-forming border demarcation, it is these requirements that hold here. The delimitation, then, becomes apparent from the answers to three questions:

1 *How is the object delimited in time and space in a contactual universe, so that its particular processing of the border with nature is thereby expressed?* The park

and garden as physically delimited areas belong to the long cultural history of mastery over nature, as well as being closely connected to the history of housing construction and – to use modern terminology – real-estate development; the modern city park is a part of a more recent, particularly European, history, as mastery over nature through an aestheticization of the natural space, and through a reorganization of time and space that places greater weight on social categories (nature connected to public space and leisure time) than on natural categories (the changing of the day and year). The individual park's physical borders with the surrounding urban space are directly determined by what a city can make available as public space for recreation, combining aestheticized nature with technology (e.g. drainage) and economic means (e.g. purchase of land space). The park's physical borders are therefore also its textual borders.

2   *How is the object delimited so that a particular use of the body is thereby expressed?* From its earliest days, the city park has offered us both physical and mental health: relaxation, physical excercise, casual clothing. Simultaneously, the park's aesthetics is an invitation to the individual to experience indirect mastery over nature by moving his or her own body around. The park is a place to discover that one's body is *my* body, and that one is physically present in an unconstrained social community. This is why there are certain rules that set borders for bodily sovereignty: don't block anyone's way, don't indulge in sex on the lawn, don't spend the night in the park, etc. The opposition between the body as nature and the body as culture is harmonized in the park. Again, the park's textual borders follow its physical ones.

3   *How is the object delimited so that it enters into a narrative mediation process?* The cultural history of the park and the garden has always been a history of the mediation between culture and nature. The park has formed an image of nature that we use to define our place in nature. In Europe, that place became quite strong with the arrival of the Renaissance and the seventeenth-century garden. The city park, on the other hand, is less a natural image than a function of the city itself – hygienic, aesthetic and social–psychological. The dangers lurking in the park at night do not spring from nature, but are generated by the city itself.

The park does not depict nature in its original state, but rather imitates gardens, landscapes, or images of these, because its function is not to mediate culture and nature, but to *displace* the opposition between nature and culture to the opposition between the urban dweller's collective natural and cultural need for air, light, and 'being oneself' on the one hand, and the city's man-made obstacles to these necessities. This opposition is now *mediated* in the park's physical experience of simultaneous privacy and community, simultaneous personal freedom and confinement to a demarcated area, and this process occurs on an individual's own conditions.

The park thus contributes to obscuring the fundamental border between nature and culture, and finally serves to remove us from those elements of nature that are beyond our control. The park takes part in two stories: the story of urban alienation from the relation with nature, in which the park is both a result of this relation and a means to overcome it (cf. Schmitt 1990); and the story of the emergence of the modern individual subject who subordinates nature to the individual's choices, responsibilities and experiences (cf. Green 1990). Through this, the park becomes a model or, in Lotman's terminology, a secondary sign-system.

A demarcation that fulfils this criterion does not contribute to delimiting each park as a specific text, but rather establishes a broader historical border around the park as cultural phenomenon, open to understanding its historical (pre)conditions and seeing its gradual removal from the nature it depicts, to an increased dependence on the less visible function as just one recreation area among others in an urban culture.

The park border as text can therefore follow its physical limits within the city's area, as long as we conduct a synchronous analysis of the park's signs, codes and structures in relation to time and space and physical behaviour. We will continue with this analysis. But a diachronic analysis of its role in the regrouping of the culture's perceptions of nature and its role as a cultural model requires that the borders be extended. The same holds true for a synchronic analysis of the park's role as social space in relation to other urban recreation areas. One cannot make a delimitation that is common for all relevant elements of a city park's role as text.

Cultural processes

The next step in analysing the delimitation of the text concentrates on the text's role in the cultural exchange processes that we use to process the border with nature. These processes are in general characterized by three types of activities.

The first of these activities is the *material* production process, in which objects and materials are produced and consumed using tools ranging from stone axes to robots. This process defines the borders of a culture's social contactual universe, and places each individual object in a particular contactual universe. It ensures that the cultural processes can be reproduced or *repeated*. Only when material events do not simply occur, but allow themselves to be repeated, do they become part of a production process. This integration can take place through technological development.

The city park also results from a material production process. Parks are constructed and maintained using familiar technology and labour methods that have proven effective in logging, mining, agriculture and (rail-)road construction. The ground is drained and cranes are brought in to plant, relocate and remove large trees, so that the park may function as was initially intended. Therefore the 'production' of the park as material phenomenon does not shift the borders of human control over nature, and the park's border is not fenced off by material obstacles, nor by guards, keys, or passwords to protect secret and possibly dangerous technology. The border is, first and foremost, determined by symbolic criteria, defined by a simple opposition in meaning: 'entrance' (door, gate, opening) versus 'non-entrance' (hedge, fence, wall), and institutional criteria (appropriation of funds, pricing, expropriation, etc.). This material production of the park is not relevant to its particular cultural identity, but is a material precondition for it. Had we analysed a nuclear power plant, our findings would have been quite dissimilar.

Another type of activity is the *semiotic* production process. With indexical, iconic and symbolic signs and the codes that govern their uses, we delimit what can be perceived within a culture, so that it can refer to something else. This process, in other words, ensures that phenomena are identified as something specific and can thus be *recognized* as such. The border for recognition lies in control over the codes: cryptic writing becomes legible as soon as the code is broken.

To what does the city park refer that we can identify and recognize, and which signs and codes dominate this process? The park has, in James Gibson's words (1979: 221), a layout that appeals to particular aspects of the semiotic skills that the park's visitors possess. The park in its spatial design is, as mentioned earlier, an *iconic* sign for the idealized landscape. This iconic quality ensures that it can be recognized instantly through its imitation of a scenic landscape, and that it dominates over the arbitrary or conventional, since the *symbolic* sign plays only a lesser part here: entrance to the park requires no fee, except perhaps a so-called symbolic contribution; and once inside, one can find only a few practical verbal directions, some rules of conduct, a few names carved into the trees, and some signs conveying messages like 'Wet paint', 'Ice cream'.

Indexical signs are, on the other hand, employed in a special way. They are used so that the *designations* dominate over the *reagents* (see Chapter 3, p. 32ff.). Naturally, we guide ourselves by reagents such as smell, sight and sound – we stand up from the park bench to catch sight of a bird we have heard, and move out of the way for a person we know will soon pass us from behind by the sound of footsteps on the path. This, however, has much less relevance to the park specifically than to our general orientation within the surrounding world. Since the park is intended to *function as* rather than *be* nature, the reagents for natural processes are recoded. By planting perennials, mowing the lawn, and clearing fallen leaves, the reagents for the changing seasons are reduced; and by harmonizing colours, differences in size, and the balance between rock, water and plants, the reagents for nature's own processes are reduced. Instead, these phenomena function primarily as designations which lozalize a non-urban space within the city in relation to human presence: 'Look, this is nature.' Further, the reagents of human design (the placing of the trees, the curves of the pond, the twisting of the paths, the colour of the fence and benches, etc.) imitate the reagents of nature's forces and thus become, first and foremost, man-made designations that also say, 'Look, this is nature.'

Simultaneously, the reagents for the city's presence are removed as much as possible: within the park, the noise emanating from the streets outside is muffled, and the cars racing past are almost out of sight. This means that it can also be difficult to find signs which localize and mark the park's borders, and one's own location in the park as a whole. This is so, even though there may be road signs and maps; such signs usually direct visitors around the park rather than directing them out of it. Most designations merely localize the space as non-urban; they do not clearly delimit the borders of the park, and invite one to enter rather than exit.

This layout provides a special semiotic appeal to the park's users. The reduction of symbolic signs, which rest on and dictate collective consensus, loosens the stable everyday semiotic conventions. Here there are no strict rules imposed on visitors, nor are they required to pay an entrance fee, talk or speak in a particular way, or use specific formal signs and codes, let alone dress codes. The particular quality of the iconic signs, depicting a landscape that has been adapted to fit the dimensions of the human body, grants easy access to thoughts, images and daydreams that immediately satisfy physical pleasures and fill the closed space with infinite possibilities, an experience of infinity that is reinforced by the park's poorly marked outer edges, deluding us into believing the park experience to be without beginning or end.

As Bühler and Piaget have emphasized, it is a necessary condition for our continued existence as physical subjects that we *always* use indexical signs to localize ourselves in the surrounding world and thereby determine its realistic character (Larsen 1991b, 1994a). The remaking of this fundamental process, here placed under individual control, constitutes the basic appeal of the park. Because the reagents' role is de-emphasized, it need not be fatal to overlook or misinterpret one or more reagents. Here, we can simply apologize after accidentally colliding with someone; the same would not be true had we been run over by a car in the street. The greater priority given to the designations, along with the removal of clear border markers, enables the individual freely to produce his or her own localizing designations. The paths do not clearly refer to something, but simply point to something indefinite that none the less remains within the framework of the reliable and easily interpreted iconic sign-system.

Each individual can delimit his or her own contactual universe, at his or her own free will, simply by moving his or her own body, sit down, or leave a scene at any point in time. This corresponds to Bateson's notion of games as explained above (p. 179f.). The park as a complex sign for naturalized individual freedom is therefore valid only for time-delimited visits, even though the park appeals to the visitor to forget the limits of time and space. But when other localities take over the park's function, e.g. through tourism, which offers landscapes elsewhere and turns them into parklike sceneries of larger dimensions, and when different leisure activities and places compete with the park, then its borders can be as easily forgotten.

Thus we reach the cultural process's third type of activity, which consists of an *institutional* organization of phenomena so that they can be collectively *acknowledged* to have a certain status and value. Written and unwritten laws play a role here, as do transgressions of such laws, which demonstrate that any acknowledgement has its limits and can be punished by expulsion from the institutionalized community.

In the city park, what must be acknowledged to make an important text in our culture is the mediation between nature and culture it offers. Many parks contain conventional symbolic signs that provide a collective inter-pretational framework for the individual material experience of being in the park. Contributing to this symbolic experience are monumental gates, sta-tues and memorials to great heroes of the past, and parts of the park that date back to the seventeenth-century garden. But these stand in clear con-trast to the park's own sign-system, which is centred on the individual visitors and their inividual and casual strolling. The symbolic signs are more likely to be the surviving remains of earlier phases of the park's history rather than integrated elements of a modern city. Neither have the park's iconic qualities been successful in upholding its particular status as text in the urban culture, imitating an aspect of nature we now have easy access to elsewhere.

More important are the indexical signs that support the park's function as public space for expression of individually guided physical behaviour, regard-less of whether this behaviour relates to nature or not. When a society insti-tutionalizes leisure time through common rules, as has been the case since the nineteenth century, it must simultaneously provide a common, i.e. public, leisure space, a place where one can lay down that there are no institutiona-lized rules for behaviour, save for unwritten behavioural norms. Here, an annual carnival would no longer suffice; rather, what is needed is a fixed place where one can always go and always do whatever one feels like doing (cf. Larsen 1997d).

The park, and increasingly the street, have become such spaces, primarily to those who have both work and leisure time, broadly speaking the middle class (Larsen 1997d). But public space is, like the street, difficult to control, particularly at night, when the park has neither a formal nor an informal institutionalized status. The scenic landscape's offer of urban mediation between the need for experience of individual self-expression and the growing formal organization of everyday life lost its indisputable collective validity around 1925, when functionalist urban planning took shape. Other public leisure areas, both within and outside the city limits, become equally impor-tant but alternative possibilities for mediation: clubs, cafés, shopping malls, theme parks, etc., all of them products of mass-consumption culture. The park's identity as privileged city space is no longer acknowledged to the same extent, and its written and unwritten rules are constantly broken: as people walk in the park they pick flowers they are not supposed to, homeless people spend the night in the park, and the park attracts drug dealers, muggers and rapists.

In the first instance, the park gained its identity as textual entity in the urban culture through semiotic production, particularly tied to its iconic and indexical qualities. Secondarily, its particular textual characteristics are confirmed through the urban culture's institutionalized organization of time as leisure time. Only to a modest extent is the park defined as a specific text through a specific inherent form of material production process. But without all three types of cultural processes, the park would not exist. When the park's role as iconic sign is pushed into the background and its role as nature-neutral public space is emphasized, an understanding of the park as cultural text will require other defining and demarcating features, in which the semiotic properties we have highlighted remain valid, though seen from a new perspective: the development of space for leisure as a specific form of mass-consumption.

Conventions and processual codes

The three types of cultural processes are realized by codes that connect signs, their objects and sign users (see Chapter 2). These codes include, first of all, *conventions*: rules that can be changed through a conscious effort from within the culture, e.g. eating habits, fashion, traffic signals, sexual habits. Semiotic analyses of modern cultural phenomena have primarily been concerned with conventions such as the examples mentioned. In the city park, important conventions are intertwined and connected to spontaneous physical behaviour; this is manifested in the dress code, to name one example. With clothing conventions ranging from casual dress to toplessness, the park's users turn their bodies into signs for 'relaxed naturalness'. Conventions have changed over time and differ from country to country; illuminatingly, this holds true particularly for conventions governing the amount of flesh that may be revealed.

Second, the codes include the actual *processual codes*; these cannot be changed unless the cultural text concerned, and perhaps the entire culture to which it belongs, changes as well, e.g. when the codes for the relationship between religion and justice or between gender and society are changed. Particularly relevant to the city park are the processual codes that regulate the relationship between space and the sensory apparatus, which defines the scenic landscape and the body's place within it, and the relationship between labour and leisure, which defines the park as a social space. These processual codes govern the relationship with nature in, respectively, perception and the labour process. The scenic landscape transforms space, using the human body as yardstick, and the separation of labour and leisure transforms time into a social category in relation to the human body's needs.

Basic requirements

When delimiting the park as a cultural text, we described the three preconditions that must be met for the formation of culture to result in specific human cultures. These three requirements mark the principal borders of a culture. They form a broader foundation for the individual texts and are well known from many cultural analyses of time and space, of body and subject, and of action and narrative in modern Western culture. We will, therefore, add here only a few final comments on these requirements:

1 *Time and space*: The spatial perception which supports the park as text is the mechanical perception of nature's three-dimensional space, separate from time. Space is static; its events and phenomena follow patterns of action and reaction, and it can be placed under rational control. Time is structured by the opposition between organic and natural time and between mechanically and socially categorized time. The park is nature that has been manipulated to satisfy social needs for specific human experiences.
2 *Body and subject*: The human subject is generally perceived as a subject with a physical behaviour that obeys its conscious intentions which, in the park, take the form of moving around following the individual's spontaneous desires.
3 *Action and action model*: The narrative structures organizing such a subject's identity-building emphasizes the individual's attempts to 'become oneself', and to 'have the situation under control', regardless of whether these attempts are successful or not. A walk in the park is an encounter with nature, shaped so that we are reconciled with the culture for which we are responsible but which, at the same time, threatens our control over ourselves and our surrounding world.

The contents of these preconditions indicate a phenomenon's cultural affiliations, its cultural identity. Cultural phenomena which, as the park, rest on these preconditions belong or can belong to the same culture. This is one reason why the nature depicted by the park does not provide an alternative to the city, as had been originally intended by its planners and builders, but is in fact part of the city itself and can, based on the same sign-structure, shift its function from imitating nature to providing an open public space for self-expression. Other phenomena with other preconditions will therefore conflict with or remain outside of the culture concerned. What is most relevant to us is not the relatively well-known content of the three preconditions, but the way in which they not only mark the border between culture and nature but, as stated previously, the border between what belongs to a particular culture and what is alien to it. This border is marked differently, depending on which of the three preconditions it deviates from.

1   What is outside a culture may be regarded as *extracultural*, i.e. outside the human surrounding world in the form familiar to us. None of the three preconditions apply in this case: the extracultural cannot be localized in time and space, nor can it be connected to familiar forms of physical behaviour and subjectivity, or to familiar narratives and stories. It is simply unrecognizable. The invention and development of technologies such as the microscope and binoculars have contributed to shifting the border between the cultural and the extracultural, possibly in the form of a hypothesis of what the extracultural is and what it means. At a given point in time, such a technology is able to indicate new temporal and spatial conditions for observation, and bring about a particular and possibly new form of physical behaviour, e.g. by giving greater priority to sight or by determining the subject's role in relation to objective observation. Technology can also develop new narratives as action models, serving as a 'manual' revolutionizing the more limited way in which reality was earlier viewed. Such extremes do not apply in the park.

2   What is outside a culture may be regarded as *anticultural*, belonging to another culture opposed to the given culture. This holds in particular for cultures which possess stories or perceptions of body and subjectivity that are in conflict with a given culture's tales and ideas of subjectivity, but they do not necessarily conflict with other temporal and spatial concepts. On a large scale, this holds true of the oppositions of the cold war, and on a smaller scale for crime in the park.

3   What is outside a culture may be regarded as an *alternative culture* in relation to a given culture by embodying another culture which is simply different from the given culture, and which may be a positive or negative ideal for changing the given culture, possibly through migration into and out of that culture. Typically, alternative cultures contain the same stories and the same subjects, but localize them more or less vaguely in alternative temporal and spatial zones. One example is immigration to Western Europe from non-European sites in the hope to escape from impeding temporal and spatial structures at home but without changing their basic narratives or concepts of body and subject. Another is urban dwellers who move to the countryside striving to avoid the city's temporal and spatial structures, be they regarded as mechanical–rational or as flickering scenes of nomadic life. In its early days, the city park represented such an alternative to urban culture.

4   What is outside a culture may be regarded as a *subcultural* phenomenon in relation to a given culture, thereby occupying a peripheral yet relatively well-delimited corner of the given and dominant culture, which itself can be placed peripherally in relation to other, more dominant cultures. This cultural echelon allows exchanges between the different cultures.

Subcultures formed by ethnic minorities, youth, or other distinct groups can cross the interior boundaries of the dominant culture and may then assume the role of anticultural or alternative-cultural groups. These subcultures typically invest other stories and perhaps other subjects into the same temporal and spatial structure as that which reigns in the dominant culture. As an open social space, the park provides a meeting place for various subcultures, each delimiting their space and physical subjectivity with different indexical signs.

A delimitation of the cultural text in relation to these cultural fringes completes our cultural-semiotic analysis. The park has changed through history: originally intended simply to imitate nature, it became a privileged cultural text in the urban culture, and then (using many of the same signs) became part of the city's delimitation of public space for spontaneous self-expression, while simultaneously collecting both anti- and subcultural features.

Cultural borders and cultural change

Culture is formed along the borders of what we perceive to be nature. Encounters with landscapes, familiar as well as unknown, serve to reinforce this border to us and revive the three fundamental requirements for culture-forming border-drawing. Mediation means here that not everything which functions as nature is called nature by us, and not everything which we call nature actually functions as such. The only certainty is that nature in some way or another always participates in the culture's semiotic processes. Culture never stops telling tales about this, or it would not be culture.

We can now specify the three requirements for culture's delimitation in relation to its natural basis. If these conditions remain unsatisfied, a culture cannot be generated in such a way that it is embodied in particular actions and norms, conventions and codes, and therefore cannot be generated at all as a specifically human culture:

1 *Time and space*: The border must be drawn so that the culture's sign-systems can localize phenomena in time and space within a contactual universe in which they can be exchanged.
2 *Body and subject*: The border must be drawn so that bodies become subjects that can engage in discourse on intersubjective conditions.
3 *Action and action model*: The border must be drawn so that bodies are brought into relation with one another and other time/space phenomena, and embodied in actions and processes that allow culture's basic models to receive a narrative structure.

These foundational requirements also entail views on cultural dynamics. Cultural change follows from a new way of localizing phenomena in time and space (e.g. the relation between natural and supernatural); from a breaking up of the interrelationship between body and subject (e.g. the shaping of the modern individual before and after the French Revolution); and from the change of normative actions (e.g. the growing importance of ethical values in environmental politics). Cultural transformations are most radical when all three aspects are subject to change simultaneously. Cultural conflicts are most radical when issues derived from one or more of the three requirements are opposed: for example, the clash between indigenous cultures and immigrant cultures in the same social space. In an era of globalization such conflicts will be ubiquitous and will shape the life conditions of most humans for many years to come. Whether good or bad, this will be the cultural reality of the twenty-first century. We need to develop tools to analyse this situation. Cultural semiotics is one such tool.

Glossary

The glossary contains the key concepts discussed in the book. Concepts that appear as independent entries are italicized, followed by '(s.v.)', as are names that are listed in the biographies.

Abduction, deduction, induction Following *Charles Sanders Peirce* (s.v.), these three notions define the three basic types of inference. *Abduction* (also called retroduction and hypothesis in Peirce) is a weak inference leading to an open hypothesis concerning a surprising and apparently inexplicable phenomenon. Peirce presents this simple example:

> All the beans from this bag are white
> These beans are white
> These beans are from this bag

The example shows what it means for an inference to be weak: the stock of beans might consist of 100 open bags of beans and the one referred to might be any of them.
Deduction is exemplified by Peirce as follows:

> All the beans from this bag are white
> These beans are from this bag
> These beans are white

Finally, *induction* is illustrated thus:

> These beans are from this bag
> These beans are white
> All the beans in this bag are white

According to Peirce, the research process follows this scheme: Hypothesis (abduction), deduction and induction: (1) An unexpected phenomenon is observed. In order to explain it a hypothesis is established (the abductive stage of the research process). (2) Through analysis the researcher makes explicit all the phenomena that are necessarily derived from the hypothesis (the deductive stage). (3) An inductive procedure (samples, tests, interviews, polls, etc.) reveals whether the consequences detected by analysis actually obtain.

Abstractive relevance   The process of perception through which a given phenomenon acquires a specific identity. In the process we select the features relevant for the identification by making an abstraction of the rest. The relevant features constitute a relatively distinct system attributing a stable identity to the phenomenon in spite of its different manifestations. A thing that changes because it is used or an ageing person can still be considered to be the same thing and person respectively. The process depends to a certain extent on the *context* (s.v.). In certain contexts we focus only on features that allow us to identify a sound as a human voice as opposed to a mechanical sound; in other contexts we may observe only features characterizing the sound as a manifestation of Danish, not of another language or of animal 'speech'. The concept is coined by *Karl Bühler* (s.v.) and is part of the basis for the definition of *distinctive features* (s.v.).

Affordance   The structured possibilities for perception and movement offered by the *surrounding world* (s.v.) to a human observer. They constitute the objective foundation for the structures we project on to the surrounding world in order to orient ourselves and to move (*James Gibson* (s.v.)).

Arbitrary, arbitrariness   Arbitrary means deliberate or conventional. *Ferdinand de Saussure* (s.v.) makes a distinction between three types of arbitrariness. (1) The most important concerns the relation between the expression and the content of individual verbal signs which is simply called *arbitrary*. Being arbitrary means that there is no 'natural' reason why the sequence of *phonemes* /r-o-l-i/ in Danish means 'quiet' and Swedish means 'funny'; in both languages this relation relies entirely on the convention that defines respectively Danish and Swedish. The convention may only change from one language to another, but not from one individual to another; it is intersubjectively compulsory. (2) The relation between the sign as a whole and the object it refers to is sometimes labelled *radically arbitrary* by Saussure. This type of arbitrariness indicates that sign and object have no necessary immanent relation. A more usual term is *unmotivated* (s.v.). (3) The relationship respectively between signs, between content elements or between expression elements is characterized as either absolutely arbitrary or relatively arbitrary. Signs or sign-elements that enter the same *paradigm* (s.v.) are called *absolutely arbitrary* because the form of one element from the paradigm does not determine other paradigmatic elements. The occurrence of one or more singular forms in a paradigm does not determine what the plural forms look like. If signs or sign-elements occur in a syntactic chain they are *relatively arbitrary*, because the occurrence of one element partly determines the following elements (after three consonants at the beginning of a

syllable in Danish you must have a vowel, but it could be any vowel).
(See *combination*.)

Articulation, double articulation, first and second articulation   The
distinction between the first and second articulations of language was
introduced by the French linguist André Martinet in *Éléments de linguistique générale* (1960). The first articulation divides the acoustical manifestation of language in the *smallest meaning-carrying units* (words, *morphemes*
(s.v.)), whereas the second articulation produces a division in the *smallest
meaning-differentiating units* (*phonemes* (s.v.)), that is units without meaning
but serving the function of marking differences in meaning, as for example the vowels in *stool, steel, style*. According to Martinet and most other
linguists, the specificity of language and its power as a semiotic system
rely on the fact that it possesses both articulations; the effect of especially
the second articulation is that language with a very limited number of
phonemes can construct a practically infinite number of meanings.

Biosphere   The entire universe of living organisms and their interaction
(see *semiosphere*).

Code, structural code, processual code   A rule according to which
given elements are selected and combined to generate new elements.
Structural codes are codes by which elements make up static systems and
are often called the *structure* (s.v.) of the system. A distinction is often
made between *digital* codes and *analog* codes. Digital codes structure elements according to absolute differences (either–or relations), as for example between *phonemes* (s.v.) defined by *distinctive features* (s.v.); analog
codes organize elements through gradual approximation (more-or-less
relations), as for example a green colour that can be mixed to become
more and more similar to the colour of grass. *Processual codes* are the rules
by which such structures are interrelated. Meaning is generated when
structural codes for elements of expression and for elements of contents as
separate systems interact with processual codes for the relation between
expression and content and thus generate signs.

Combination   According to *Roman Jakobson* (s.v.), one of the two fundamental operations of speech. From this point of view a verbal *utterance*
(s.v.) is produced in a *coded* (s.v.) operation through a selection from a
paradigm (s.v.) of elements defined by mutual *similarity* (s.v.) and *difference*
(s.v.). They are selected in order to be combined into a *syntagm* (s.v.),
where they are connected by *contiguity* (see *contact*). The combination is
governed by rules of combination, so-called syntactical rules. The following exemplifies both the selection from the paradigm and the combination into a syntagm:

in the morning	the women	are always awake
during the day	the girls	rarely snooze
in the evening	the men	often slumber
at night	the boys	never wake up

For Jakobson the poetic function of language projects the paradigmatic principle of selection on to the syntactic dimension of combination, making the interplay between similarity and difference also the predominant principle for the combination, as for example in proverbial phrases like *easy come, easy go*. Here the similarity of the two syntactical units on the expression plane and the differences on the content plane are more important than the sequential order (see *contact* and *metaphor*).

Commutation, commutation test   According to *Louis Hjelmslev* (s.v.), a commutation is a correlation on one of two planes of languages related to a correlation on the other plane, for example the correlation between /h/ and /c/ in *hat* and *cat* is related to a correlation between the contents of *hat* and *cat*. A commutation is observed through the commutation test – when the exchange of an element on one plane generates a difference on the other. The exchange of /h/ for /c/ in *hat* produces a difference on the content plane. Through the commutation test elements of a paradigm are identified. Hjelmslev also claims that an exchange of elements on the content plane shows a commutation on the expression plane. If we have the combination of *human + child + female* and change *female* for *masculine*, then the expression plane will change *girl* for *boy*.

Conceptual stage   The build-up of a *surrounding world* (s.v.) by abstract relations between phenomena, as for example mathematical calculi and other logical operations. The third step in the cognitive development based on the *senso-motoric* (s.v.) and the *symbolic* stage (s.v.) (*Jean Piaget* (s.v.)).

Contact, contactual universe   Contact occurs when signs, sign users and the objects referred to are situated and interrelated in the same physical space, called a *contactual universe*. Their interrelationship is established by the *designator function* (s.v.) (*Karl Bühler* (s.v.)). A more common term for contact is *contiguity*, as in the definition of the indexical *sign* (s.v.), of metonymy as opposed to *metaphor* (s.v.), and of *combination* (s.v.) as opposed to selection. In these instances the simultaneous presence of elements in the same contactual universe is necessary for the production of meaning: the metonymy presupposes contiguity between whole and part in order for us to say *I take a glass* instead of *I take a glass of beer*; the indexical sign presupposes the co-presence of sign and object in the same material universe; and the combination works because of the co-presence of signs in the same syntactical sequence.

Content, figuræ of content, content form, content substance   In structural linguistics the distinction between content and expression is essential to the description of language. Following *Louis Hjelmslev* (s.v.), it is the very first division to be performed by the linguist. According to *structuralism* (s.v.), it is important to regard the content as a structure of the same type as the *expression* (s.v.), that is as made up of minimal units, *figuræ of content*, and therefore analyse them in the same way. First Hjelmslev makes a distinction between the formal organization of the content, the so-called *content form*, and the *content substance*. The content form is the way in which the minimal semantic units, the *figuræ* of content, are interrelated into a system. Each natural language may structure the surrounding world or the social experience differently. Hjelmslev's example has become a classic:

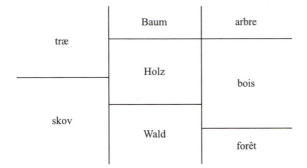

Here, the content form of each language is defined by the boundaries between the semantic boxes, whereas the content substance is made up by the individual entities of each box referring to phenomena in the surrounding world. The demonstration of the specific lexical structure of different languages seems obvious. However, it is difficult to see that the following claims made by Hjelmslev and other structuralists are justifiable: (1) in natural languages the substance presupposes the form; and (2) form can be analysed without taking the subsance into account. The figura of content is a conception that is created as an analogue to the *figura of expression* (s.v.), that is the expression units below the sign level used as building blocks of the sign. But it is highly questionable to assume the existence of content below the sign level.

Context   The concrete setting or situational environment of a *sign* (s.v.) or a *text* (s.v.) comprising more than the semiotic systems to which the sign or the text belongs. A literary text is embedded in a social context constituted by verbal, visual, auditive, gestural and other signs (see *co-text*).

Context of effective definitions   The explicit conditions for the construction of a certain phenomenon to define it as a specific *structure* (s.v.) (a population may be structured according to political affiliation and thus on political grounds). From this point of view a given phenomenon may be characterized by several types of structures depending on the conditions for the construction of structures (Raymond Boudon) (opposed to the *context of intentional definitions* (s.v.)).

Context of intentional definitions   The implicit assumptions concerning the immanent identity of an object that make us interpret the *structure* (s.v.) of the object as the expression of that identity. This point of view implies that one structure only is the true structure of a given phenomenon. Thus the members of a nation may be structured according to income, to age, etc., but only one structure which organizes them according to the essential properties of the nation will be the true one (Raymond Boudon) (opposed to *context of effective definitions* (s.v.)).

Convention, conventional   The cultural code we can make conscious and change through deliberate choice (eating habits, class-room behaviour, ways of communication, etc.). In *Charles Sanders Peirce* (s.v.) *conventional* means that the sign–object relationship is constituted by *habits* (s.v.) (see also *arbitrary* and *speech acts*).

Co-refer, co-reference   The precondition for the understanding of meaning is that elements that build up the structure of meaning not only produce specific meaning but also share a reference to a presupposed *life world* (s.v.) that contains conceptions shared by the sign users (of time and space, of subjectivity, of motivations for action, etc.). The elements are said to *co-refer* to such a universe.

Co-text   The concrete setting or situational environment of a *sign* (s.v.) or a *text* (s.v.) comprising only the semiotic systems to which the sign or the text belongs. The co-text of the words of a novel is the other verbal signs of the novel (see *context*).

Culture, cultural semiotics   Culture is the process by which human beings define and operate a *limit* in relation to the natural foundation of our lives and to what we conceive of as the non-human part of our surrounding world. This process unfolds through intertwined sub-processes: *material* production, *symbolic* production and *institutional* organization, sub-processes that build up a delimited *coded* (s.v.) and *conventional* (s.v.) cultural *universe* (s.v.). Every cultural universe is based on *presuppositions* concerning time and space, body and subject, actions and models of actions which allows us, through the sub-processes, to specify the universe as a universe for human culture: if we cannot articulate time and space in such a way that bodies can be situated as subjects interrelated in time and space through actions with a shared acceptability, the sub-processes do not generate culture. *Cultural semiotics* investigates the cultural process, its presuppositions and the structure of the cultural universe, taking the symbolic processes as its point of departure.

Deduction   (see *abduction*).

Deixis   The *designator function* (s.v.) of verbal language as carried out by specific verbal *designator elements* (s.v.), as for example pronouns, adverbs, tense. Through deixis a verbal *utterance* (s.v.) is anchored in the *enunciative now* (s.v.) (on indices and indexical signs, see *sign*).

Designation   (see *sign*).

Designator element   Any element in a given semiotic system that carries out *designator functions* (s.v.) in a particular text. Different designator elements can manifest the same designator function, as for example the function to indicate the presence of a thing in our material environment (real designator function): in this case, the designator element in a gestural sign system may be the index finger, in a verbal sign system the word *there*, in a cinematographic sign system the zoom, in other visual sign-systems an arrow.

Designator function   The function of delimiting a shared space where sign, object and sign users are situated in relation to each other. All semiotic systems must be able to perform this function in order to *refer* (s.v.) and to communicate. However, they use different *designator elements* (s.v.). The designator function shows three aspects attributing a different status to the shared space: through the *real* designator function sign, object and sign users are situated in the same *material* space (for example carried out by a gestural designator element like the *index finger*); through the *discursive* designator function the three components are situated in relation to an already delimited *text* (s.v.) (for example carried out by a verbal designator element such as 'As referred to *above*' or the abbreviation '(s.v.)', both referring to the same text as that of the designator element itself); through the *ideal* designator function the three components are situated in relation to *essentially different* discursive universes (for example carried out by cinematographic designator element *change of colour* to indicate a shift from dream to reality or from memory to the actual presence). Through these three functions a semiotic system is capable of delimiting (1) the space where the sign users are actually present, (2) what can be repeated and thus given a certain cohesiveness, and (3) universes with different ontological status.

Diagram   The second of *Charles Sanders Peirce*'s (s.v.) three subdivisions of the iconic sign (see *image*, *metaphor* and *sign*). A diagram is characterized by the common relations it holds with the object or the state of affairs it refers to. Both a city map and a statistical curve showing the change of GNP over time represent a similarity with the object in terms of quantitative scale, for example 1:100 (1 cm on the map corresponds to 1 m of the object; 1 cm on the curve corresponds to £100 million). The statistical curve demonstrates that diagrams are not built on similarity or shared proportions alone, but also to a large extent on conventions, and that different notational systems to a certain degree may represent the same object (a plan of house and a three-dimensional model may refer to the same house).

Dialogue   Exchange of *meaning* (s.v.) between two parties by use of sign. A dialogue is most often seen, and rightly so, as involving interpretational (non-strategic) human communication; the mating behaviour of birds and the dance of bees near the hive are also instances of dialogue.

Difference   A necessary condition for the function of signs as signs is that they can be distinguished from each other. In the most general and flexible semiotic systems, as for example natural and artificial languages, the difference between signs and sign-elements constitutes cohesive systems that can be described as *structures* (s.v.), at least on the expression plane (see *phonemes* and *distinctive features*). To a certain extent this is also the case on the content plane, although the systems of content units are less rigid (see *content*). The constitutive role of the difference led *Ferdinand* *de Saussure* (s.v.) to maintain that the (verbal) sign is primarily characterized by being what the surrounding signs are not.

Discourse, discourse analysis   A discourse is a semiotic act that locates meaning in a time–space situation where somebody produces *meaning* (s.v.) for somebody. At the same time the discourse distributes the role of the *subjects* engaged in the production of meaning and delimits the institutionalized *universe* (s.v.), where the meaning is recognized as a shared meaning. The discourse is the manifestation of the *intentionality* (s.v.) of meaning production, that is of the fact that consciousness is oriented toward the world around us. A *discourse analysis* aims at analysing *utterances* (s.v.) and other semiotic acts in relation to the features that constitute them as discourses. Discourse analysis will emphasize language as speech (versus a static system) and as the enunciation (versus the utterance) (see *enunciation* and *speech act*).

Giving the warning *Watch out!* is a discourse. The discourse analysis examines how it is anchored in time and space (is the warning uttered near me, here and now, by whom and to whom?). Furthermore, it investigates the distribution of roles between the person giving the warning and the person or persons to whom it is addressed (is the shouting person reliable, is she or he entitled to shout at me, is it addressed to me or not, whose intentions are expressed by whom?). Finally, the discourse delimits the validity of the warning (is it a joke or a serious warning, is it a line said on stage or by the spectator next to me?).

Apart from this semiotic conception there are other conceptions of discourse: *linguistical*, emphasizing discourse as a verbal sequence larger than a sentence and containing references to the situation in which it is realized (*Émile Benveniste* (s.v.)); *literary*, regarding discourse as the specific literary mode of representation implying narrators, points of view and modalities (irony etc.) as opposed to the *story* (s.v.) (*Gérard Genette* (s.v.), *Roland Barthes* (s.v.)); *sociological*, viewing discourse as a synthesis of action and ideology expressing power relations (*Michel Foucault* (s.v.)); or *conceptual*, seeing discourse as the ideal non-manipulated dialogue concerning a shared ethical or epistemological foundation for interpretations of human experience (*Jürgen Habermas* (s.v.)).

Distinctive feature   Term introduced by B. Trnka and later *Roman Jakobson* (s.v.) to designate the components of the *phonemes* (s.v.) according to his analysis. Phonemes manifested in the syllabic chain make up a sequence, whereas the distinctive features occur simultaneously in clusters; a phoneme is defined as such a cluster. Moreover, the distinctive features are defined on the basis of the production of concrete sounds in the human articulatory apparatus (mouth, nose, throat, lungs). Jakobson and his colleague Morris Halle assume that the distinctive features of all phonemes are constituted by twelve binary oppositions, as for example vocalic/non-vocalic, consonantic/non-consonantic, nasal/oral, voiced/unvoiced, etc. In Chomsky and Halle's *The Sound Pattern of English*

(1968), the number of distinctive features rose to 37, and recent research has questioned the possibility of describing all distinctive features as oppositions. A particular phoneme, as for example /m/, is defined as non-vocalic, consonantic, non-compact, nasal and dark, whereas /d/ and /t/ with shared distinctive features are defined as opposites, /d/ being voiced, /t/ unvoiced. Distinctive features are also used more broadly to characterize the defining properties of a phenomenon.

Enunciation   The act of producing an *utterance* (s.v.). Through its enunciation any utterance will always be anchored, *simultaneously*, in relation to the *subject* producing the utterance, to the *now* of the uttering and to the *object* referred to. This simultaneity constitutes the *now of the enunciation*. When the enunciation is foregrounded, the utterance is not only seen in relation to the object, as in logical theories of true statements or in the common-sense conception that talking only means talking *about* something. The utterance is always integrated in *speech acts* (s.v.) in a *discourse* (s.v.).

Euclidian space   The spatial *surrounding world* (s.v.) in so far as we conceive it as a quantitative phenomenon, independent of human presence, as for example distance measured according to the metric system. Different from the *topological space* (s.v.) and the *imagined space* (s.v.) (*Jean Piaget* (s.v.)).

Exchange   The cultural act by which phenomena are transmitted in such a way that the parties engaged in the process obtain an individual and collective identity that is visible to the other cultural actors. Gift-giving and the transfer of symbols of power are examples of exchange (*Marcel Mauss* (s.v.), *Claude Lévi-Strauss* (s.v.)).

Expression, figura of expression, expression form, expression substance   *Louis Hjelmslev* (s.v.) takes over the distinction between expression and *content* (s.v.) from *Ferdinand de Saussure* (s.v.), but in a more rigorous definition. He adds to Saussure's simple opposition that between form and substance, both on the expression plane and the content plane. The *expression form* is the expression as constituted by the systematically articulated differences as sound (*phonemes* (s.v.)) or writing (graphemes). The decisive point is that expression is seen as a *structure* (s.v.) of differences. The *expression substance* is the material in which the expression form is manifested, for example ink, acoustic waves, wax marks, etc. Hence, the same form can be manifested in difference substances (the same goes for the relation between content form and content substance). The *figuræ of expression* are the units of expression below the sign limit serving only a meaning-differentiating function, as for example phonemes (see also *figura*).

Extension, extensional   The extent of that to which a concept or a semantic unit *refers* (s.v.) (the extension of the concept *bird* is the class of organisms defined as birds, but not of all other phenomena which rightly or wrongly are labelled as birdlike) (opposed to *intension* (s.v.)).

Figura   *Louis Hjelmslev*'s (s.v.) term for the units below the sign limit from which the (verbal) signs are constructed. On the *expression* (s.v.) plane the figuræ are the *phonemes* (s.v.) and the *distinctive features* (s.v.). At least in the case of verbal language such figuræ of expression can be clearly defined. As for the *content* (s.v.) plane, it is far less plausible, if relevant and indeed possible, that we could operate with units below the limit of the sign. Frequent examples of figuræ of content are *masculinity* and *femininity*. It seems, however, obvious that they are themselves signs. Hence, we do not find that the distinction between figura and sign can be maintained on the content plane.

Function   In *Louis Hjelmslev* (s.v.) the notion of function is crucial. He defines it as a relation of dependence between two elements that can be observed through scientific description. Hjelmslev holds the relation between expression form and content form to be a function, called denotation, which defines the verbal sign.

Habit   *Charles Sanders Peirce* (s.v.) often defines the logical *interpretant* (s.v.) of a *sign* (s.v.) as the translation of the sign into a new sign. This definition is important because it emphasizes that interpretation implies a permanent connection and translation between different semiotic systems (for example depending on different senses). If this conception is not supplemented it might, however, lead us to assume an overall unbroken and infinite process of interpretation in contradiction with our habitual and delimited acts in most situations. Therefore, Peirce introduces the notion of the finite (final or ultimate) logical interpretant which is not in itself a sign but a *habit* or a readiness to act in a certain way under certain circumstances if prompted by a particular goal. The importance of habits in human behaviour is obvious. Society and culture would collapse without habits. But Peirce, following Darwin, also assumes that habits evolve in nature.

Homonym   When the oral expression of two different words happens to be identical they are said to be homonymic: 'The *deer* in the woods are *dear* to me.' The opposite of homonym is *synonym*.

Homophony   (see *polyphony*).

Icon   (see *sign*).

Image   Here an *image* belongs to *Charles Sanders Peirce*'s (s.v.) tripartite subdivision of the iconic signs (see *diagram*, *metaphor* and *sign*). The image is defined by having *properties* in common with the object it refers to. Thus *image* is a technical term for a particular sign type. Therefore, it covers a series of phenomena we do not usually call images, as for instance a colour sample, and, along with similarities, images, like portraits, also contain diagrammatical (and thereby conventional) features in relation to the portrayed object, as for instance scale.

Imagined space   The spatial *surrounding world* (s.v.), in so far as we conceive it as a net of mutually related positions that become spatial only when we actually occupy them, as for example the relation between up and down, right and left – we do not know what *up* or *left* is if we cannot imagine what it is to be *down* or to the *right*. Different from the *topological space* (s.v.) and the *Euclidian space* (s.v.) (*Jean Piaget* (s.v.)).

Indices (see *sign*).

Induction (see *abduction*).

Intension, intensional The defining properties of a certain phenomenon as expressed in the *meaning* (s.v.) of signs that refer to it (the intension of *bird* is the features that constitute the meaning of what the identity of a bird is; they may also, as for example in *metaphors* (s.v.), apply to other phenomena than birds) (opposed to *extension* (s.v.)).

Intentionality, intention A basic *distinctive feature* (s.v.) of human consciousness. That our consciousness is intentional means that it will permanently be oriented *toward* something and thereby be conscious *about* something. However, this does not mean that objects of intention are real. Consciousness can be oriented toward dreams, fictions, illusions, etc. What it does mean is that consciousness is never empty but constantly engaged in a meaning-creating sign-process. *Intention* is also used more narrowly as the deliberate expression of voluntary acts.

Interlinguistic A term used by *Roman Jakobson* (s.v.) together with the terms *intralinguistic* (s.v.) and *intersemiotic* (s.v.) to differentiate ways in which meanings are transmitted and interpreted. Interlinguistic transmission is a translation from one natural language to another.

Interpretant (*(1) Immediate, dynamical, final interpretant, (2) emotional, energetic, logical interpretant, (3) intentional, effective, cominterpretant.*) Generally speaking the interpretant is the third element in *Charles Sanders Peirce's* (s.v.) presentation of the *sign* (s.v.), which is regarded as a mutually interrelated triad of sign/sign vehicle, object and interpretant. Peirce states in his best-known sign-definition that the sign 'addresses somebody, that is, creates in the mind of that person an equivalent sign, or perhaps a more developed sign. That sign which it creates I call the *interpretant* of the first sign' (Peirce, 228). Here the interpretant is seen as a new sign released by the first sign, as for example when we understand what somebody else has said to us. In this case the words we hear are the first signs referring to an object we can identify, whereas our understanding of the sign is the interpretant. This way of looking at the sign-process, or semiosis, underlies an important point in Peirce: semiosis is transfer and expansion of knowledge between parties in a dialogue.

Peirce worked on the notion of the interpretant throughout his life, and his papers contain numerous sketches of various classifications. Only the three most important and elaborated are mentioned here. Each of them is built on a tripartition of the interpretant:

1   The distinction between *immediate, dynamical* and *final interpretant* shows the position of the interpretant in different stages of the process of investigation and understanding. The *immediate* interpretant is the interpretant given in and by the sign itself. The immediate interpre-

tant is the meaning-potential of the sign before its actual interpretation (see *system-objects*). The *dynamical* interpretant is the result of an
actual interpretation, for example our actual understanding when
reading a sequence of signs, or the slobber of a dog smelling the
food. The dynamical interpretant is often to a large extent determined by the meaning-potential of the sign itself (the immediate
interpretant); but additional meanings are easily produced, e.g.
from the experience of the interpreter (the interpretation of a bodily
symptom made by a lay person will differ from that of a medical
doctor). The *final* interpretant is the interpretant that will remain
unchanged during any further investigation and interpretation,
even if this process went on for ever. The outcome would be a valid
and stable interpretational habit (see *habit*).

2   A different set of distinctions holds between *emotional, energetic* and
logical interpretant. We have an *emotional* interpretant if the sign is
interpreted as a quality or in a feeling. Such interpretations entail no
analyses, not even a consciousness about a distinction between sign,
object and interpretant; the interpreter is, as it were, one with the
interpretation. Many aesthetic experiences may belong to this type of
interpretant, but any interpretation can contain an emotional interpretant. We have an *energetic* interpretant when the sign's interpretant
gives rise to physical activity, for example a foot on the brake when
the traffic light turns red. We have a *logical* interpretant when a sign is
interpreted in being translated to another sign, as for example when
we define a *bachelor* as an *unmarried man*. This process may go on
indefinitely because the interpreting signs call for another interpretation in a new sign, etc. Therefore Peirce introduces an ultimate logical
interpretant which is not a sign itself but an interpretational habit.

3   The distinction between the *intentional interpretant, the effective interpretant*
and *the cominterpretant* is based on a conception of the semiosis as a
dialogical phenomenon. The *intentional* interpretant is the interpretant
intended by the sign utterer to be understood by the receiver, whereas
the *effective* interpretant is the interpretant actually chosen by the
receiver. If the intentional and the effective interpretant are identical,
or if they can be made identical through dialogue, the *cominterpretant*
occurs as the identity between the interpretation of the parties
engaged in a dialogue. Strictly speaking, we do not have two interpretants of the sign in question but only one, and the two parties are
to be seen as one with regard to the interpretation in question.

Intersemiotic   The exchange and translation between semiotic systems of a
different nature, for example between our perception of the world around
us and its linguistic articulation. Different semiotic systems do not produce identical differentiations and articulations of given phenomena.
The facial muscular system allows for about 25,000 different facial

expressions, and although we are hardly able to distinguish between all of them, we are at least able to perceive more nuances than we can express linguistically in explicit terms (but verbal creativity will then do part of the job). Intersemiotic translation is, however, not only a way of refining our perception and understanding of the surrounding world. It is a pre-condition for meaning altogether to occur. It is only in the combination of different semiotic systems that meaning is produced: if somebody talks to us in a language absolutely unknown to us without any gestures, facial expressions or pointing to objects, even an endless flow of words would not help us. Only when speech is connected with known non-verbal *iconic* and *indexical signs* (s.v.) and thus given an intersemiotic dimension, will we begin to grasp the language spoken to us (see *interlinguistic* and *intra-linguistic*).

Intertextuality   The fact that verbal and non-verbal *texts* (s.v.) are inter-related in various ways: they may share *codes* (s.v.) and *conventions* (s.v.), they may allude or refer directly to each other, or they may enter in a direct dialogue with each other through quotations. Intertextuality may be the effect of a direct influence from one text upon another, but may also rely more generally on the fact that the texts belong to the same culture.

Intralinguistic   What belongs to the same natural language, especially the translation between its signs, as for example in definitions: an intralin-guistic translation of a *fifth* is *a tone on the fifth degree from another tone counted as the first* (see *interlinguistic* and *intersemiotic*).

Layout   The organization of our *surrounding world* (s.v.) in relation to a human observer using mainly the sight (*James Gibson* (s.v.)).

Life world   Our *surrounding world* (s.v.) as it appears to us in immediate experience, that is as it appears when we take it for granted as it is. The immediacy of the experience is determined both by the given cultural *codes* (s.v.) and *conventions* (s.v.) and by our biologically shaped senses.

Linguistic sign   The linguistic sign differs significantly from most other signs (1) in being *unmotivated* (s.v.) and *arbitrary* (s.v.), (2) in having an expression with a *double articulation* (s.v.) and (3) in being distinguished from other signs, both on the expression and the content plane, primarily because of a relation of difference and similarity to other signs (or sign-components). Linguistic signs are not identical with words, because words may be composed of several *morphemes* (s.v.) (see also *sign* (s.v.)).

Meaning   The content of a *sign* (s.v.) or a *text* (s.v.). When the traffic light is green, it means *Go*. When the outline of a female body is shown on a door it means *Ladies' room*. When the king in a game of chess cannot avoid being checkmated, it means *Game lost*. Meanings emerge from the double determination of signs and texts: they are defined both *structurally* (see *structure*) and *pragmatically* (see *pragmatics*). Structurally, a sign must be distinguishable from other signs (we must be able to distinguish the green of a traffic light from the amber or the stereotypical outline of a woman from that of man). Pragmatically, there must be conventions or codes at hand for the use of the sign (it has been decided that *green* means *Go*, the rules of chess have been developed and agreed upon over time, and the use of words most often relies on unconscious *habits* (s.v.)).

Mediation   A collective process of meaning production by which a given *culture* (s.v.) synthesizes basic but contrasting meanings in a narrative, thereby making this narrative interpret the foundation of the culture (see *Claude Lévi-Strauss*).

Medium   That aspect of the surrounding world that allows for unimpeded passage of sense-impressions as opposed to *surface* (s.v.) and *substance* (see *James Gibson*).

Metalanguage   A language used to refer to or to 'talk about' another language. The theory of metalanguages is developed and refined in logic and mathematics. A metalanguage is most often conceived of as a scientific language used to describe and analyse a language of logically lower rank, the object language of the metalanguage, but also a descriptive language, as the grammar of a natural language is a metalanguage that defines the possible and acceptable combinations of the elements of the natural language. *Louis Hjelmslev* (s.v.) makes a distinction between a metalanguage or metasemiotic and a connotative language or semiotic: the former has another language or semiotic as its content plane, whereas the latter has another language or semiotic as its expression plane.

Metaphor   According to *Charles Sanders Peirce* (s.v.) a subdivision of the iconical sign (see *image*, *diagram* and *sign*) defined by its capacity to represent 'a parallelism in something else'. This is a broader notion of metaphor than the usual one, including for example a measuring apparatus that operates by transforming a certain input to readable signs in another medium. In this sense the measurable effect of an earthquake on the Richter scale is a metaphor for the event (and at the same time an *indexical sign* of it; see *sign*). According to *Roman Jakobson* (s.v.) a metaphor is a rhetorical figure based on *similarity* (s.v.) between two semantic fields. Thus a metaphor is a radical and condensed manifestation of one of the two fundamental structural principles of language: *selection* (s.v.) based on similarity (and contrast), and *combination* (s.v.) based on contiguity (see *contact*). A traditional metaphor such as 'the dawn of life' is a parallelism between the sequence of day and night and the sequence of life. One element from one of the semantic fields is transferred to the other to express a similarity between the two types of sequences.

Modalities   Since Aristotle logic has dealt with modal propositions (Latin *modus* = mode (of being)), that is the relation of logical propositions to reality and/or recognition. In modal logic distinctions have been made between possible and impossible, probable and improbable, necessary and contingent propositions. Modal logic has played an important role in the history of philosophy and laid the ground for many controversies. Modern logic and philosophy are also deeply involved in modal logic.

In linguistics *mode* indicates the attitude of the speaker in relation to the reality referred to in the utterance, for example expressed in the form of the verb: indicative, subjunctive, imperative. A particular group of verbs has been singled out as *modal verbs*: *will, shall, can, may, must, ought.* Such verbs do not refer to acts as such but to preconditions for acting or not acting: possibility, necessity, etc. Close to modal verbs proper are verbs like *hope, dare, wonder, want.* In linguistics modality can also comprise a syntactical construction like 'Maybe it is the case that . . .' or 'If we imagined that . . .'

In *narratology* (s.v.) *Algirdas Julien Greimas* (s.v.) has developed *Vladimir Propp*'s (s.v.) analyses of folktales and introduced modalities in the analysis of narrative acts with a special emphasis on the importance of *desire* or *will, knowledge* and *ability.* Continuing from Greimas and modern modal logic Lubomir Dolezel has stressed the four modal systems of a text: (1) the *alethic* (Greek *aletheia* = truth) concerning what is possible, impossible and necessary in the represented universe; (2) the *deontic* (Greek *deon* = obligation) concerning what is permitted, prohibited and obligatory; (3) the *axiological* (Greek *axios* = value) concerning what is good, bad or indifferent; and, finally, (4) the *epistemic* (Greek *episteme* = knowledge) concerning what is known, unknown, presumed, doubtful. In principle any analysis of narrative acts will comprise all four systems.

Model A concept in *cultural semiotics* (s.v.) of a *text* (s.v.) that refers to another text in such a way that it retains the culture-specific *distinctive features* (s.v.) of the text referred to. A scientific description of the characteristics of a given society related to food, eating, digestion, table manners, etc. as manifested in texts in different semiotic systems will be a model for these texts and the way they are interrelated. The model is also called a *secondary* modelling system, whereas the texts referred to are called a *primary* modelling system (*Jurij Lotman* (s.v.)).

Morpheme The smallest meaning-carrying linguistic unit and thus a *lingustic sign* (s.v.). A word like *im-prove-d* contains three morphemes with different functions and properties.

Motif In the study of literature this term is used for a frequently recurring complex of action-generating factors or an often-described typical carcater or situation (the revenge of the loser, the moon or the serenade under the window of the beloved). In *narratology* (s.v.) the term *motif* refers to the motivation for action or to particular recurring typical narrative segments (treason, escape, fight, etc.).

Motivated A sign is motivated when the expression plane shows a similarity to the object referred to by the sign, for example onomatopoeia, such as *boom* or *cock-a-doodle-doo* (opposed to *unmotivated*). The fact that onomatopoeia varies from one language to another (*cock-a-doodle-doo* is called *kykliky* in Danish), and therefore determined by the *second articulation* (s.v.) of the language in question, led *Ferdinand de Saussure* (s.v.) to claim that the linguistic sign is primarily unmotivated but that it may contain secondary motivated features.

Narratology   The structural study of the textual representation of action. In western culture Aristotle's *Poetics* offers the earliest example of an analysis of such representations. In the twentieth century *Vladimir Propp* (s.v.) has presented pathbreaking formal analyses of Russian folktales. Later the analysis of myth by *Claude Lévi-Strauss* (s.v.) has been influential, together with the works of *Roland Barthes* (s.v.) and *Algirdas Julien Greimas* (s.v.). Earlier in this century the Dane Axel Olrik also made an important contribution to the study of narratives in establishing his so-called epic laws. In addition, Bengt Holbek's more recent dissertation *Interpretation of Fairy Tales* deserves to be mentioned.

Narrator   The narrative instance that is responsible for what is narrated – 'said' (the voice). The credibility of the narator is crucial for the reader's evaluation of the statements of the text. As a personal narrator, or a narrator on the same level as the characters, the narrator may be identical with one of the characters or relate the events as if he were on the same level as the characters; or, as transpersonal narrator, the narrator may transcend the level of the characters. Often identified with *point of view* (s.v.).

Nominalism   A philosophical position claiming that signs are purely conventional and independent of the phenomena in the surrounding world they refer to. Theories and the languages they are based upon are abstract constructions (opposed to *realism* (s.v.)).

Object – dynamical, immediate   In *Charles Sanders Peirce*'s (s.v.) semiotics the object is integrated in the definition of the *sign* (s.v.) itself, which thereby is seen as a triadic phenomenon. His position is opposed to *Ferdinand de Saussure*'s (s.v.) and the continental tradition he inspired (*Louis Hjelmslev* (s.v.), *Algirdas Julien Greimas* (s.v.) and others) but in line with *phenomenology* (s.v.) and the influence it exercised on semiotics. Peirce makes a distinction between two objects. The *immediate* object is the object as it is represented in and by the sign. A person as we see her in a photo is the immediate object, represented in and by the photo as a sign of her. The *dynamical* object is the object that exercises an influence on and determines the sign, and thereby also its immediate object. The actual individual represented in the photo is the dynamical object of the sign, because she has actually determined it. We only come to know the dynamical object through the sign, that is through its immediate objects. Peirce's distinction is influenced by Kant's dinstinction between 'the thing for us' and 'the thing in itself'. Peirce, however, regarded the relation between the two objects as dynamic: through ongoing research we can actually know more and more about the dynamical object. In the hypothetical case of complete knowledge of the object through an infinite research process, the distinction between the two objects would disappear (see *phenomenology*).

Ostensive definition Pointing to or showing the object to be defined. *Charles Sanders Peirce* (s.v.) holds the so-called collateral experience, that is experience that combines several fields of experience, to be necessary for the interpretation of the sign. If sign users do not have a certain amount of immediate knowledge of the objects of the *life world* (s.v.), signs will not be capable of referring and conveying meaning. Language acquisition cannot take place unless the child is able to combine the sounds of speech with other sense-impressions in order to establish certain signifying and interpretative habits.

Paradigm According to *Louis Hjelmslev* (s.v.), a class of elements that can occupy the same positions in a chain but not at the same time: thus singular and plural marker (in English 'zero' and -*s*) belong to the same paradigm (see *combination* and *syntagm*).

Phenomenology One of the most important philosophical movements of the twentieth century, based on the work of *Edmund Husserl* (s.v.) and with a major impact also outside philosophy on linguistics, aesthetics and psychology. The basic idea is that any reflection on the world around us has as its point of departure the way in which its objects appear in our experience based on *intentionality* (s.v.). Consciousness is intentional by being permanently oriented toward objects, whether real or imagined. An empty consciousness is no consciousness. Objects and consciousness are mutually related from perception to action, and this interrelationship is what is manifested in signs and sign-processes. Such processes are dealt with in the works of the phenomenological canon, especially emphasizing the limits of the way in which signs *refer* (s.v.) and *represent* (s.v.), their function as *indexical signs* (s.v.) and the role of the *body* in sign-processes. Moreover, phenomenology operates with various categories of *object* (s.v.) (real objects, intentional objects, etc.). The differences between these categories contribute to the definition of the sign-process in relation to perception, communication and recognition. Therefore the semiotic perspective is essential to phenomenology, both in Husserl and in the works of later phenomenologists (for example *Maurice Merleau-Ponty* (s.v.), *Paul Ricœur* (s.v.) and *Alfred Schütz* (s.v.), or the critics of phenomenology such as *Jacques Derrida* (s.v.)). In linguistics phenomenology has inspired, for example, *Roman Jakobson* (s.v.), *Karl Bühler* (s.v.) and *Viggo Brøndal* (s.v.).

Phoneme The smallest independent, meaning-differentiating unit of verbal language. The phoneme is built up of *distinctive features* (s.v.) and is differentiated through the *commutation test* (s.v.).

Point of view The ideological and/or perceptual position in a narrative from where the textual *universe* (s.v.) is overlooked, both in terms of the values operating in the universe and in terms of the boundaries of the fictional universe. Also called 'perspective', 'vision', 'focal point'. This position may be personal, that is, occupied by one or more of the characters, or restricted by their possible experience and value-systems; or the point of view may be transpersonal or omniscient beyond the level of the characters. Often identified with *narrator* (s.v.).

Polyphony   Term used by Mikhail Bakhtin to characterize *texts* (s.v.) that express themselves in several voices, each representing a different world-view. Opposed to *homophonic* texts in which one world-view is expressed in such a way that it dominates or even excludes others.

Pragmatics, pragmaticism, pragmatism   Pragmatics in the broadest sense identifies the *meaning* (s.v.) or signification of things with the actions they generate. In *linguistics* pragmatics is the study of the use of language in communicative and other acts. Pragmatics not only takes into account the norms of the grammatical systems but also the norms of communicative processes and the situational, psychological and cultural factors that determine the use of language (see *speech act*). In *Charles Sanders Peirce* (s.v.) *pragmatism*, later called *pragmaticism*, constitutes a scientific approach to semiosis, identifying the meaning of a concept with the possible actions and attitudes that can be inferred from the definition of the concept as its probable effects or, in more general terms, the *habits* (s.v.) a sign implies, including interpretative habits.

Reagent   (see *sign*).

Realism   A philosophical position claiming that signs refer to and presuppose the actual properties of things in the surrounding world they refer to. Theories and the languages they are based upon give real recognition (opposed to *nominalism* (s.v.)).

Reference, referent   The referent of a sign is the *object* (s.v.) which in the given situation is represented by the sign in the text containing the sign. The reference is the sign's relation to this object. In some semiotic theories reference and referent are regarded as integral parts of semiotics (e.g. *Charles Sanders Peirce* (s.v.) and the *phenomenological* (s.v.) tradition); in other theories they are excluded (e.g. *Ferdinand de Saussure* (s.v.) and, to a large extent, the continental tradition) (see also *extension*).

Representamen   In *Charles Sanders Peirce's* (s.v.) semiotics it is a term that occurs in two oppositions. (1) Representamen is opposed to the term *replica*, an opposition that corresponds to that of *type* versus *token*. A replica is the concrete sign, for example the sound of an *a*, whereas a representamen is the norm or the rule which the replica must observe in order to be a token of the representamen as type, for example the *phoneme* /a/ as a cluster of *distinctive features* (s.v.). (2) In some instances Peirce distinguishes between representamen and sign as two different sign-vehicles (i.e. the first component of the triadic *sign* (s.v.)). In this case a sign is a representamen with a mental *interpretant* (s.v.), whereas a representamen is not necessarily a sign. He gives the following example: 'If a sunflower, in turning toward the sun, becomes by that very act fully capable, without further condition, of reproducing a sunflower which turns in precisely corresponding ways toward the sun, and of doing so with the same reproductive power, the sunflower would become a Representamen of the sun. But *thought* is the chief, if not the only, mode of representation' (Peirce, 2.274). Although the distinction does not play a significant role in his work, the quotation shows Peirce's preoccupation with the sign-processes of nature.

Representation (representing or standing for an object to an interpretant) The basic idea of semiotics is that a sign is a sign because of its capacity to represent. This conception is crucial whether the sign is seen as a dyadic relation between expression and content (for example *Ferdinand de Saussure* (s.v.), *Louis Hjelmslev* (s.v.), *Algirdas Julien Greimas* (s.v.)) or as a triadic relation between sign (vehicle), object and interpretant (*Charles Sanders Peirce* (s.v.)). In the first case the expression is the representation of the content, in the second the sign (vehicle) represents or stands for the object in relation to the interpretant. Semiotics shows that relations of representation are more complex and more widespread than generally accepted: the footprint represents the animal to the hunter's thought, the red spots represent the measles to the doctor's. The lawyer represents his client to judge, court and law, the member of parliament represents his constituency and party to parliament. The archeological relics represent a lost building to the expertise of the archaeologist, and the model of the building in a museum represents a hypothesis of the former structure of the building to the visitors.

Schema The *code* (s.v.) relating consciousness and *surrounding world* (s.v.) in perception and interpretation (*Alfred Schütz* (s.v.), *Jean Piaget* (s.v.)).

Selection (see *combination*).

Semiosphere A *universe* (s.v.) defined by the semiotic competence of living organisms. Different organisms live in partly different semiospheres. The human semiosphere is defined by our simultaneous use of indexical, iconic and symbolic *signs* (s.v.) in *discourses* (s.v.).

Senso-motoric stage The build-up of a *surrounding world* (s.v.) from the actual presence of the body in a *contactual universe* (s.v.). The first step in the cognitive development followed by the *symbolic* (s.v.) and the *conceptual stage* (s.v.) (*Jean Piaget* (s.v.)).

Sign – iconic, indexical, symbolic The distinction between the three types of sign – iconic, indexical and symbolic – is introduced by *Charles Sanders Peirce* (s.v.), and, like many contemporary semioticians, he held this to be his most important sign typology. The distinction is based on the relation between the sign and its *dynamical object* (s.v.): if a sign acts as sign for its dynamical object because of its *similarity* (s.v.) to it, it is an *iconic* sign. The similarity is *conventional* (s.v.) in the sense that it obeys certain criteria that are predefined with a particular descriptive purpose, but nevertheless, the similarity exists whether it is interpreted or not. The convention determining the description semiotizes the elements and structural features shared by sign and object, but it does not generate them. Peirce subdivides the iconic signs into *images* (s.v.), *diagrams* (s.v.) and *metaphors* (s.v.).

If a sign operates because of a relation of contiguity to the dynamical object (see *contact*), it is an *indexical* sign. Peirce distinguishes between two groups of indexical signs. *Reagents* are affected by their object by a causal relation. The trees bent by the wind are reagents of the force and direction of the wind. Of course, the sign–object relation will have to be interpreted in order for the sign to act as a sign, but the relation itself exists whether the trees function as a sign or not. *Symptoms* (s.v.) and *tracks* (s.v.) belong to the reagents. The other group is made up of *designations*. In contradistinction to reagents, the sign–object relation of designations does not originate in the object but in the designations themselves. A street sign in Boston carrying the name 'Broad Street' designates the object, one of the main streets of the city, and it is because of this street sign (or other name-giving signs) that the street is Broad Street. The designation directs the attention to the individual thing designated but in a conventional way, whereas the reagent is caused by its object (see *designator element* and *designator function*).

The *symbolic* sign (see also *symbol*) is only connected with its dynamical object through a habit of denomination or interpretation. It is related to its object neither through similarity nor contiguity. *Linguistic signs* (s.v.) are the prototypical symbolic signs. They function as denominations of classes of things or state of affairs, not of individual objects. But the entire tripartition of signs also operates in natural languages. First, we have the deictic elements of language (pronouns, adverbs, etc., see *deixis*) and the deictical function of language is indispensable for *speech* (s.v.) to be performed. Second, we have denominations that seem to refer to classes of thing but rather function as proper names (the sun, the moon, etc.), that is as indexical signs pointing to individual things. Third, we have onomatopoeia like *cuckoo*, which is an iconic sign for the referent, but also changes from one language to another and thus pertains to the conventional and symbolic nature of language (see *motivated*).

Peirce's distinction is important because it underlines that the sign-function is operating in the entire *biosphere* (s.v.), not only among humans, and that the symbolic signs only function in a permanent interaction with iconic and indexical signs.

Similarity According to *Charles Sanders Peirce* (s.v.), and to the tradition of philosophy at large, association based on *similarity* is one of the two fundamental psychological principles of association shaping the overall human experience of the surrounding world and the knowledge generated by the connections we construct between the objects of our experience. The other principle is association based on *contiguity* (see *contact*). Peirce adds association motivated by interest as a third principle. Moreover, his distinction between the *iconic*, the *indexical* and the *symbolic sign* (s.v.) is also based on these principles: if the sign is related to its object by similarity it is iconic, if by contiguity it is indexical, and if by habit it is symbolic. *Roman Jakobson* (s.v.) also underlines similarity and contiguity as the two fundamental and contrasting principles for the production of oral and written texts. He uses the opposition to separate different forms of aphasia and to set up the distinction between *metaphor* (s.v.) based on similarity and *metonyms* based on contiguity (see *contact*). Similarity cannot function as the only classifying criterion because everything is similar to or shares properties with something else in some respect. Therefore, similarity will always have to be specified as a similarity in a certain respect, that is according to explicit descriptive principles of comparison and its purpose (see *context of effective definitions*).

Speech *Ferdinand de Saussure* (s.v.) distinguishes between two types of linguistics: a linguistics of language (*une linguistique de la langue*), that is of language as system, and a linguistics of speech (*une linguistique de la parole*), that is of the concrete use of language in communication and action. Saussure concentrated almost entirely on the study of language as system because he supposed that this approach alone enabled him to reveal the essential features of language, whereas speech was characterized by individual and accidental properties. More recently linguistics, particularly *pragmatics* (s.v.), has taken up the systematic study of speech (see *speech act*).

Speech act Viewing speech as a specific type of action has a long history. Classical rhetoric analysed how speakers act upon their listeners to make them react as they want and contained practical devices for speakers. In the twentieth century *John Austin* (s.v.), inspired by the late Wittgenstein, among others, examined different types of verbal *utterances* (s.v.) as different ways of acting (see also *enunciation* and *discourse*). He singles out, for example, 'promise', 'warn', 'claim', 'advise', 'threaten', 'apologize', etc. Futhermore, Austin distinguishes between different aspects of the utterance: the *locutionary* aspect (Latin *locutio* = speech) or the statement; the *illocutionary* aspect (Latin *in* + *locutio* = address) or the enunciation; the *perlocutionary* aspect (Latin *per* + *locutio* = through speech) or the effects of the utterance.

In any address to others (or to oneself) all three aspects occur simultaneously. First, we have the *statement*, for example the assertion that something is the case (reference + predication: 'it is true that P'). Second, we have the *enunciation* (s.v.), which indicates the habitual act the speaker is supposed to perform in and by what he says ('I warn you that . . . ', 'I hereby claim that . . . ' and also 'I baptize you . . . '). Speech acts are *conventional* (s.v.) in the sense that we are able to recognize them as different types of act (promising and baptizing are different from threatening). Moreover, we often know intuitively if the conditions for their performance are met. Finally, we have utterances that are concrete speech acts performed in a communicative and referential *context* (s.v.) and containing a perlocutionary aspect: the utterance is the expression of particular, individual intentions and produces certain *effects* on the addressees. The difference between the illocutionary aspect and the perlocutionary aspect is clear when, for example, the utterer is insincere, is lying in order to move the listener to perform certain acts under false pretensions. Here, the contrast between the disguised individual purpose belonging to the perlocution (a threat disguised as a promise of the type 'an offer you can't refuse') and the conventional meaning of the speech act as uttered in and by the enunciation (a promise) is a precondition for the insincerity to produce the intended effect (see also *pragmatics*).

Speech-act theory from Austin to *John Searle* (s.v.) is only about fifty years old. It has been and remains a fruitful but turbulent field of research, inviting philosophers, linguists and text theoreticians to cooperate – and to disagree.

Story In the study of literature a concept covering the totality of narrated events in a narrative text. The story is often opposed to the *discourse* (s.v.).

Structure, structuralism In a narrow sense a *structure* is a net of relations between mutually interdependent elements that make up a totality that gives a certain phenomenon its identity which is said to be its structure. In a broader sense it is any static organization of a phenomenon and its components that can be defined in a *context of effective definitions* (s.v.). In this case structure, or the structural code, is the rule that defines the organization (see *code*). *Structuralism* is the study of phenomena defined as structures. Its scope varies with the notion of structure (static, dynamic, narrow, broad, etc.) and is based upon the field of research it belongs to (linguistics, anthropology, etc.).

Surface That aspect of the surrounding world that marks the boundary between *medium* (s.v.) and *substance*. The perception of the surrounding world is a perception of surfaces (see *James Gibson*).

Surroundings The totality of phenomena making up the physical space of an organism whether it can perceive them or not. The *biosphere* (s.v.) is a part of that space (opposed to *surrounding world*).

Surrounding world (Umwelt) The part of the *surroundings* (s.v.) that an organism can perceive and interpret with its senses and its semiotic competence. Also called *Umwelt* (*Jakob von Uexküll* (s.v.)). The surrounding world is shaped as a totality stored in the memory of the organism and projected on to the surroundings as a *schema* (s.v.) guiding the behaviour of the organism in the surroundings. The *life world* (s.v.) and the *semiosphere* (s.v.) are parts of the surrounding world or Umwelt.

Symbol In semiotics symbol may acquire two contrasting definitions. In the tradition following *Ferdinand de Saussure* (s.v.) the symbol is opposed to the *sign* (s.v.): the sign is *arbitrary* (s.v.), the symbol is *motivated* (s.v.) although it also contains arbitrary features. For Saussure and *Louis Hjelmslev* (s.v.) the blindfolded goddess with a balance in her hand is the symbol of justice because her attributes are motivated. In the tradition following *Charles Sanders Peirce* (s.v.) the symbol, as opposed to the icon and index (see *sign*), is the *unmotivated* (s.v.) and *conventional* (s.v.) sign with a relation to the *object* (s.v.) based on a *habit* (s.v.).

Symbolic stage   The build-up of a *surrounding world* (s.v.) by relations between signs and phenomena that are not necessarily co-present with the sign. The second step in the cognitive development based on the *senso-motoric* (s.v.) and the *conceptual stage* (s.v.) (*Jean Piaget* (s.v.)).

Symptom   In *Charles Sanders Peirce* (s.v.) a subgroup of indexical *signs* (s.v.) that are part of and co-present with the object (see *track*). In antiquity the study of medical symptoms, symptomatology, was the earliest stage of semiotics.

Syntagm   An organized sequence or chain of linguistic signs. Also used to describe a sequence of non-verbal signs, as for example cinematographic signs (see *combination* and *paradigm*).

System-object   A delimitation of a phenomenon in the surrounding world based on the assumption that it is structurable but before any specific structure has been defined (Raymond Boudon). Identical with immediate *interpretant* (s.v.).

Text   On a scale from the broadest to the narrowest conception of text we find four different notions that are pertinent to different semiotic schools or disciplines:

1   The most narrow notion is often foregrounded by linguists who regard the text as an entity consisting of one or more linguistic signs.

2   According to a less narrow notion, texts are defined as all phenomena that communicate a message through digitally or analogically coded signs (see *code*). Here the communicative act is the core. From this perspective traffic lights, paintings and folk costumes are texts as they transmit intended and/or traditional information. This notion of text is particularly relevant in cultural semiotics and anthropology.

3   A broader notion of text also accepts non-intended and genetically programmed transmission of messages between organisms as texts, for example birds' mating dance.

4   The broadest notion of text includes all relations in the universe, also inorganic, as possible semiotic relations and thus manifested as texts, as for example when features of a landscape are interpreted as traces from the last glacial period. This all-embracing notion of text is relevant, too, as long as we keep in mind that sign (vehicle) and object are functional entities that only exist in connection with the interpretant and thus in an interpretation. The world at large can be interpreted as a text, and our survival depends on our capacity to continue to interpret it as such; but before it is interpreted it is not a text. There are no contradictions between the four notions, only a different degree of broadness.

Topological space   The spatial *surrounding world* (s.v.) in so far as we conceive it on the basis of the actual presence of our body, for example the space as shaped by relations like *close* versus *distant*. Differs from the *imagined space* (s.v.) and the *Euclidian space* (s.v.) (*Jean Piaget* (s.v.)).

Track   An important type of indexical *sign* (s.v.) that is actually produced
by the object and may lead to it through interpretation, for example the
interpretation of the track of animals by the hunter, or the search for
tracks to be interpreted by the detective.

Universe   As a technical term *universe* indicates different coexisting fields of
human reality with different modes of being (see *modalities*). We may
separate a shared universe of experience determined by our body and
our senses in which we act from a fictional universe, which is a possible,
mind-dependent world existing on the basis of a text or a corpus of texts
as the only access to the fictional universe (see also *contact, designator
function, life world, semiosphere, surrounding world*).

Unmotivated   A sign is unmotivated when its expression plane does not
show a similarity to the object referred to by the sign: the sequence of
phonemes /g-r-a-s/ has no likeness to the greenery in the garden (opposed
to *motivated* (s.v.)). The unmotivated relation between the sign and the
non-linguistic object is a precondition for the claim that the linguistic sign
is constituted by an *arbitrary* (s.v.) relation between expression and content (*Ferdinand de Saussure* (s.v.)).

Utterance   The concrete and individual production of a text, particularly a
verbal text (see *discourse, enunciation, speech act*).

Biographies

The following are short biographies of important semioticians from the twentieth century referred to in the book. The reader is referred in general to the Glossary. Only a few explicit references are given below.

Austin, John L. (1911–60) English philosopher of language whose *How to Do Things with Words* (1962) is one of the most important contributions to the development of the *speech-act analysis* (s.v.). He demonstrates that every utterance is a communicative act. Its meaning is not only determined by the state of affairs it concerns, but also by the grammatical and situational factors that make it a specific type of act.

Barthes, Roland (1915–80) French semiotician and literary scholar. On the one hand, Barthes tried to make semiotics a branch of structural linguistics and to employ its rigorous formal analytical apparatus. In particular he adapted Ferdinand de Saussure's and Louis Hjelmslev's theories to the analysis of cultural sign-systems at large, both verbal and non-verbal, especially the visual (*Mythologies* (1957), *Éléments de sémiologie* (1964)). On the other hand, in a series of works on the aesthetic experience, Barthes also focused on the essential sensual quality of meaning production as it emerges in the momentaneous sense-experience (*Le plaisir du texte* (1973), *La chambre claire* (1980)).

Bateson, Gregory (1904–80) English anthropologist. He contributed to the development of cybernetics (the doctrine of mechanical systems and system control) and applied it to studies of communication theory and psychology. In these areas he took a special interest in complex communicative acts that involve several layers of meaning (play) or make our capacity to control complex meaning collapse (schizophrenia). *Steps to an Ecology of Mind* (1972) is an important collection of his articles.

Benveniste, Émile (1902–76) French linguist. Benveniste was one of the pioneers of structural linguistics in France. His works on the enunciative processes of language are highly pertinent to semiotics. He scrutinizes in particular the way time and subjectivity are manifested in language systems. Important articles are published in *Problèmes de linguistique générale* I (1966) and II (1974).

Brøndal, Viggo (1887–1942)   Danish linguist and Romance philologist. Inspired by phenomenology, philosophy of language and the *structuralism* (s.v.) of Ferdinand de Saussure, he attempted to work out a structural linguistics. But in contrast to Saussure and his followers, his starting-point was not the immanent structure of language, but the relation between language, mind and the *surrounding world* (s.v.). The structure of language with all its particular elements is, in its totality, a concrete and specific formation that shapes the way consciousness orients itself toward reality and transforms it into meaning (*Parties du discours* (1928, 1948), *Essais de linguistique générale* (1943)). Although Brøndal was opposed to Louis Hjelmslev's formalistic theory of language they co-founded Le Cercle Linguistique de Copenhague (1931) and its journal *Acta Linguistica* (1939).

Bühler, Karl (1879–1963)   Austrian philosopher, linguist and psychologist. Bühler's major work is *Sprachtheorie* (1934). Here he developed a communication model, the so-called *Organon model*, which is not founded on formal relations but on the sign and its representation of objects and state of affairs in relation to sender and receiver. This model forms the basis of the communication model later introduced by Roman Jakobson. Language is the medium, or *organon*, that makes represented objects communicable and, through its deictic sign-functions, enables the representations to be anchored in the concrete communication situation. Bühler influenced the linguistics of the Prague School, and he also worked with the sign-systems and communication of animals.

Derrida, Jacques (1930–)   French philosopher in the phenomenological tradition. He is engaged in an ongoing criticism of any philosophy based on the assumption that consciousness and world, sign and thing, concept and object can at any point be seen as a unity. His philosophy focuses on the difference and the emergence of differences. Language is a process, called writing, that generates meaning through a permanent production of differences. Major works are *De la grammatologie* (1967) and *L'écriture et la différence* (1967) containing, among other things, a criticism of *structuralism* (s.v.) in linguistics, philosophy and anthropology, a discussion later to be continued in a criticism of *speech-act analysis* (s.v.) in John Austin and John Searle.

Eco, Umberto (1932–)   Italian semiotician. Eco has developed a rich cultural semiotics on the basis of modern European linguistics and semiotics with extensive historical references to the philosophy and language theories of the Middle Ages. In his *La struttura assente* (1968) he has demonstrated the usefulness of applying semiotics in cultural analysis of various verbal and non-verbal text types, often foregrounding the indirect and subtle manifestations of meaning. Later, for example in *A Theory of Semiotics* (1976) and *Semiotics and the Philosophy of Language* (1984), and *Kant e l'ornitirinco* (1997), he confronts the foundational problems of general semiotics. It will be difficult to find any semiotic problem that Eco

has not touched upon and given a new perspective in theoretical, historical and fictional texts as well as in essays on cultural criticism. His works
have inspired many semioticians across the divides between schools and
disciplines.

Foucault, Michel (1926–84) French historian of mentalities. Foucault has
especially concentrated on *discourses* (s.v.), that is extensive historical
systems of meaning that institutionalize the connection between knowledge and power in a cultural epoch as manifested in its dominating social
practices – teaching, organization of prisons and hospitals, practical
approaches to health and to sexuality. Discourses are located in partly
disconnected and contradictory layers in a cultural epoch. Foucault
focuses particularly on the exclusion and inclusion of phenomena on
the margins of historially specific social and cultural norm-systems.
Major works are the early *Les mots et les choses* (1966) and the later
Histoire de la sexualité in several volumes (1976 and later).

Genette, Gérard (1930–) French literary critic. His work has been a major
contribution to literary studies in the field of discourse analysis dealing
with structures of time and sequential structures and with narrator and
point of view (*Figures* III (1972)).

Gibson, James (1904–79) American perception psychologist. In a series of
empirical studies Gibson examines the role of the senses, sight in particular, for the construction of our *surrounding world* (s.v.) centred on the
moving human body (*The Ecological Approach to Visual Perception* (1979)).

Greimas, Algirdas Julien (1917–92) Lithuanian–French semiotician. He
founded the Paris School and was its leading figure until his death. This
school developed European *structuralism* (s.v.) to a general semiotics with
a global impact. In his important *Sémantique structurale* (1966) Greimas
broadened the scope of Louis Hjelmslev's structural linguistics to include
a general semantics and thereby gave the structural theory and analysis
of text a decisive impetus, both inside and outside Europe. The first step
was his analysis of the minimal units of meaning and their organization in
the so-called elementary structure of signification together with his analysis of the narrative process. Inspired by Vladimir Propp, this process
was seen as a series of transformations governed by actors that operate in
myths, fictional narratives and in the texts of mass culture.

Habermas, Jürgen (1929–) German sociologist and philosopher. The
leading figure of the Frankfurt School. Among Habermas's numerous
works on social philosophy his discussions of forms of communication
and discourses are of particular interest for semiotics. Guided by the
ideal of a communication without supremacy and in a critical presentation of *speech-act analysis* (s.v.) (especially John Searle) he formulates a
theory about the universal conditions for communicative action, that is a
collective endeavour to reach agreement. *Discourses* (s.v.) are regarded as
institutionalized forms of communication containing the ideal conditions
for the possibility for such an agreement (*The Theory of Communicative*

Action (1984, German 1981)). He has also published critical analyses of the works of Michel Foucault and Jacques Derrida, among others (*Die philosophische Diskurs der Moderne* (1985)).

Hjelmslev, Louis (1899–1965) Danish linguist. He transformed Ferdinand de Saussure's structural linguistics into a rigorous formalistic theory of language, glossematics. Its basic claim is that language is a general semiotic structure of relations between elements, their status as elements of content or of expression being a side-issue (*Prolegomena to a Theory of Language* (1943, 1953) and the more popular introduction *Language* (1963, 1973)). Glossematics has been the single most important contribution to general semiotics and has had a global impact, especially through the work of Algirdas Julien Greimas and the Paris School. Together with the Festschrift *Recherches structurales* (1949), Hjelmslev's *Essais linguistiques* (1959) and *Essais linguistiques* II (1973) have become part of the international semiotic canon. Although Hjelmslev was hostile toward Viggo Brøndal's philosophical approach to linguistics, they co-founded Le Cercle Linguistique de Copenhague (1931) and its journal *Acta Linguistica* (1939).

Husserl, Edmund (1859–1938) German philosopher and the leading figure of phenomenology. His most important early work is *Logische Untersuchungen* (1900–01), in which he discussed the thesis that the consciousness is always oriented toward an object, and that the world is only accessible to us as a *surrounding world* (s.v.) that appears for the consciousness. The task of phenomenology is to describe objects as they appear for us, both in relation to pre-existing structures of meaning in the cultural universe and in relation to the world of real objects that appears to us. Two consequences are relevant to semiotics: (1) as object-oriented, our consciousness is always engaged in an interpretative process with the object, i.e. in sign-processes; (2) meaning is structured as hierarchically organized elements enabling us to organize and evaluate the objects of the surrounding world and change our focus on them. Husserl has exercised a decisive influence on European linguistics and semiotics with a sceptical attitude to the pure formalism of *structuralism* (s.v.), for example linguists like Roman Jakobson, Karl Bühler and Viggo Brøndal, the entire Prague School and philosophers like Maurice Merleau-Ponty and Paul Ricœur.

Jakobson, Roman (1896–1982) Russian–American linguist. Although firmly rooted in structural linguistics, Jakobson has worked in almost all fields of twentieth-century linguistics and semiotics: from phonology via folklore and literature to cultural phenomena generally, always maintaining a methodological and theoretical perspective of general importance. Having been a leading figure in Russian Formalism, he became a key person in the Prague School – he co-authored its programme in the late 1920s and contributed pathbreaking phonological analyses with empirical, theoretical and philosophical perspectives. Having left

Europe, he continued his work in the USA from the 1940s onwards, now with a more pronounced semiotic approach, partly influenced by Charles Sanders Peirce's semiotics. Best known in a semiotic context is his work on the poetic language and on translation between semiotic systems (*Fundamentals of Language* (1956), *Selected Writings* II, III and VII (1971 and later)).

Lacan, Jacques (1901–81)   French psychoanalyst. In a radical reinterpretation of Freud's psychoanalysis Lacan launches the idea that the unconscious is a structure of the same nature as language and therefore governed by an ongoing production of differences with the phallus as the basic differential instance. Important articles are collected in *Écrits* (1966).

Lévi-Strauss, Claude (1908–)   French ethnologist. Inspired by the works of Roman Jakobson and the Prague School, Lévi-Strauss introduced the methods of *structural linguistics* (s.v.) into ethnology. He developed an analysis of myths and narratives in regarding them as an ongoing process of mediation between a culture's fundamental but contrasting categories of meaning. Important articles are published in *Anthropologie structurale* (1958) and *Anthropologie structurale* II (1973).

Lotman, Jurij (1922–93)   Estonian semiotician. Lotman was the creative centre of the Tartu School that made Soviet semiotics internationally known. On the basis of linguistics, ethnology and the study of literature Lotman developed a cultural semiotics. According to his theory, a culture is an open hierarchy of texts functioning as *models* (s.v.) of the culture they belong to. In being models they retain the *distinctive features* (s.v.) of the culture in question and thereby also define its boundaries to non-cultural or alternative cultural areas (*Universe of the Mind* (1990)).

Mauss, Marcel (1872–1950)   French anthropologist. Mauss's broad analyses of pre-industrial cultures provide their structure and function with a theoretical and topical perspective. His importance for semiotics is mainly due to his analyses of gift-giving, of the notions of person and self and of conceptions of the body. Claude Lévi-Strauss has edited a volume of his essays, *Sociologie et anthropologie* (1950).

Merleau-Ponty, Maurice (1908–61)   French phenomenologist. He increased the emphasis of early phenomenology on the structure and function of consciousness to include the role of body on the threshold between experience and meaning as a space for the emergence of meaning before consciousness occurs. Major works are *Phénoménologie de la perception* (1945) and *Signes* (1960).

Peirce, Charles Sanders (1839–1914)   American philosopher, mathematician, logician, scientist and for many contemporary semioticians the founder of modern semiotics. Although without an academic career, he was known and respected in his lifetime, especially in the fields of logic and mathematics. He saw himself first of all as philosopher, logician and semiotician. To him these three disciplines, together with mathematics, constituted different aspects of the same phenomenon.

According to Max Fisch (Fisch 1986) the development of his thought describes three movements. The first movement is opened by a lecture series at Harvard in 1866 and the articles 'On a New List of Categories' (1867), 'Questions Concerning Certain Faculties Claimed for Man' (1868), 'Some Consequences of Four Incapacities' (1868) and 'Ground of Validity of the Laws of Logic' (1869). Here we find the germ of Peirce's semiotics: the categories of Firstness, Secondness and Thirdness (a replacement of Kant's twelve categories), the criticism of intuitive knowledge (against Descartes) and the thesis that all knowledge is conveyed by signs.

The second movement takes shape together with Peirce's first formulation of the *pragmatic* (s.v.) theory of meaning in six papers from the journal *Popular Science Monthly* (1877–78) called 'Illustrations from the Logic of Science'. The two best known are 'The Fixation of Belief' and 'How to Make Our Ideas Clear'. The basic viewpoint is that the meaning of concepts is identical with the perceivable and practical effects that can be imagined as the possible consequences of their definitions.

The third and last movement runs from 1898 to his death in 1914. This includes most of Peirce's writing on semiotics. Philosophical pragmatism had gradually become popular, first of all because of Peirce's influential friend, the psychologist William James. In an attempt to distance himself from the popular version, he reformulated his own position as pragmaticism. In a lecture series at Harvard, 'Lectures on Pragmatism' (1903), and in the papers 'What Pragmatism is' (1905) and 'Issues of Pragmaticism' (1905) he defended a more strict scientific approach. He connected semiotics with his pragmatic philosophy of science and makes clear that it belongs to philosophical *realism* (s.v.).

Crucial for contemporary semiotics is Peirce's claim that signs are dynamical entities that not only transmit but also generate meaning. Semiosis, that is sign and interpretation as process, is a process interrelating three factors: sign (vehicle) (see *representamen*), *object* (s.v.) and *interpretant* (s.v.). From the dynamical viewpoint it follows that signs do not make up a class of objects (as for example verbal signs), but a triadic relation that makes it possible for any phenomenon to function as sign that represents an object to an interpretant. Hence Peirce's semiotics grasps the world in three dimenions: as qualities; as dyadic relations, that is as contrasting and colliding forces; and as signs, habits and rules.

Piaget, Jean (1896–1980)   Swiss psychologist. Piaget formulated a cognitive and developmental psychology foregrounding the child's appropriation of the *surrounding world* (s.v.) through symbolic constructions. These are founded in our bodily presence but are transformed in a process of increasing abstraction (*La psychologie de l'enfant* (with Bärbel Inhelder (1966)). He took early an interest in Ferdinand de Saussure's theory and later he published on methodological and epistemological perspectives of *structuralism* (s.v.) (*Le structuralisme* (1968)).

Propp, Vladimir (1895–1970)   Russian folklorist, belonging to the group of Russian formalists. In his seminal *Morphology of the Folktale* (1928) he defined the general narrative structure of the folktale and had a decisive influence on structural narratology after World War II, for example Algirdas Julien Greimas and Claude Lévi-Strauss.

Ricœur, Paul (1913–)   French philosopher. Ricœur has been working, theoretically and practically, with hermeneutics especially in the fields of language philosophy, linguistics, psychoanalysis and narratology (*De l'interprétation* (1965), *Le conflit des interprétations* (1969), *Temps et récit*, I–III (1983–85)). In contradistinction to formalistic and static conceptions of language, as expressed in *structuralism* (s.v.), he emphasizes language as event in space and time and interrelating language, its users and reality.

Saussure, Ferdinand de (1857–1913)   Swiss linguist. Saussure gained very early an international reputation as philologist after his studies in Germany. He stayed for several years in Paris before he settled in Geneva. But only when his student's notes from his late lectures (1907–11) were published posthumously in *Cours de linguistique générale* (1916) did he become the founding father of *structuralism* (s.v.) in modern linguistics. He insisted on lingustics as an autonomous scientific enterprise focusing on the immanent relations of language. In *Cours* he also outlined a general semiotics, called semiology, on the basis of linguistic key concepts such as synchrony and diachrony, language as system and speech, the arbitrary sign, system, form, value – concepts that have had an enduring impact on twentieth-century linguistics, especially in Europe, and later on became semiotic fundamentals in otherwise opposed semiotic schools and movements.

Schütz, Alfred (1899–1959)   German sociologist and phenomenologist. Schütz applied the phenomenological notions of time and subject to the historical and individual experience in everyday life of the socially formed *surrounding world* (s.v.). His major work is *Der sinnhafte Aufbau der sozialen Welt* (1932).

Searle, John (1932–)   American philosopher of language. Searle continues John Austin's *speech-act analysis* (s.v.) in an attempt to systematize the different ways speech acts are deliberately oriented toward a receiver (*Speech Acts* (1969), *Expression and Meaning* (1979)). He formulated a severe criticism of Jacques Derrida's conception of meaning as a permanent production of differences, claiming that it removes purposiveness and responsibility from communication.

Sebeok, Thomas A. (1920–2001)   Hungarian–American linguist and anthropologist. Sebeok took a particular interest in the borderline between the humanities and the sciences. He focused on animal communication and neurobiological communication processes (*Perspectives in Zoosemiotics* (1972)), along with intensive work on the key notions of general semiotics. As editor of the official journal *Semiotica* of the International Association for Semiotic Studies and editor of numerous anthologies, he contributed more than most semioticians to the international institutionalizing of semiotics as a field of research. Selected papers have appeared in *Contributions to the Doctrine of Signs* (1976) and *The Sign and its Masters* (1979).

Uexküll, Jakob von (1864–1944)   German biologist. Uexküll viewed the relation between organisms and the surroundings as a process of sign-generation and sign-exchange with the *surrounding world* (s.v.), or Umwelt, as the pivotal term, that is the part of the surroundings that an organism can perceive and interpret with its senses and its semiotic competence as a totality. Important papers have been published in *Kompositionslehre der Natur* (1980).

Bibliography

Aarestrup, Emil (1962 [1826]). *Digte* I–II. Copenhagen: Hans Reitzel.

Alphand, Adolphe (1867–73). *Les promenades de Paris* I–II. Paris: Rottschild.

Aristotle (1926a). *The 'Art' of Rhetoric* (The Loeb Classical Library). Transl. John Henry Freese. London: William Heinemann.

— (1926b). *The Nichomachean Ethics* (The Loeb Classical Library). Transl. H. Rackham. London: William Heinemann.

— (1932). *The Poetics; 'Longinus' on the Sublime; Demetrius on Style* (The Loeb Classical Library). 2nd edn. London: William Heinemann.

Austin, J. L. (1962). *How to Do Things with Words*. Oxford: Oxford University Press.

Bal, Mieke (1985 [1977]). *Narratology*. Toronto: Toronto University Press.

Bally, Charles (1969 [1939]). 'Qu'est-ce qu'un signe?' *A Geneva School Reader in Linguistics*, Robert Godel. (ed.) Bloomington: Indiana University Press, 87–100.

Barthes, Roland (1975 [1973]). *The Pleasure of the Text*. New York: The Noonday Press.

— (1986). 'The Death of the Author', R. Barthes, *The Rustle of Language*. Oxford: Blackwell, 49–55.

— (1988 [1966]). 'An introduction to the structural analysis of narratives', *The Semiotic Challenge*. Oxford: Blackwell, 95–135.

Bateson, Gregory (1972). *Steps to an Ecology of Mind*. London: Paladin.

Benveniste, Émile (1974 [1966]). *Problems in General Linguistics*. Coral Gables: University of Miami Press.

Blumenberg, Hans (1986). *Die Lesbarkeit der Welt*. Frankfurt am Main: Suhrkamp.

Boudon, Raymond (1968). *A quoi sert la notion de structure?* Paris: Gallimard.

Brask, Peter (1979). 'Model Groups and Composition Systems', *Danish Semiotics*, Jørgen Dines Johansen and Morten Nøjgaard (eds). Copenhagen: Munksgaard, 177–271.

Bremond, Claude (1966). 'La loquie des possibles narratifs', *Communication* 8, 60–76.

Brøndal, Viggo (1943 [1933]). 'Langage et logique'. *Essais de linguistique générale*. Copenhagen: Munksgaard, 49–71.

— (1948 [1928]). *Les parties du discours*. Copenhagen: Munksgaard.

Brooks, Peter (1984). *Reading for the Plot. Design and Intention in Narrative*. New York: Alfred A. Knopf.

Bruner, Jerome S. (1966). 'On Cognitive Growth', *Studies in Cognitive Growth*, Jerome Bruner et al. (eds). New York: John Wiley, 1–61.

Bühler, Karl (1978 [1927]). *Die Krise der Psychologie*. Frankfurt am Main: Ullstein.

— (1990 [1934]). *Theory of Language*. Amsterdam: John Benjamins.

Burkert, Walter (1979). *Structure and History in Greek Mythology and Ritual* (Sather Classical Lectures 47). Berkeley, Los Angeles, and London: University of California Press.

Carroll, Lewis (1965). *The Annotated Alice*. Harmondsworth: Penguin.

Chomsky, Norman and Morris Halle (1968). *The Sound Pattern of English*. New York: Harper and Row.

Clare, John (1984). *Selected Poems*. London: Everyman.

Clarke, David (1990). *Sources of Semiotic. Readings with Commentary from Antiquity to the Present*. Carbondale: University of Southern Illinois Press.

Conrad, Joseph (1987 [1902]). *Heart of Darkness*. New York: Bantam Books.

Cooper, Barry (1981). *Michel Foucault. · An Introduction to his Thought*. New York: Edwin Mellen.

Cosgrove, Denis (1993). 'The Picturesque City: Natures, Nations and the Urban since the 18th Century', *City and Nature. Changing Relations in Time and Space*, Thomas Møller Kristensen, Svend Erik Larsen, Per Grau Møller and Steen Estvad Petersen (eds). Odense: Odense Universitetsforlag, 45–58.

Coulthard, Malcolm (1985). *An Introduction to Discourse Analysis*. New York: Longman.

Culler, Jonathan (1976). *Structural Poetics*. Ithaca: Cornell University Press.

— (1983). *On Deconstruction*. Ithaca: Cornell University Press.

Danesi, Marcel (1994). *Messages and Meanings. An Introduction to Semiotics*. Toronto: University of Toronto Press.

Danesi, Marcel and Donato Santeremo (eds) (1992). *Introducing Semiotics*. Toronto: Canadian Scholars' Press.

Deely, John (1982). *Introducing Semiotics. Its History and Doctrine*. Bloomington: Indiana University Press.

— (1990). *Basics of Semiotics*. Bloomington: Indiana University Press.

Derrida, Jacques (1978 [1967]). *Writing and Difference*. Chicago: Chicago University Press.

Dijk, Teun A. van (ed.) (1985). *Handbook of Discourse Analysis*. Vol. 1: *Disciplines of Discourse*; vol. 2: *Dimensions of Discourse*; vol. 3: *Discourse and Dialogue*; vol. 4: *Discourse Analysis in Society*. New York: Academic Press.

Dolezel, Lubomir (1976a). 'Narrative modalities', *Journal of Literary Semantics* 5/1, 5–14.

— (1976b). 'Narrative Semantics', *Journal for Descriptive Poetics and Theory of Literature* 1 : 129–51.

Dos Passos, John (1979 [1930]). *The 42nd Parallel*. New York: Signet.

Dreyfus, Hubert and Paul Rabinow (1982). *Michel Foucault: Beyond Structuralism and Hermeneutics*. Brighton: Harvester.

Ducrot, Oswald (1971). *Dire et ne pas dire*. Paris: Herman.

Eco, Umberto (1984). 'Dictionary versus Encyclopedia'. *Semiotics and the Philosophy of Language*. Bloomington: Indiana University Press, 46–86.

— (1990). *The Limits of Interpretation*. Bloomington: Indiana University Press.

— (1992). *Interpretation and Overinterpretation*, S. Collini (ed.). Cambridge: Cambridge University Press.

— (1997). *Kant and the Platypus*. New York: Vintage Books.

Eco, Umberto and Thomas Sebeok (eds) (1983). *The Sign of Three. Dupin, Holmes, Peirce*. Bloomington: Indiana University Press.

Elam, Keir (1980). *The Semiotics of Theatre and Drama*. London: Methuen.

Emmeche, Claus and Jesper Hoffmeyer (1991). 'From Language to Nature', *Semiotica* 84, 1/2, 1–42.

Emerson, Ralph Waldo (1967 [1836]). *Nature. The American Tradition in Literature* I. New York: Norton, 1067–98.

Fisch, Max H. (1986). *Peirce, Semeiotic, and Pragmatism*, K. L. Ketner and Chr. J. W. Kloesel (eds). Bloomington: Indiana University Press.

Fiske, John (1990). *Introduction to Communication Studies*. 2nd edn. New York: Routledge.

Fohrmann, Jürgen and Harro Müller (eds) (1988). *Diskurstheorien und Literaturwissenschaft*. Frankfurt am Main: Suhrkamp.

Forster, Edward M. ([1927] 1962). *Aspects of the Novel*. Harmondsworth: Penguin.

Foucault, Michel (1981 [1970]). *The Order of Discourse*, R. Young (ed.). *Untying the Text*. Boston: Routledge & Kegan Paul.

Freud, Sigmund (1953–54 [1900]). *The Interpretation of Dreams. The Standard Edition of the Complete Psychological Work of Sigmund Freud* (S.E.), vols IV and V. London: The Hogarth Press.

Frye, Northrop (1957). *Anatomy of Criticism*. Princeton: Princeton University Press.

Gadamer, Hans-Georg (1997 [1960]). *Truth and Method*. London: Sheed & Ward.

Galilei, Galileo (1953). *Opere*. Milan: Ricciardi.

Genette, Gérard (1972). *Figures III*. Paris: Editions du Seuil.

— (1980). *Narrative Discourse*. Ithaca, NY: Cornell University Press.

Gibson, James (1979). *The Ecological Approach to Visual Perception*. Boston: Houghton Mifflin.

Glacken, Clarence (1967). *Traces on the Rhodian Shore*. Berkeley: University of California Press.

Goodman, Nelson (1968). *Languages of Art*. London: Oxford University Press.

— (1972). 'Seven Strictures on Similarity'. *Problems and Projects*. Indianapolis: Bobbs-Merrill, 437–50.

— (1978). *Ways of Worldmaking*. Indianapolis: Hackett Publishing Company.

Green, Keith (ed.) (1995). *New Essays in Deixis*. Amsterdam/Atlanta: Rodopi.

Green, Nicholas (1990). *The Spectacle of Nature*. Manchester: Manchester University Press.

Greimas, Algirdas Julien (1983 [1966]). *Structural Semantics*. Lincoln: University of Nebraska Press.

— (1977 [1969]). 'Elements of a narrative grammar', *Diacritics* 7, 23–40.

— (1987 [1970]). *On Meaning*. Minneapolis: University of Minnesota Press.

Grice, H. Paul (1975). 'Logic and Conversation'. *Syntax and Semantics* III. New York: Academic Press, 41–58.

Grzybek, Peter (1989). *Studien zum Zeichenbegriff der sowjetischen Semiotik*. Bochum: Brockmeyer.

Habermas, Jürgen (1971 [1969]). *Knowledge and Human Interests*. Boston: Beacon Press.

— (1979) 'What Is Universal Pragmatics?', Jürgen Habermas, *Communication and the Evolution of Society*, Thomas McCarthy (ed.). Boston: Beacon Press.

— (1983) 'Interpretative Social Science vs Hermeneuticism', *Social Science as Moral Inquiry*, N. Haan, R.N. Bellak, P. Rabinow and W.M. Sullivan (eds). New York: Columbia University Press.

— (1987a [1981]). *The Theory of Communicative Action* I–II. Cambridge: Polity Press.

— (1987b [1985]). *The Philosophical Discourse of Modernity*. Twelve Lectures. Cambridge: MIT Press.

— (1993). *Justification and Application. Remarks on Discourse Ethics*. Cambridge: MIT Press.

Hawkes, Terence (1989). *Structuralism and Semiotics*. Berkeley: University of California Press.

Helbo, André et al. (1991). *Approaching Theatre*. Bloomington and Indianapolis: Indiana University Press.

Hénault, Anne (1992). *Histoire de la sémiotique*. Paris: Presses Universitaires de France.

Hess-Lüttich, Ernst and Roland Posner (eds) (1990). *Code-Wechsel*. Opladen: Westdeutscher Verlag.

Hjelmslev, Louis (1961 [1943]). *Prolegomena to a Theory of Language*. Revised English edn. Transl. Francis J. Whitfield. Madison: University of Wisconsin Press.

— (1959 [1954]). 'La stratification du langage'. *Essais linguistiques*. Copenhagen: Nordisk Sprog og Kulturforlag, 36–68.

— (1959). *Essais linguistiques* (Travaux du Cercle Lingustique de Copenhague XII). Copenhagen: Nordisk Sprog og Kulturforlag.

— (1970 [1965]). *Language. An Introduction*. Madison: University of Wisconsin Press.

Hoffmeyer, Jesper (1996). *Signs of Meaning in the Universe*. Bloomington: Indiana University Press.

Holbek, Bengt (1987). *Interpretation of Fairy Tales*. Helsinki: Academia Scientarum Finnica. FF Communications No. 239.

The Holy Bible: Authorized King James Version (1974 [1611]). New York: Meridian/New American Library.

Homer (1980). *The Iliad*. Transl. Robert Fagles. Intro. and notes Bernard Knox. New York: Viking Penguin.

Honneth, Axel and Hans Jonas (eds) (1991). *Communicative Action. Essays on Jürgen Habermas's The Theory of Communicative Action*. Cambridge: Polity Press.

Iconicity. Essays on the Nature of Culture. Festschrift for Thomas Sebeok on his 65th Birthday, P. Bouissac, M. Herzfeld and R. Posner (eds). Tübingen: Stauffenburg Verlag.

Innis, Robert (1982). *Karl Bühler. Semiotic Foundations of Language Theory*. New York: Plenum.

— (ed.) (1985). *Semiotics. An Introductory Anthology*. Bloomington: Indiana University Press.

— (1994). *Consciousness and the Play of Signs*. Bloomington: Indiana University Press.

Jakobson, Roman (1960). 'Linguistics and Poetics'. *Selected Writings*, III. The Hague: Mouton, 18–51.

— (1965). 'Quest for the Essence of Language'. *Selected Writings*, II. The Hague: Mouton, 349–59.

Jakobson, Roman and Morris Halle (1956). *Fundamentals of Language*. The Hague: Mouton.

Jaworski, Adam and Nikolas Coupland (eds) (1999). *The Discourse Reader*. London: Routledge.

Johansen, Jørgen Dines (1986a). '"Il ne faut pas oublier le pain". Meaning and Linguistic Form', *Journal of Pragmatics* 9, 567–90.

— (1986b). 'The Place of Semiotics in the Study of Literature', *Semiotics and International Scholarship – Towards a Language of Theory*, Jonathan D. Evans and André Helbo (eds). Dordrecht: Elsevier, 101–26.

— (1986c). 'Sign Concept, Meaning and Study of Literature'. *Pramatics and Linguistics*. Odense: Odense University Press, 95–102.

— (1988a). 'What is a Text? Semiosis and Textuality: A Peircian Perspective', *Livstegn*, no. 5, I. Bergen, Norway, 7–32.

— (1988b). 'The Distinction between Icon, Index, and Symbol in the Study of Literature', *Semiotic Theory and Practice*, Berlin: Walter de Gruyter, 497–504.

— (1989). 'Hypothesis, reconstruction, analogy: On hermeneutics and the interpretation of literature', *Semiotica* 74, 3/4, 235–52.

— (1990). 'The triple status of a fictional universe of discourse'. *Proceedings of the XIIth Congress of the International Comparative Literature Association*, vol. 5 *Space and Boundaries in Literary Criticism.* Munich, 77–82.

— (1991c). 'Literature: Collective memory – collective fantasy'. *Face* 1, São Paulo, 35–59.

— (1992a). 'Desire: Representation and Repetition in Literature'. *Orbis Literarum* 47, 257–87.

— (1992b). 'Code and Reference. Bertrand Russell and Roman Jakobson on cheese'. *Cruzeiro Semiotico* 14, 65–74.

— (1993a). *Dialogic Semiosis.* Bloomington: Indiana University Press.

— (1993b). 'Let sleeping signs lie: On signs, objects, and communication', *Semiotica* 97, 3/4, 271–95.

— (1996a). 'Iconicity in Literature', *Semiotica* 110, 1/2, 37–55.

— (1996b). 'Arguments about icons', *Peirce's Doctrine of Signs. Theory, Applications, and Connections.* Vincent M. Colapietro and Thomas M. Olshewsky (eds). Berlin/New York: Mouton de Gruyter, 273–82.

— (1996c). 'Sign structure and sign event in Saussure, Hjelmslev, and Peirce', *Peirce's Doctrine of Signs. Theory, Applications, and Connections.* Vincent M. Colapietro and Thomas M. Olshewsky (eds). Berlin/New York: Mouton de Gruyter, 329–38.

— (1998a). 'A Semiotic Mapping of the Study of Literature', *Sign System Studies* 26. University of Tartu, 274–98.

— (1998b). 'Analogy and Fable in Poetry and Fiction', *RSSI (Recherches Sémiotique/ Semiotic inquiries)* 17, 1–3, 255–69.

— (1998c). 'Hjelmslev and Glossematics', in *Semiotik/Semiotics. A Handbook on the Sign-Theoretic Foundations of Nature and Culture*, Roland Posner (gen. ed.). Berlin: Walter de Gruyter, 2272–89.

— (1999). 'A diagrammatic modelling of semiosis', *Semiotica* 126, 1–4, 41–73.

Johansen, Jørgen Dines, A. Helbo, P. Pavis and A. Ubersfeld (eds) (1991). *Approaching Theatre.* Bloomington: Indiana University Press.

Johansen, Jørgen Dines and Svend Erik Larsen (1990). *Theatrical Codes.* Video film, 27 min. Odense University: Center for Literature and Semiotics.

Kelly, Michael (ed.) (1994). *Critique and power. Recasting the Foucault/Habermas debate.* Cambridge: MIT Press.

Kroeber, Alfred and Clyde Kluckhohn (1952). *Culture. A Critical Review of Concepts and Definitions.* Cambridge: The Peabody Museum/Harvard University Press.

Lacan, Jacques (1966). *Écrits.* Paris: Seuil. (Part of the book translated as *Ecrits. A Selection.* New York: Norton, 1982.)

Lakoff, George (1987). *Women, Fire, and Dangerous Things. What Categories Reveal about the Mind.* Chicago: University of Chicago Press.

— (1988). 'Cognitive Semantics', *Meaning and Mental Representations*, Umberto Eco, Marco Santambrogio and Patrizia Violi (eds). Bloomington: Indiana University Press.

— (1993). 'The Contemporary Theory of Metaphor', *Metaphor and Thought*, 2nd edn. A. Ortony (ed.). Cambridge: Cambridge University Press, 202–51.

Lakoff, G. and M. Johnson (1980). *Metaphors We Live By*. Chicago: University of Chicago Press.

Lakoff, George and Mark Turner (1989). *More than Cool Reason. A Field Guide to Poetic Metaphor*. Chicago: Chicago University Press.

Larsen, Svend Erik (1984). *Sémiologie littéraire*. Odense: Odense University Press.

— (1987). 'A Semiotician in Disguise: Semiotic Aspects of the Work of Viggo Brøndal', *The Semiotic Web '86*, Th. A. Sebeok and Jean Sebeok (eds). Berlin/New York: Mouton de Gruyter, 47–102.

— (1988). 'Gods, Ghosts, and Objects', *Semiotica* 70, 1–2, 49–58.

— (1991a). 'Un essai de sémiotique transatlantique', *Sens et réalité* (*Langages* 103), J.-C. Coquet and Jean Petitot (eds). Paris: Larousse, 7–22.

— (1991b). 'Urban Indices', *Semiotica* 86, 3–4, 289–304.

— (1991c). 'The Logic of Cultural Exchange', *Within the US Orbit*, Rob Kroes (ed.). Amsterdam: VU University Press, 91–100.

— (1992). 'Il y a forme et forme ou Lévi-Strauss à Prague'. *Degrés* 71, d-d20.

— (1993a). 'Patriarchal Hierarchies. Hjelmslev's Glossematics', *Semiotica* 94, 1–2, 35–54.

— (1993b). 'Contemplation and Distraction: A Visual Analysis of Two Urbanized Natural Sceneries', *City and Nature. Changing Relations in Time and Space*, Thomas Møller Kristensen, Svend Erik Larsen, Per Grau Møller and Steen Estvad Petersen (eds). Odense: Odense University Press, 79–96.

— (1994a). 'Body, Space and Sign', *Gramma* 2, Thessaloniki, 77–91.

— (1994b). 'Nature on the Move: Meanings of Nature in Contemporary Culture', *Ecumene* I, 3 (London), 283–300.

— (1994c). 'Déspatialisation et respatialisation', *Figures architecturales/Formes urbaines*, P. Pellgrino (ed.). Paris: Anthropos, 167–73.

— (1994d). 'Representation and Intersemiosis', *Peirce and Value Theory*, H. Parret (ed.). Amsterdam: John Benjamins, 255–76.

— (1994e). 'Et in Arcadia ego. A Spatial and Visual Analysis of the Urban Middle Space', *Advances in Visual Semiotics* (*The Semiotic Web 1992–93*). Berlin/New York: Mouton de Gruyter 537–57.

— (1996). 'Stories of Nature: The Urban Subject between Word and Nature', *Word Subject Nature*, T. Rachwal and T. Slawek (eds). Katowice: Wydawnictwo Uniwersytetu, 11–24.

— (1997a). 'Metaphor – A Semiotic Perspective', *Danish Yearbook of Philosophy* 31, 137–56.

— (1997b). 'Der Prospect Park in Brooklyn: Natur in der Stadt', *Zeitschrift für Semiotik* XIX, 1–2, 83–96.

— (1997c). 'Interplay of Images', *Cultural Dialogue and Misreading*, Mabel Lee and Meng Hua (eds). Sydney: Wild Peony Press, 304–12.

— (1997d). 'La rue entre ville et nature', *La rue – espace ouvert*, Svend Erik Larsen and Annelise Ballegaard (eds). Odense: Odense University Press, 14–63.

— (1998a). 'Ferdinand de Saussure und seine Nachfolger', *Semiotik/Semiotics. A Handbook on the Sign-Theoretic Foundations of Nature and Culture*, Roland Posner (gen. ed.). Berlin: Walter de Gruyter, 2040–73.

— (1998b). 'Semiotics', *Concise Encyclopedia of Pragmatics*, Jacob Mey (ed.). Oxford: Elsevier, 833–46.

— (2000). *A Roundtrip from Structure to Code* (*Kurseinheit 2: European Paradigms of the Humanities*). Hagen: Fern-Universität Hagen.

— (ed.) (1997). *Gärten und Parks* (*Zeitschrift für Semiotik* XIX, 1–2). Tübingen: Stauffenburg Verlag.

Lévi-Strauss, Claude (1967 [1958]). *Structural Anthropology*. New York: Basic Books.

— (1983). *Structural Anthropology* II. Chicago: Chicago University Press.

Lotman, Jurij (1990). *Universe of the Mind*. London: Tauris.

Lotman, Jurij and Boris Uspensky (1978 [1971]). 'On the Semiotic Mechanism of Culture', *New Literary History* IX, 2, 211–31.

Lucid, Daniel P. (ed.) (1977). *Soviet Semiotics*. Baltimore: Johns Hopkins University Press.

Lyons, John (1977). *Semantics* 1–2. Cambridge: Cambridge University Press.

MacDonell, Diane (1986). *Theories of Discourse*. Oxford: Blackwell.

Manual (1992). *New Jersey Driver Manual*. Trenton: Dept. of Law and Public Safety.

Martinet, André (1964 [1960]). *Elements of General Linguistics*. Chicago: University of Chicago Press.

Mauss, Marcel (1950). *Sociologie et Anthropologie*. Paris: Presses Universitaires de France.

Merchant, Carolyn (1990 [1980]). *The Death of Nature*. San Francisco: Harper.

Merleau-Ponty, Maurice (1982 [1945]). *Phenomenology of Perception*. London: Routledge.

Morelly, Abbé (1950 [1755]). *Code de la Nature*. Paris: Raymond Clavreuil.

Morris, Charles (1971). *Writings on the General Theory of Signs*. The Hague: Mouton.

Olmsted, Frederick Law (1981). *Landscapes into Cityscapes. Frederick Law Olmsted's Plans for a Greater New York City*. New York: Van Nostrand Reinhold.

Peirce, Charles S. (1931–58). *Collected Papers of Charles Sanders Peirce*, 8 vols, ed. by Charles Hartshorne, Paul Weiss and A. W. Burks. Cambridge, MA: Harvard University Press (also on CD-ROM at InteLex Corporation, Charlottesville 1992).

— (1975–79). *Contributions to The Nation*, I–III, K. Ketner and J. Cook (eds). Lubbock: Texas Tech Press.

— (1976). *The New Elements of Mathematics*, I–IV, C. Eisele (ed.). The Hague: Mouton.

— (1977). *Semiotics and Significs: The Correspondence between Charles S. Peirce and Victoria Lady Welby*, Ch. S. Hardwich (ed.). Bloomington: Indiana University Press.

— (1982–). *Writings of Charles S. Peirce: A Chronological Edition*, M. Fisch, C. Kloesel, E. Moore et al. (eds). Bloomington: Indiana University Press (planned to be in 30 volumes; six have been published).

— (1992–98). *The Essential Peirce* 1.2, Nathan Houser (gen. ed.). Bloomington: Indiana University Press.

— (n.d.). Unpublished manuscripts. Indiana University. (References to MS with number, year and pagination as in the files of the library.)

Perinbanayagam, R.S. (1991). *Discursive Acts*. New York: Aldine de Gruyter.

Petitot, Jean (1986). 'Structure', *Encyclopedic Dictionary of Semiotics*, Thomas A. Sebeok (gen. ed.), vol. 2. Berlin/New York: De Gruyter, 991–1022.

Pettersson, Anders (1990). *A Theory of Literary Discourse*. Lund: Lund University Press.

Piaget, Jean (1962). *Plays, Dreams and Imitation in Childhood*. New York: Norton.

Piaget, Jean and Bärbel Inhelder (1948). *La représentation de l'espace chez l'enfant*. Paris: Presses Universitaires de France.

Piaget, J. and B. Inhelder (1969 [1948]). *The Psychology of the Child*. London: Routledge and Kegan Paul.

Pinxten, Rik (1976). 'Epistemic Universals', *Universalism and Relativism in Language and Thought*, Rik Pinxten (ed.). The Hague: Mouton, 117–75.

Polkinghorne, Donald (1988). *Narrative Knowing and the Human Sciences*. New York: State University of New York Press.

Posner, Roland (1991). 'What is Culture?', *Términos de comparación*, Lisa Block de Behar (ed.). Montevideo: Academia National de Letras, 27–63.

Propp, Vladimir J. ([1928] 1968). *Morphology of the Folktale*. 2nd edn. Austin: Texas University Press.

Racine, Jean (1960). *Théâtre complet*. Paris: Classiques Garnier.

Renkema, Jan (1993). *Discourse Studies. An Introductory Textbook*. Amsterdam: John Benjamins.

Ricœur, Paul (1974 [1969]). 'Structure, Word, Event', *The Conflict of Interpretations*. Evanston: Northwestern University Press, 79–96.

— (1984–88). *Time and Narrative*, I–III. Chicago: Chicago University Press.

— (1991). *Reflection & Imagination. A Paul Ricoeur Reader*, Mario Valdés (ed.). New York: Havester/Wheatsheaf.

Rosenbaum, Bent and Harly Sonne (1979). *The Language of Psychosis*. New York: The University of New York Press.

Ryan, Marie-Laure (1991). *Possible Worlds, Artificial Intelligence, and Narrative Theory*. Bloomington: Indiana University Press.

Saussure, Ferdinand de (1972 [1916]). *Cours de linguistique générale,* Tullio de Mauro (ed.). Paris: Payot.

— (1959). *Course in General Linguistics*. Transl. Wade Baskin. Glasgow: Fontana/Collins.

Schmitt, Peter J. (1990 [1969]). *Back to Nature. The Arcadian Myth in Urban America*. Baltimore: Johns Hopkins University Press.

Schütz, Alfred (1955). 'Symbol, Reality, and Society', in *Symbol and Reality*, Lyman Bryson et al. (eds). New York: Praeger, 135–203.

Schütz, Alfred and Thomas Luckmann (1973). *The Structures of the Life-World*. Evanston: Northwestern University Press.

Schuyler, David (1986). *The New Urban Landscape. The Redefinition of City Form in Nineteenth-Century America*. Baltimore: Johns Hopkins University Press.

Searle, John (1969). *Speech Acts*. Cambridge: Cambridge University Press.

— (1979). *Expression and Meaning*. Cambridge: Cambridge University Press.

Sebeok, Thomas (1976). *Contributions to the Doctrine of Signs*. Bloomington/Lisse: Indiana University Press/Peter de Ridder Press.

— (1979). *The Sign and its Masters*. Austin: University of Texas Press.

— (1991). *A Sign is just a Sign*. Bloomington: Indiana University Press.

— (1991). 'In What Sense Is Language a "Primary Modeling System"?', *On Semiotic Modeling*, Myrdene Anderson and Floyd Merrell (eds). Berlin: Mouton de Gruyter, 327–39.

— (1994). *Signs. An Introduction to Semiotics*. Toronto: Toronto University Press (Toronto Studies in Semiotics).

— (ed.) (1960). *Style in Language*. Cambridge, MA: MIT Press.

Singer, Milton (1984). *Man's Glassy Essence*. Bloomington: Indiana University Press.

Thompson, Stith (1966). *Motif-Index of Folk-Literature*. Bloomington: Indiana University Press.

Tinbergen, Nicolas (1951). *Social Behaviour in Animals*. London: Chapman and Hall.

de Troyes, Chrétien (1992). *Erec et Enide*, Jean-Marie Fritz (ed.) (Lettres gothiques). Paris: Librairie Générale Française.

Uexküll, Jacob von (1980). *Kompositionslehre der Natur*. Berlin: Propyläen.

— (1982 [1940]). 'The Theory of Meaning', *Semiotica* 42, 1, 25–82.

Voltaire [François de] (1923). *Zadig and Other Romances*. Transl. H.I. Woolf. London: Routledge and New York: Dutton.

Wilden, Anthony (1972). *System and Structure*. London: Tavistock.

Index

Page references in italics indicate figures or tables